THE LOVERS' SPREAD: A TAROT GUIDE TO RELATIONSHIP COMPATIBILITY

MerrieOak Publishing

Also by Eleanor Piper

TAROT BOOKS
The Yes / No Tarot Oracle

NOVELS
The Grim – a novella

SHORT STORY COLLECTIONS
Between Stops

Note: Any person who chooses to base their decisions on oracular readings does so at their own risk. The author and the publisher are not liable for how readers may choose to use or interpret the information given in this book.

The Lovers' Spread: A Tarot Guide to Relationship Compatibility

Eleanor Piper

The Lovers' Spread:
A Tarot Guide to Relationship Compatibility

Originally published by Authors' Online 2012
This edition by MerrieOak Publishing, 2015

Copyright © Eleanor Piper 2009
Cover art and diagram © Siobhan Smith 2009
Cover design © Jamie Day 2009

All rights reserved. No part of this publication may be reproduced, stored in a retrieval system, or transmitted in any form or by any means, electronic, mechanical, photocopy, recording or otherwise, without prior written permission of the copyright owner. Nor can it be circulated in any form of binding or cover other than that in which it is published and without similar condition including this condition being imposed on a subsequent purchaser.

A CIP catalogue record for this book
is available from the British Library

ISBN 978 0 9931600 1 1

MerrieOak Publishing
England

This book is also available in e-book format
ISBN 978 0 9931982 1 2

CONTENTS

1. Introduction	1
2. The Lovers' Spread	3
3. How to Lay the Cards	4
4. Author's Note	10
5. The Meanings:	
The Fool	11
The Magician	14
The High Priestess	17
The Empress	21
The Emperor	24
The Hierophant	28
The Lovers	32
The Chariot	37
Strength	41
The Hermit	44
The Wheel of Fortune	48
Justice	52
The Hanged Man	57
Death	62
Temperance	67
The Devil	72
The Tower	77
The Star	80
The Moon	85
The Sun	90
Judgment	94
The World	99
Ace of Wands	102
Ace of Cups	107
Ace of Swords	112
Ace of Pentacles	117
Two of Wands	122

Two of Cups	129
Two of Swords	135
Two of Pentacles	142
Three of Wands	148
Three of Cups	154
Three of Swords	160
Three of Pentacles	167
Four of Wands	174
Four of Cups	181
Four of Swords	189
Four of Pentacles	194
Five of Wands	204
Five of Cups	212
Five of Swords	218
Five of Pentacles	224
Six of Wands	229
Six of Cups	236
Six of Swords	244
Six of Pentacles	251
Seven of Wands	258
Seven of Cups	262
Seven of Swords	267
Seven of Pentacles	272
Eight of Wands	277
Eight of Cups	281
Eight of Swords	286
Eight of Pentacles	290
Nine of Wands	294
Nine of Cups	299
Nine of Swords	302
Nine of Pentacles	307
Ten of Wands	313
Ten of Cups	318
Ten of Swords	321

Ten of Pentacles	325
Page of Wands	328
Page of Cups	332
Page of Swords	336
Page of Pentacles	341
Knight of Wands	345
Knight of Cups	348
Knight of Swords	352
Knight of Pentacles	355
Queen of Wands	358
Queen of Cups	361
Queen of Swords	365
Queen of Pentacles	370
King of Wands	375
King of Cups	380
King of Swords	385
King of Pentacles	389
6. Afterword	394

Love is selfless.

INTRODUCTION

Will I fall in love?

Will I find a person who can make me happy?

Is the time right to have a relationship?

Are we right for each other?

You probably had a question like this in mind when you picked up this book. I hope it will help guide you to your answers.

The Lovers' Spread: A Tarot Guide to Relationship Compatibility has been designed so that anyone can use it. You don't need to be an expert on the Tarot (although I hope that experts will also enjoy this book), all you need is a deck of Tarot Cards and off you go.

If you don't have a deck of Tarot Cards, you probably know someone who does. It is surprising the number of people who have an interest in fortune telling. Perhaps a friend of yours bought a deck out of curiosity during their teens, or perhaps their interest in the Tarot runs deeper than that?

If you don't have easy access to a deck, you should be able to find one at your local bookshop, most are happy to order a deck for you if there isn't one on their shelves.

This book gives a layout (or spread) for the Tarot Cards, which can help to divine the dynamics at play within a relationship, or for a potential relationship. In other words, it gives an oracular method of discovering whether one person is suited to another.

As with all fortune telling methods, the way you approach the process of casting, reading, and interpreting the messages of the cards can affect what information they will actually give. If you treat it as a game, they'll play with you. If your thoughts are unfocused or clouded by motive, they'll likely be obscure and abstruse in return. Approach the cards with a clear head and a calm heart, and you'll probably get an open, clear message in return.

Of course, sometimes it is not right for us to know the way of things, so be aware that the reading you get may be literal truth (rather than a metaphorical or symbolic meaning), or the cards and your subconscious may be using alternate interpretations to lead you astray. This is why it is frequently useful to seek the advice of a professional Tarot Card Reader who will be used to dealing with divination and Oracle.

For the most part, you should get out of the reading what you put in.

On the next page I'll outline the spread, the order in which the cards are laid, and the individual meanings of the cards.

It is then your turn to interpret how the meanings interact, in order to build up a whole picture: one that shows what part you are likely to play in any relationship that evolves; what part the other person is likely to play in any relationship that evolves; how you are likely to interact with one another; and whether there are any outside influences or people who could cause problems for the relationship.

Enjoy.

THE LOVERS' SPREAD

This spread should only be drawn once per relationship.

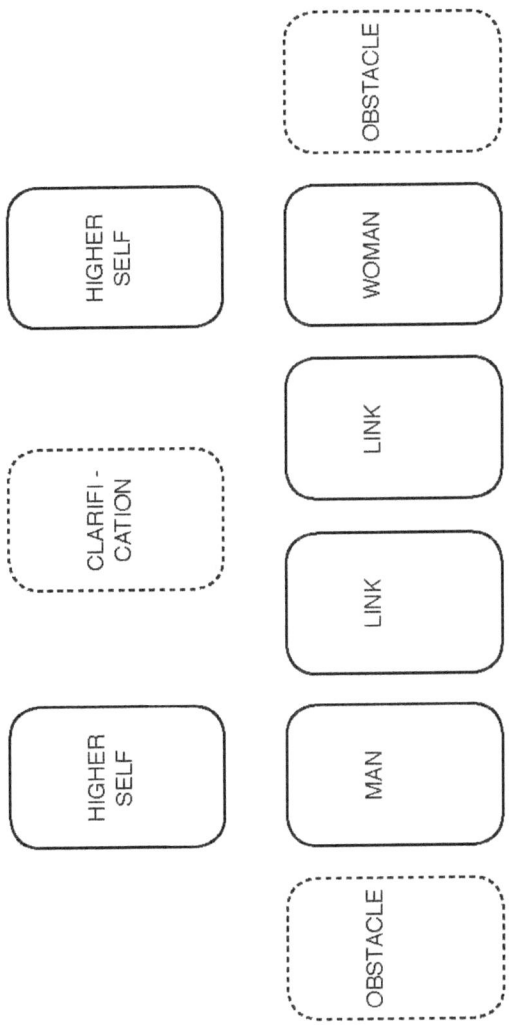

Within this spread your personal card is the *querent* card the other person's card is the *love interest* card;

there are two divine influence cards – one each – which is the *Higher Self/Influences/Themes* card; there are two emotional needs/behaviour cards – one each – called the *querent's link* card and the *love interest's link* card respectively.

The rest of the cards are optional: the first is the *clarification* card; the next optional card is the *querent's obstacle* card; and the last optional card is the *love interest's obstacle* card.

See below for details on how to go about laying the cards in the spread.

HOW TO LAY THE CARDS

This spread is intended to be cast with the cards in their upright positions. Should a card turn up in its reversed position, read it as you would an upright card.

NB: Those who are familiar with the Tarot and who work regularly with the reversed positions could adapt the reading to reflect the altered meaning for the cards affected if they feel it is right to do so.

*

Sit down in a comfortable position, and centre yourself.

Try to stop thinking about the laundry, and just get to a point where all thoughts stop.

If you are having difficulty with this, concentrate on your breathing: breath through your nose, drawing the breath down to your diaphragm and lower back allowing your chest to fill from the bottom upwards. Your upper chest should not move visibly until the very end of the inward breath. Take a slow, deep breath in, hold it a moment, then slowly breath out, hold it; slow, deep breath in, hold it a moment, then slowly breath out, hold it; etc. (If you get light headed or feel sick at any point go back to your normal breathing immediately!)

You can also imagine a diffuse (clear blue, golden, or white) light around you, bathing you gently in its cool, relaxing glow.

This should give you something to concentrate on, help relax you, and get you into a meditative state – which is what you are trying to achieve.

Once you are calm, pick up the cards and shuffle them face down until you feel that the Tarot deck is as it wants to be. As you shuffle the cards, visualize the person that you are interested in having a relationship with. Try to stay calm and centred while you do this.

When it feels right to you, lay out the cards face up, in The Lovers' Spread:

The first card you lay is your personal card. If you are a man, lay it to the left of centre, if you are a woman lay it to the right of centre - as shown in the diagram of The Lovers' Spread. (If you are in lesbian or gay relationship, lay the male card for whichever of you has the most masculine energy, and the female card for whichever of you has the most feminine energy. As above, start with your personal card.)

The *querent* card
This first card is the *querent* card.

It describes your role in life, who you are, what you are like.

Don't look at the meaning until the whole spread is laid out.

When you do check it, if it seems totally out of keeping with who you are it is possible that the cards are unwilling to share information with you at this time. But do remember, we are dealing with symbols and metaphor here. Somehow it should be describing at least one part of your nature – the part of you that you will be bringing most of into the world during this relationship that you crave (or that you are already involved in).

If the card doesn't match you at all, and you get the feeling that the cards are being unwilling to share, put the deck away and leave it. You aren't ready to know right now.

The *love interest* card

The second card you lay is for the person you are interested in having a relationship with, or who you are already having a relationship with. If this person is male, lay the card (leaving enough space for the link cards) to the left of your *querent* card, or if they are female lay it to the right of your querent card (leaving enough space for the link cards). The example given in the diagram of The Lovers' Spread shows how.

This card is the *love interest* card.

It describes that person's role in life, who they are, what they are like.

The *querent's Higher Self/Influences/Themes* card

The third card you lay is your divine influences card; you lay it directly above your personal (querent) card. It might help to think of it as a fate card, or Karma card.

This card is the *querent's Higher Self/Influences/Themes* card.

It describes what is happening to you in your inner emotional and mental life, and that which keeps being brought into your life, a theme if you like – it hints at what your spiritual self is trying to teach you.

Outside events and influences are going to come in and highlight this theme.

Internally it is something subconscious that you need to explore and express in order to feel more complete, satisfied or fulfilled in your life.

In a way it is one version of destiny, in that it is an inner prompting that cannot be denied; and if you do deny that part of yourself, you are likely to be beset by metaphorical "demons" until you start to take notice of the message that you are trying to send yourself about achieving your highest good.

The *love interest's Higher Self/Influences/Themes* card

The fourth card you lay is your love interest's divine influences card; you lay it directly above their card (the love interest card).

This card is the *love interest's Higher Self/Influences/Themes* card.

It describes what their spiritual self is trying to teach them; their inner emotional and mental life, and the themes and external influences that will impact them in order to highlight what they need to explore during their life in order to achieve their highest good.

The *querent's link* card

The fifth card you lay is your personal link card; you lay it directly beside your querent card, facing towards your love interest's personal card (leaving enough space for their link card to be laid next to it).

This card is the *querent's link* card.

It describes what you are looking for from the other person in a relationship and how you relate to them. Your emotional wants and your emotional behaviour.

The *love interest's link* card
The sixth card you lay is your love interest's link card; you lay it directly beside their love interest card, facing towards your querent card – so that it sits between your link card and their love interest card.

This card is the *love interest's link* card.

It describes what they are looking for from you in a relationship, and how they relate to you. Their emotional wants and their emotional behaviour.

The *clarification* card
Now, put the deck to one side and check the meaning of the cards you've laid so far.

If you need clarification of whether you and the person you would like to have a relationship with should try to make a go of it or not, then proceed to lay the clarification card.

It should be obvious from the meaning of the other cards whether it is needed or not.

This card is the *clarification* card.

If the clarification card refuses to give a clear answer, well, then that's the way it is. You probably aren't supposed to know the ultimate outcome at this time.

In addition, the clarification card doesn't provide a time scale (usually), so it may indicate that a union will be good, but not mention that it will only be short, or it may indicate that a union will be bad, but not say that the union will be a long-term one that is highly beneficial in teaching you life lessons but which ends abruptly and badly.

So take care with your interpretation – are you being too literal, or are you being too metaphorical? These cards can be tricky.

There are still two more optional cards that may need to be drawn. These are the obstacle cards.

The *third party/obstacles* cards

If there is an obvious obstacle in the link card that you have drawn for yourself, then a card should be drawn and placed on the opposite side of your querent card.

Alternatively, if you get an uneasy feeling, or the impression that another card wants to be drawn in respect of either the querent card and/or the love interest card, then lay another card in the appropriate spot – as above. It may even jump out and put itself there…

You should do the same thing for the love interest if their link card indicates problems, or if you get the feeling that a card needs to be there.

This card is your *third party/obstacles* card.
Or
This card is your *love interest's third party/obstacles* card.

The third party/obstacles card will show if there is anyone who is causing one or other (or perhaps both) of you problems, and trying to prevent you from being together.

If either of these obstacle cards is present, there is a good chance that the relationship will not work because of the added stress placed on whichever of you is affected by it, and your partner's reaction to your resulting behaviour (or vice versa). A breakdown of the relationship isn't always inevitable, and the relationship may proceed well despite the interference.

But if there is an obstacle card be aware that the relationship will not be an easy ride no matter what the other cards indicate.

This spread should be a useful intuitive divination tool for anyone who is considering a relationship, or anyone who is currently in a relationship and who wants to understand more about the dynamic which they and their partner share.

I hope that those of you who are professional Tarot readers will find this book and the spread described useful for enhancing your work.

AUTHOR'S NOTE

For me this book was both a labour of love, and fun to write. I trust that you will get the same sense of fun and insight into partnerships as you use the book.

The Lovers' Spread reading can provide you with insight into a relationship you are considering or that you have already embarked upon.

But (remember this, it's important), each of us has our own path to follow, our own lessons, our own destiny; and ultimately, ONLY *YOU* can feel in your heart which person you are meant to spend time with – long or short.

No one has the right, or the knowledge required, to tell you how to live. So, either use the guidance given, or ignore it and do what you feel is right for you.

Actions lead to consequences.

THE MEANINGS

ZERO – The Fool

As the querent: You live your life your way, and no one is going to tie you down. You hate restriction and will break free of any situation that seems static or limiting. Your life is a path that only you can walk. As soon as you accept that other people need their freedom too and stop demanding that they follow you your life will get easier.

In a love match you are looking for someone who will let you go your own way and do your own thing. Make sure the other person has the same outlook on life or you are both going to get very disappointed or hurt. Remember, if you make a commitment to someone it is not fair to walk out after five minutes because they crowd you. Take time to look at what you are getting into. You need to consider the long term and the consequences of your actions as they impact on someone who loves you. This is not a time to rush in blindly.

As the love interest: This person doesn't respond well to authority, and they value freedom. Don't expect them to devote their lives to you, they won't.

They can be a lot of fun to be with; they are a breath of fresh air. But this person tends not to look before they leap and may rush into a relationship with you that they are not suited to.

If you don't mind them being out at all hours, travelling the world without you, day dreaming when they are with you, suddenly changing all your carefully laid plans at the last second in favour of some hair-brained adventure that you are certain will never work; if you don't mind this then you could have a lot of fun together. They will be deep, honest, open and totally unpredictable.

If this person is working as a bank teller when you meet them, don't be fooled: they'll probably quit next week in favour of macramé class. You might want to ask to see their C.V. – it'll give you an idea of their life style.

As the querent's Higher Self/Influences/Themes: The world is always presenting you with new situations and adventures, challenges for you to meet on your own terms. Because you are open to change you seem to be experiencing a lot more variety in life than most people, and many of the changes are driven by you, whether you admit it or not. Somehow most everything that happens to you turns out to be for the best – even if it is terrifying at the time, you have a sense of being looked after.

Other people may not be so adaptable or willing to cope with the constant changes and challenges that are a feature of your life. If the person who loves you isn't a free spirit it is going to take quite a lot of talking to get them to understand how your life works, and if they try to tie you down chances are the world will start impacting negatively on both your lives. Your freedom to grow and learn has to be accommodated or come first ahead of the relationship.

As the love interest's Higher Self/Influences/Themes: This person's life is an unpredictable mess, and they seem to be as much responsible for it as external events.

They seem to take all the random changes and

adventures easily in their stride – stuff that makes a normal person blanch and run for their mother has this person fetching their crampons and windcheater. They take insane risks, and if everything goes wrong they just shrug their shoulders, smile and set out for the next horizon. They will be happy and feel safe in the tornado ride that is their life, you may not be.

The chaos that impacts their life will sweep you away, no matter how much of a rock you think you are.

If you take up with them you will be forced to learn a lot about life, and while the unpredictability may be nice, you'll have your heart in your throat as often as not.

If you are strong enough to cope, then this will be a very rewarding journey together.

As the querent's link card: You are looking for something new and exciting that will add meaning to your life. Constant change is the name of the game, something extraordinary every day. A new journey with every sunrise. If the other person can't give you this, or help you find this, then you are going to get bored. Check their personal and Higher Self cards for compatibility with your breezy nature. If it's not there you might want to pause and think a moment before rushing in the way you always do.

As the love interest's link card: A wayward spirit this one. Seeking change and inspiration. They may want you to travel with them to really strange places at the drop of a hat. Or they may want to go alone – and who knows when, or *if*, they'll come back.

If you are changeable as the sea, mysterious as a

dream, and unable to settle ever, with the ability to show them something unique or teach them something new and wonderful every other day in a new location, then you are probably their ideal partner.

Alternatively, if you are able to help them pack and plan and wire them funds when they run out, and enjoy the slideshow when they return, and inspire them about where to go and what to see next, and run the home and your life as a couple successfully without them – and make sure they remember to take the anti-venom and extra-woolly socks, then they'll likely be content to return to your side during the brief breaks in their adventure that they call life. Can you cope with that?

As clarification: You are being unrealistic and naive about the situation. Move on.

As a third party/obstacles: A person who you underestimate badly. You think they are an idiot, perhaps too gullible and trusting. But this person is very deep and knows all about beginnings and endings even if they aren't sure where they are in their journey right now. Ask yourself, why did this person set out on their own? They may well have taken everything of value with them when they left.

Look again at the person you are interested in, are they really who you think they are?

I – The Magician

As the querent: A person who is sure of themselves and in control of their life. You are a person who is active and makes things happen according to your plans and goals. You like to use communication to your advantage. You like to be in control and make the decisions with regard to things that affect your life.

Remember, love is about partnership and sharing. Ensure you allow the other person their freedom, and give weight to their opinions. Fan their spark, don't squash it.

As the love interest: A person who is sure of themselves and in control of their life. A person who is active and makes things happen according to their plans and goals. A person who uses communication to their advantage.

They are likely to be the one who is seen to run the relationship by the outside world. Very likely they will be the one in control, or in the position of dominance, in the relationship – or at the very least they will want to be the active decision maker of the pair.

As the querent's Higher Self/Influences/Themes: Your life is influenced by your higher intentions. Life is likely to be very directed, and you have a sense of destiny. This doesn't mean it will be an easy ride for you – more likely you will be driven harder to work to achieve something with your life. Your goals are likely to come first and your relationships second (unless the relationship is your goal – but this is unlikely unless your personal card or your link card indicates relationship as your goal).

You are likely to be able to talk your partner into following you on your life journey, but talk isn't sufficient in the long run. Ensure you give them the support they need, and provide the little things that let them know they are loved – personal, well thought-out gifts – something that will have a positive emotional meaning for them. When you make love to them, make sure you concentrate on them and your shared union, rather than allowing your mind to lose itself in other matters.

<u>As the love interest's Higher Self/Influences/ Themes</u>: The person's life is influenced by their higher intentions. Life is likely to be very directed, and this person has a sense of destiny. This doesn't mean it will be an easy ride for them – more likely they will be driven harder to work to achieve something with their lives.

Their goals are likely to come first and their relation-ships second (unless a loving relationship is their goal – but this is unlikely unless their personal card indicates love/relationship as their goal).

Be prepared to help them in whatever they do – either with the actual work/quest, or by providing a comfort-able environment as a foundation from which they can fly.

<u>As the querent's link card</u>: You want everything: someone with talent, money, perfect skin. What's on offer might seem to be perfect, but are you really making the right choice? Alternatively, you want perfection, but how perfect does someone have to be before you will accept what's on offer? Flaws are part of the rich tapestry of life.

You want someone who is savvier than you. But don't be blinded by bluff and a smart mouth. Knowledge is all very well, but wisdom, responsibility and an understanding of consequences are needed for the long haul. Are you really only after a one night stand? Is that all they want?

As the love interest's link card: This person is trying to work out whether you are the bee's knees or the world's greatest con-artist. They've been burnt before and they really don't deserve to be taken for a ride again. They need a hero or a heroine.

If you can fit on the pedestal that they have built things might be okay, but unless your personal card and your Higher Self card indicate perfection, your love interest may wake up one day and realize the grass is greener in someone else's bed.

As clarification: Be absolutely certain whether this is what you need. Not what you want, what you need. This is no time for playing games. If you have the slightest hesitation, walk away.

Between you, you can create reality – a very powerful combination for good or ill. If you do fight, it will get extremely nasty.

Check the link cards against the Higher Self cards again…is there warning or benevolence here?

As a third party/obstacles: They are in control of the situation. Forget your love interest and move on.

Even if you stand and fight you are likely to lose unless *all* the cards for yourself, your love interest, and particularly the clarification card show that the two of you belong together. You will need to find a way of sneaking off in the night if the two of you really do want to be together as this third party won't want to let go, and they'll be darned difficult to shake off if they decide to try to stop you.

II – The High Priestess

As the querent: You are on a very deep journey,

bringing your unconscious and intuitive knowledge to the surface. A calm person with an inner calling. Your intuitive inner wisdom is always your best guide, go with your gut in all things. Just be aware that you do not yet have all the facts, and it will take time for the core truths to be brought into the light. Sometimes your life can be very difficult as the universe continues to reveal new truths about the way things are and who you are.

Because your inner journey is your life, it may not be possible for you to walk hand in hand with any lover other than god/goddess. Sometimes emotion drowns you with its potency. Other people may never understand how you feel or the way you live. Spend some time on the mountain or in the wasteland – don't kill yourself trying to live an ordinary life.

As the love interest: This is an important person for you, although you may not know it. They are extraordinary, and you can glimpse the disturbing fields of the night sky reflected in the deepest ocean through their smallest motion when you least expect it. This person is a teacher, not by what they say, but by who they are and what they do. A deep individual, wise beyond their years; if you choose not to listen to what they have to say that is your choice, do not put the consequences on them, they gave you fair warning.

As the querent's Higher Self/Influences/Themes: Life chucks all kinds of curveballs at you, and it will continue to beat on you until you grasp its deepest lessons. Do not expect to know what's right first time around, there is always another layer to peal away before you get to the truth. If you allow emotion to cloud your judgment all that is left is gut reaction, which is not always the wisest course. You need to uncover your inner truth before you will be able to relate to another person on the deepest level. Find yourself, only then can you process how you feel. If you try to live vicariously through another person you will cause yourself and them pain.

As the love interest's Higher Self/Influences/ Themes: If you make assumptions about why things happen in this person's life, you will be wrong. This isn't about knowing right from wrong, this is about them gaining wisdom. Other people and events swamp them with emotion, they feel what is right even if they can't explain it. They are on a deep journey and if you try to distract them you will both suffer; life has a way of forcing the issue when this card is exalted. Follow them, walk beside them, or step out of the way.

As the querent's link card: You represent a divine mystery to them. And you need a divine mystery in return. You need the sticky, convoluted, passion of pure emotion. You yearn for what they represent; but what you need from them is only just on the edge of your grasp, brushed by the tips of your fingers. It must be frustrating, this endless wanting. You desire the unfathomable.

Secret lust, hidden passion: an affair.

As the love interest's link card: The need for deep passion, romance and mystery in love is strong here.

Intuitive knowledge of the divine in love is required by this person's other half. If you have no idea what I am talking about then there is a good chance you will not satisfy each other in bed, as neither of you will understand or give what the other needs and wants.

This person expects you to work with them to fathom the depths and awe of physical, mental and emotional union. If you are someone whose touch can be light as a feather, but whose waters run deep, then they will be magnetized by you. If you instinctively know what they want without them having to utter a word – then a) you must be psychic, and b) you are exactly what they are looking for.

This person is strongly intuitive, and your role in their life is to be a lightning conductor for them - a bridge between their occult/subconscious and their mundane/ conscious. Expect them to know you better than you know yourself.

As clarification: There are a lot of secrets here. Whether they are good or bad is unknown; each of you is keeping your own counsel to protect the people around you. The only thing you can rely on is your gut instinct, the other person isn't talking.

If you are happy to live in an environment like this then that's your choice, if not you should walk away.

This relationship is founded on intuition. What you share is only verging on the conscious. Trust your gut.

As a third party/obstacles: This person knows far more than they are telling. Did they leave because of infidelity, or are they still seeing your partner behind your back? This person is emotionally unstable and has questionable morals, they won't follow any "rules" in their quest to regain/defend that which they see as rightfully theirs.

You need to be suspicious and careful in all your dealings; the truth won't be pleasant.

III – The Empress

As the querent: You are someone who revels in fields of lush grass, orchards ripe with fruit, waters teaming with fish – anywhere natural and bountiful. You want to live next to, or with, nature.

You almost definitely want a family, lots of plump children playing in the gardens around you. And you won't have to wait for the kids either. Once you find your partner you'll be hard put to prevent them from arriving every five minutes. Prepare for triplets.

If, in the very unlikely event, you are unable to have children for some reason, then you will find adoption rewarding. You might even consider sponsoring a child or two in the third world.

As the love interest: This person is going to have children, lots of them. They may even have some when you first meet? If you want to be with them you are going to need to like kids.

This person loves creativity, art, gardening, pottery – anything linked to the fertile earth. They will need greenery and the influence of nature in their surroundings. Their house is likely to be filled with plants, animals, children. They may well be an excellent cook. They are likely to work outside or with children or animals, or be deeply involved with art and creating with their hands…if not, then it will likely be their dream to do something of that kind in the future. Chances are they'll be able to make a secure home life as a result of their success in the field they have chosen.

This person will have the ability to surprise you in unexpected ways. You may never fully understand what makes them tick.

As the querent's Higher Self/Influences/Themes: If you approach life in a positive way, the universe will support and nurture you – helping you find the nourishment and reserves you need to fulfil your projects; when you work in tune with the positive gestational forces you will be at your most productive.

If, however, you approach life in a negative way, you will suffer extremes of destruction, desolation, and barren isolation.

It is very important that you find your centre and concentrate on the beauty of creative, nurturing effort as soon as possible in your life. Be yourself, not some mannequin pulled by the strings of other people's pain, fear and ideas of how to live. The rat race is not for you.

As the love interest's Higher Self/Influences/Themes: This person seems to emanate the universal female creative principle. Whether they are a man or a woman, the universe surrounds them with opportunities to create, nurture, and birth things into the world. If they are a positive person they will be extremely productive in their creativity.

There will be an element of safety and security about this person's life – a divine force looks after their needs. That's not to say there won't be hard times, but the outcome will be one of success most times.

If nature is dealing some harsh blows to this person it is because they need to look at the path they are following – chances are they are not being true to their inner angel. If bad luck is to blame, then frequently their best survival tactic is to immerse themselves in art; creation for the sake of it. Something positive will result.

As the querent's link card: You have a deep need for family, for security, for the art and beauty in loving. You desire the fertile sward. You are not afraid to wade into the thick of things and get messy; you may even prefer this type of hands on approach.

What you really want is a supportive partner who will nurture you and your goals.

You are a creative person who can produce great things in the right environment. When you feel needed and loved you are at your best.

As the love interest's link card: This person needs family and a stable loving relationship more than anything. The drive to nurture and mother is strong, and at their innermost level their whole life is about creation – of children, art, gardens…They have an earthy nature and love to watch the sunrise; the light emerging from the black abyss of night is a metaphor for everything about their lives. This person needs permanence. They make a very good life partner, even if they are exceedingly unique and unconventional in their lifestyle.

If all you are after is a one night stand, you had better make sure the contraception is up to scratch or you could be dealing with phone calls nine months down the line.

As clarification: You did want a family, didn't

you? Well, you're going to get one. This card bodes well for a committed relationship; indicating marriage, family, and fertility. Whatever activities you undertake together will bear fruit.

If you are a woman you may discover that you are going to be a mother soon.

As a third party/obstacles: Financial troubles, domestic tyranny and emotional blackmail could all be contributing to your separation from the person you love. If they have withdrawn from you it is because they need to think things through.

Perhaps the "Mother-in-Law" is the biggest hurdle you face. Alternatively you may be trying to get cosy with someone who has a same sex preference.

Talk, it's the only way you'll find out what the problems are. Whether you can solve these problems is another matter.

IV – The Emperor

As the querent: You are one of those people who are full of energy and who knows how to make things happen. You like to think of a solution to problems, applying your keen mind and logic to the task at hand.

You have a strong desire to live in an ordered world, where the rules are known, laws of conduct protect people from social faux pas and errors, where the boundaries are clear. The desire to protect those is need is also strong in you.

When your authority is challenged you can become a little overbearing and place unnecessarily harsh restrictions and limitations on the offender – this is a trait you would do well to try to soften. Children in particular are likely to try to rebel against the structure you place around their lives – this is a natural part of growing up: testing the boundaries – and they may accuse you of being a tyrant. Make sure the punishment fits the crime in these cases…check the level of punishment severity with your significant other before you start laying down the law.

As the love interest: This person likes to apply their mind to the task of bringing order out of chaos. They have the energy and drive to turn ideas into concrete reality, as they are not afraid to knuckle down to the hard work involved in such activities, and they are good at motivating groups of people to help them in their work.

A responsible person who enjoys stability. They will welcome knowing the facts up front so that they can plan accordingly and get some solid foundations in place.

This person respects authority, and probably wields it themselves. They will get upset if they discover the authority they put so much store in is not actually worth as much as they believe, nor given the same respect by others as they place in it themselves.

As the querent's Higher Self/Influences/Themes: There is a strong need for you to bring order and structure to your life. The universe will be constantly teaching you about the need for discipline and adherence to the "rules" of society. You may not see much point in pandering to the needs of others or adhering to their values – but at some point you have to come to grips with the concept that some of the strictures and limitations are there for a beneficial reason. Once you have learned the whys and wherefores, then you can take the lead and go your own way. But until then it is likely that the universe will be bringing harder and harder lessons to your door to point up the fact that achievement comes from hard work, and that you need to know the rules before you can successfully break them and the mould people want to force you into.

Whatever the case, authority will play a strong role in your life, whether you clash with it or become it. Rules, laws, order, structure, logic – these are the things your life revolves around.

<u>As the love interest's Higher Self/Influences/ Themes</u>: Hierarchy, rules, and the law somehow play a big part in this person's life. Structured activities, and legal commitments will provide a sense of direction and order for them.

It could be that they are forced to take the lead in most of the situations that surround them in order that they can accomplish anything solid or lasting, and see their goals through to completion.

This person is learning that discipline and planning, adhering to structure, and using the normal channels to get things done – while time consuming – is probably the most successful approach for them. They are learning about authority, and may even be offered the opportunity to take on a leadership role.

It could be that their parents have their life planned for them, and thus they have the urge to rebel. They will likely learn that if they want to go their own way, they need to learn the rules for survival before they can really fly the nest. When they do go it alone, if they have learned their life lessons well, they should go far.

As the querent's link card: You are looking for someone who will set clear boundaries and rules for your personal life and relationship. This is because you want to know exactly where you stand.

You want someone who has an aura of power or authority about them, who can look after you and make you feel safe – possibly you seek a father figure. A ruler for your kingdom.

In short you feel the need to be with a mover and shaker, someone at the top of their game who has the respect, perhaps even worship, of their peers.

As the love interest's link card: This person wants you to talk to them about your needs, so that nothing is in doubt. If you tell them what you expect and want from them, then they will be in a position where they can work towards being able to provide that. It is possible that this person is not confident about their social abilities and hence wants the prompting.

They are looking for a leader who they can follow, who will set the goals and boundaries for the relationship clearly and logically. Someone who will provide a detailed blueprint or plan for how to proceed successfully. Someone who can keep them safe in times of hardship, and pull any strings that are required in order for life to proceed smoothly.

As clarification: It's time to make changes in your life; knuckle down, be disciplined, get practical, make things happen. The card promises victory or achievement in practical matters. It bodes well for a relationship in terms of providing a home and the physical, orderly things a family needs. But a relationship also requires emotional support, communication and work on romance, if you neglect this aspect it could lead to problems later.

If you are a man, you might be about to discover that you are a dad.

As a third party/obstacles: Someone else is pulling the strings here, and they are a powerful person. Anger, harsh words and even violence will be obstacles to harmony. Deceit could also play its part.

If there are any personal issues such as drug or alcohol abuse, jealousy, a vicious temperament, then it will be these things that are preventing you from being able to connect with the other person. Denial won't solve anything.

V – The Hierophant

As the querent: You have a strong spiritual calling and a need to understand the workings of the divine in your life, and in the lives of others around you. You may find yourself drawn to organized religion as a source of comfort and solidarity.

You are likely to find the traditions and rituals of worship comforting; they give you a necessary map by which to live, and standards and rules to follow. You like being part of a society, and you feel that others are missing out on the community they could share if they too joined in.

Communicating with God, and listening in silence to the inner wisdoms that are thus revealed, helps you to navigate the daily obstacles of life.

If organized religion is not for you, you will still have very strong links with the divine, and you are likely to want to bring sacred knowledge to society.

If you have a serious relationship with someone,

you will want to ratify the union with marriage, or the traditional wedding ceremony of the faith to which you cleve.

As the love interest: This person's spiritual life is very important to them, and they are likely to be involved in good works for the community. Religion will form an important part of their lifestyle in one aspect or another. They enjoy belonging to an organized community where the focus is on positive humanitarian growth for all.

They will have a strong set of morals and are likely to be very trustworthy.

This person values tradition, and in a relationship they will seek marriage. It is important for them that the community witnesses their commitment and sacrifice, whether that is to another or to a special cause.

This person's communication with God is important to them, and they are likely to want you to live by the same religion and values that they hold dear.

As the querent's Higher Self/Influences/Themes: The universe keeps putting you in situations that make you question the whys and wherefores of existence. Why are we here? Is there a God? What kind of God? How do I fit in?

You are likely to feel the need to study the different religions of the world. Alternatively you will find yourself faced with motivational speakers from different religions, or involved in religious culture somehow. Seems like someone or other is always banging on your door asking to speak about God.

Culture and society are both pushing you to join a religious tradition. Your inner self is also directing you to find your belief system. You may even feel a strong urge to join the priesthood.

Your inner quest for meaning is going to be the motivating and primary force in your life.

<u>As the love interest's Higher Self/Influences/ Themes</u>: This person's life is going to be dominated by religion. It could be that they are a member of the clergy, or actively involved with their local church or religious culture. Perhaps their family is strongly religious.

Whatever the case, if you aren't keen on organized religion being around this person will expose you to a lot of it, because they keep getting calls from God or God's people. It's a fact of their life that you are going to have to get used to.

Even if they aren't keen on getting ordained, or wish to escape from their morally righteous family, organized religion is going to play a big part in their lives whether they like it or not.

I'm betting that there's a good chance you are deeply involved with religion yourself if you are interested in this person.

<u>As the querent's link card</u>: You are looking for a solid relationship that sets an example of ideal family life. The public recognition and trappings of a relationship are important to you – things like engagement parties, marriage, anniversary rings; and the honouring of these traditions makes you feel safe. They give you something solid you can cling to in the dark of the night.

You want your lover to be a proper and upright citizen, who knows the right etiquette for any occasion. They will be your moral compass in many ways, and you will look to them to set the standards in your home life and your social life.

You want someone who understands how to channel the divine through into their living and loving, and who can thus raise your intimate experiences to a higher level.

As the love interest's link card: This person wants you to bring your religion and your quiet contemplation of the word into their life. They trust you to provide them with guidance and be the role model that they so desperately need.

They want someone who can make them feel loved and safe in the darkest times, and bring them joy until death do you part.

They need structure and social grounding, and they look to you to provide it. If you are involved in good works in the community that they can also become involved with they will be grateful for the chance.

This person has a need to find God in the intimacies of their life and they expect you to be their guide, their hero or heroine, their guardian angel.

They also need permanence and the physical trappings of commitment from you. If you weren't planning on an engagement ring or a big wedding then you had better reassess your plans!

As clarification: You know right from wrong, good from bad. Look for the little things that give away the underlying truth of the people involved and of the situation. Listen to your spiritual side and act accordingly.

If you know that both of you are right for each other, and the question is should you have a traditional relationship, with all parties agreed on marriage, then the answer is yes. Pop the question. Get it out in the open, at least then you'll both know where you stand.

As a third party/obstacles: Society as a whole is against this union. Whichever culture you belong to, those in authority disapprove of the relationship. You won't be able to change the minds of these traditionalists. If both of you are brave enough, you could elope and start a new life elsewhere, but you are not going to be able to be together as long as you stay put. In doing this you will lose the support of family and friends, you won't be able to go back. Fear and social/cultural differences are what is keeping you apart.

VI – The Lovers

As the querent: One of the hardest things in your life is making the choice between one thing or another, one career or a different career, one way of life versus an alternate way of life. The reason being, that to commit to one activity is to have to abandon something else – but you realize the need to make such a commitment in order to experience the activity fully. Otherwise your life would be full of tiny samplings of things – a superficial whitewash of no consequence, and what is the point in that? When you want to know something you want to know it fully.

Nothing by half measures.

As the love interest: This person makes decisions

based on their emotions, therefore logic doesn't seem to play much of a part when it comes to anything they feel strongly about. As a result they can appear to be irrational, or to make sudden and radical changes in their lives based on the flimsiest evidence. However, their process works for them, and if they didn't follow their heart in all things they would be extremely unhappy.

Everything they do, they do one hundred percent. If they make a commitment, as long as their passion and love for it lasts they will be utterly committed.

This person can be quite a handful, either socially or in bed. They can be very exciting to be around, because of their enthusiasm for the things they like.

They are a sucker for romance. If they like you they'll probably bowl you off your feet before you know what's happening.

As long as you understand that their heart will always rule their head, and that they respond on the level of emotion rather than logic, then being with them is likely to be a very rewarding experience.

If you want to keep this person grounded it is a very delicate matter, because if you handle it in the wrong way their heart will read your words and actions as a personal attack or affront and go off you very quickly indeed. Tread carefully; avoid pouring cold water on their dreams, instead try to present solutions to the problems they might encounter: for example "That's a great idea. You'll need a minus 60 sleeping bag, and a storm proof tent, and…" – it'll get them thinking whether that trip to Everest really will be so wonderful after all, because if they are going to need snow shoes to get around and frostbite proof mittens it could be that it might be a bit colder there than they would really like? Whereas if you just tell them it's cold there and they won't like it, the response would immediately be "How do you know what I'll like!" and they'll storm off in a huff – only to discover once they arrive in the foothills that you were right. But it's too late by then.

As the querent's Higher Self/Influences/Themes: Life is always throwing choices at you; do you follow the tried and tested path or chase after something new and exciting? Safety versus risk. The choices are likely to be emotionally loaded too. And whatever it is that is being presented to you is something that you will have to give one hundred percent of yourself to.

As the love interest's Higher Self/Influences/Themes: The events and situations that occur in this person's life seem to be designed by fate to force them into one or other course of action to which they have to devote themselves one hundred percent. The choices are likely to be between that which is known and considered relatively "safe", and that which is unknown, risky and exciting. The different options will have deep and conflicting emotional importance for your love interest. The way this person determines their response to such life choices will be based on how they feel. Thus their decisions will be made on the illogic of the heart rather than the logic of the head. This may make the person do seemingly crazy things, but it's the way they work, and it will be a successful strategy for them most of the time.

If they don't follow their heart the universe is likely to clobber them with harsher and harsher lessons until they are forced to respond on a level of their being that satisfies their Higher Self, creating a change in their viewpoint and response methods – this should make them a more rounded, secure and positive individual in the long run.

As the querent's link card: You seek merging in love. You want to experience as much of your lover's life as possible and probably can't bear to be parted from them for a second. It's almost a compulsion for you. This means that you may come across as overly clingy or possessive. Jealousy may be a problem for you too.

Alternatively it could be that you have almost totally submerged your personality in theirs, and can appear to be utterly under their thumb.

Your feelings for them could be overwhelming to the extent that their happiness is more important to you than your own.

The result of all this is that you may accidentally drive away the person you love by making them feel smothered.

Many people can't cope with the intensity of togetherness that you yearn for, so it would be a good idea for you to find a hobby that gets you out of the house and away from them for one night a week. This would help broaden your mind and your social sphere, and give them some much needed time to themselves.

As the love interest's link card: This person wants to spend their every waking hour with you, and will work very hard to keep you happy as they believe your needs are more important than their own. It is likely that they find their sense of identity through you and they will want to be involved in every aspect of your life.

They may be intensely jealous or possessive of you, especially if they are insecure, because they think they may lose you to someone else.

Any suggestion that you wish to be left alone will likely be interpreted as a personal attack on their heart and soul. If you do feel smothered by the intense level of contact they maintain with you, you may wish to delicately help them find an activity or social group that they can participate in – to help them find their own identity and gain a sense of self. This will also get you some time out while they are busy.

As clarification: This is an important relationship for you. But you need to make a choice. This new found love is a deep emotional connection which conflicts with a prior commitment in your life, to which you are strongly attached. Consider all the ramifications very carefully. Whichever path you choose will have long-term consequences. Ultimately your heart should be allowed to rule your head in this.

If you are having problems in a long-term relationship, this card shows that those difficulties can be resolved.

As a third party/obstacles: Any separation from your lover will be short term as long as you act to mend the break now. Your personal happiness should come first in your life – why are you allowing other things to take priority? If your lover is placing other matters or people ahead of you, you should gently remind them of love's first blush, bring the romance back into their life, and help them to understand that they need to tend to their own needs before sacrificing themselves for others who probably wouldn't do the same for them in return.

VII – The Chariot

As the querent: Conflicted, that's what you are. You are constantly struggling with yourself: your thoughts, emotions, actions. And if not with yourself, with other people or your environment.

So many things pull at you from so many different directions, it is difficult for you to decide on one set course and harness your efforts to that.

You are a pretty darned strong personality, with an iron will. You have the inner reserves to achieve great success if you apply yourself solidly to one thing. Your tendency though is to split your effort, diluting your energy and thus your success – possibly this tendency prevents you from finishing anything as you either constantly chase after the next "best thing", or find yourself pulling in different directions over what to do with regard to your current project.

With love, if you split your desire between many people you may well end up with none of them. Choose one course and stay with it if you are looking for permanence in a relationship.

The important thing, with all aspects of your life, is to go with what you need in your innermost heart – rather than do, think or feel the way other people say you should. What do they know? They are not you.

As the love interest: This person seems to spend their whole life vacillating between one thing or another, and thus gets nothing done. When they do apply themselves to a single course of action they can make Hercules look like a wimp – they can achieve anything, once they have found their direction, assuming they stick to it.

They fight with their inner nature as much as with society, and can come across as quite insecure as well as argumentative. Once they realize their inner truth and start chasing their destiny, these tendencies are likely to evaporate – until they find something new to be conflicted about!

They may be unsure of their sexuality, and rack themselves with guilt over it. They need to accept themselves for who they are and not for what society wants them to be. If you do take up with them, it is possible that they might suddenly announce that they are actually a homosexual, lesbian, heterosexual or bisexual. This isn't a reflection on you, it's just them finding themselves. Don't take it too badly, you must have suspected it? Besides, I've just warned you right here – so take a careful look before you leap.

<u>As the querent's Higher Self/Influences/Themes</u>: Life is one long struggle; just as you've got one thing ironed out, something else pops up to cause problems. This constant set of obstacles is ultimately good for you, as it will teach you new methods of dealing with and coping with circumstances. It will help you to access your inner creativity, and your emotional truth, which in turn can lead to you accomplishing much in your life. This is because your innovative approach, ability to think on your feet, and your well conceived back up plans will put you well ahead of most other people in this crazy thing we call life. You've been forced to develop these through previous experiences that life has thrown at you.

Your willpower, determination, and ability to

muster all your resources in a unified effort to tackle one goal will help you to succeed in whatever you do – but it has been a long hard lesson from the universe. Previously you would have frittered away your resources and energy and got nowhere. Now you are learning to find links between all the varied events, people and situations that surround you, and bring them together to solve the current issue you are dealing with.

One thing at a time. One direction at a time. One goal at a time.

As the love interest's Higher Self/Influences/Themes: Life throws a lot at this person, much of it conflicting. They need to learn to pull together and direct their energy into one thing at a time in order to tackle the obstacles that they encounter.

If the chaos that surrounds this person can be brought under control and set to work in their favour they will achieve much and be very successful – but first they need to learn how to spot the links between events, people and things which all form part of one big jigsaw.

As the querent's link card: You are looking for someone whose ambition drives them to success. A strong, single-minded individual who does not allow themselves to get distracted by the petty, mundane conflicts of life.

The other side of the coin is that if this person believes that they are right, they will not back down and are likely to fight tooth and nail to get what they want or think they deserve. It is their right. Victory by conquest. It may not make them easy to live with – but then, maybe what you really want is a challenge in your love and home life?

As the love interest's link card: This person wants you to lead the way, blaze the trail, take control of the direction your lives are going in. They are looking for someone who will not mess about, but who will go straight to the heart of any matter with single minded determination, and make the best that can be made from it.

Intensity, the wild ride (possibly also sparks and friction) is what this person craves. They won't settle for a mediocre lifestyle, or a mundane relationship. If they don't get their excitement and kicks from you and from hanging out with you, they are likely to leave with the next charioteer, speed freak, or adrenalin junkie, who crosses their path.

As clarification: You face an inner struggle. If you do get involved this will be a difficult relationship for both of you. Each of you is head strong and wants to be in control – you will only be able to move forwards if you do it as a team. If you have different methods of obtaining your goals, or different goals, this relationship is likely to crash and burn. If you are able to work together you will accomplish a lot, but you must take turns. Learn to compromise.

If you are dissimilar, you may as well bash your head against a brick wall, you will make no progress here.

As a third party/obstacles: Arrogance and self doubt are your inner demons. That combined with the fact that you are being railroaded, is likely to be your downfall here. Delays and obfuscation will result in you losing your temper. If a person doesn't love you, throwing a tantrum about it really won't help.

Move on with your life, forge ahead with your goals. Your love interest is torn by his or her dedication to each of the people they hold dear in their lives. They are unable, or unwilling, to devote twenty four hours a day to you. Cope with it.

VIII – Strength

As the querent: You understand that not everything in life is possible. You've had to face a lot of things that have forced you to develop an inner strength and determination that helps you get through and survive. You have the courage to face whatever life throws at you, and you have had to use it a fair bit.

You know that bullying and displays of force or power only accomplish a short term gain with long-term drawbacks. You know that such behaviour breeds enemies. Because of this you use the gentle art of persuasion to get your way, and achieve the results you want most of the time. Smiling gets you further than shouting does. And making friendly acquaintance with the right people can help you go a long way.

Sometimes your pleasant, open demeanour leads people to underestimate you, but that's just how you like it – after all if they are trying to attack you, for whatever reason, you prefer to be able to blind side them with the fatal accuracy you have an instinct for that will remove them from your picture permanently. It takes a lot to rouse you to that level of action though.

As the love interest: This person has a deep inner

strength, and the courage to face whatever life throws at them. It is likely to be a courage that they have had to develop in the face of tragedy in their lives – as a response to the experiences that they have lived through. Their childhood may not have been easy.

There is a gentleness about this person, but though they may appear soft, the gentleness is born of strength not weakness. They know the lasting value of the art of persuasion and prefer it to the short term benefits of the use of force.

If you back this person into a corner you'll get to see that the mouse you thought you were faced with is actually just the tip of this tiger's tail – they had been using velvet paws with you. If they draw their claws and bare their fangs you'll be in big trouble.

Before you start to use this person, or take advantage of their pleasant nature you might want to remember the icy glint that flashed for a moment in the depths of their eyes last time you tried it on. This person knows perfectly well where your jugular and hamstrings are located.

Love them, and they'll love and nurture you. Mess with them, and you might as well be dead – you'll probably wish you were if they decide to go to town.

As the querent's Higher Self/Influences/Themes: The universe is teaching you about strength of character and the need to control your outbursts and urges – to release your pent up tensions in a positive manner. Sport could help with this.

Your life experiences will lead you to develop an inner strength and courage, and teach you the value of persuasion over threat. You will learn how to use and express conflict in a beneficial way, rather than allowing destructive impulses to have control of you.

As the love interest's Higher Self/Influences/ Themes: This person has an inner strength and gentle calm about them born from the direct knowledge of good versus evil. They have experienced much in their life that has forced them to develop a deep inner character and courage, and an understanding of the human condition that you might not realize is there until you get to know them a lot better.

The universe will tend to bring people and events into their life that requires them to respond with gentle persuasion rather than violence or anger. How they can hold their temper in the face of some of this stuff is beyond you, but if they don't the outcome will be pretty horrible.

Don't take advantage, or rile them. Once this person has had enough they have no qualms about taking direct action to remove a source of unbearable annoyance or pain from their lives. This wouldn't be good for either of you.

As the querent's link card: You are looking for someone strong and courageous in your intimate life, who can protect you from the harshness of the outside world.

You want a person who uses persuasion rather than noise or violence to get what they want.

You need a quiet, gentle home life where ructions are few and far between.

In short, you need a rock who will provide a bastion of safety for you. It's possible you even want them to fight your battles for you?

As the love interest's link card: This person is looking for someone strong and gentle who will provide a safe shoulder or breast for them to snuggle on.

They want someone persuasive and kind.

If you are the argumentative type, you are not for them. The last thing they want is all that unnecessary upset and noise.

As clarification: What you want to do – rush in – may not be what's best for you. Now is a time to control yourself, this is not a time to give in to wild urges, and for goodness sake hold your tongue.

Gentle persuasion will get you what you want, but if you try to force the issue or lose your head in any way you will come a cropper. You don't need to pretend to be someone else to make an impression. Sexual desire is on your side, just be yourself.

As a third party/obstacles: Public humiliation will follow any abuse of power that you use in order to attempt to defeat the forces ranged against you. The people involved and the situation concerned are both out of your control and stronger than you are.

Be direct and honest in your dealings. If you start throwing your weight around or act in a cowardly or underhanded manner other people will not look on you kindly.

There is a good chance that you are pursuing the wrong goals here. Walk away and take stock.

IX – The Hermit

As the querent: You need regular alone time in order to process your inner thoughts and the lessons that life has been teaching you. You trust your inner guide to lead you through the worst storms, as the times you haven't listened have resulted in situations that could have gone a lot better.

You keep a wary eye on the events surrounding you, and tend to view newcomers with some suspicion. This is because you have been taken for a ride and had negative experiences in the past. So now you exercise prudence and caution when you spot even the faintest of warning signs.

Love involves trust and opening up to another person, and you might find this difficult at first. When you find the right partner you'll know it. Listen to what your inner voice tells you, rather than interpreting what you want to hear. Remember that the past doesn't have to repeat itself, don't let old habits and patterns rule your life.

As the love interest: This person needs time to themselves to understand how they feel about life, and to get to grips with their deep inner process. They cannot be interrupted while they are doing this, so you will need to wait patiently for them to come out of their retreat. If you can't do that, this person is not for you.

They will possibly appear shy, and they are likely to feel uncomfortable in many social situations. They are at their best with a gathering of people they trust, discussing topics that are of deep and mutual interest. This person is a serious talker; not someone who is given to idle chitchat down at the pub.

As the querent's Higher Self/Influences/Themes: Life is constantly making you look at your own existence, lifestyle, choices and personal being. The main lesson it is trying to teach you is that change is a constant, and necessary for growth; and that nothing can last forever – even the granite cliffs eventually return to the sand from which they are born.

The universe provides you with opportunities to be alone after the harshest events so that you can process your feelings and thoughts and come to terms with what has been, what has happened, and what is now.

You may feel isolated much of the time. Once you find your inner light to guide you through the darkness of the void, it will become easier for you to make contact with other people on a deep and abiding level.

Nothing is created, nothing is destroyed; the chaos and order of change – yin dancing with yang – is the truth you will glimpse and come to understand during your life's journey.

<u>*As the love interest's Higher Self/Influences/Themes*</u>*:* This person's life is about change, it is the only constant for them. It is possible that this person detests change, and the flux of their life upsets them greatly. However they must come to terms with the concepts of chaos, mutability, variation, and change as part of the process of growth that each of us encounters as we pass through our lives.

The destiny of an acorn is to create an oak tree, the destiny of an oak tree is to create acorns. If an acorn doesn't grow it will never feel the wind stir its branches or track the path of the sun with its entire being.

Love and the sharing, compromise and union that love brings will be another aspect of the learning process for this person. If they love you, you can expect them to go through a process of growth, so the person you start out with may not be the person you end up with, as like a caterpillar they will metamorphose.

As the querent's link card: You are looking for someone who is happy to get on with their own thing and spend time alone while you tend to other business.

You want someone deep and thoughtful who understands that in life all things change and that the aging process brings wisdom and is nothing to fear.

You also need them to be of a watchful and cautious nature – it is possible that your career is such that you would be seriously damaged by someone who glibly opens their mouth and spills out your intimate secrets or the first thing that comes to their mind about any aspect of your lives or beliefs.

The person you love will need to be honest and realistic, with a sound head on their shoulders.

As the love interest's link card: This person is looking for someone who is a bit of hermit – happy to exist without too much intimate human contact every second of the day. They can't handle 24 hours a day, seven days a week, they need their space. It could be that their job has them travelling a lot, or requires thinking time – perhaps they are a writer or an artist, and they have a room that is a no-go area when the door is shut?

They are looking for someone with a mature attitude to life and relationships, who can take the vagaries of life in their stride; someone with a strong philosophical or religious understanding who has the inner strength to weather any storm.

They may need you to be the light in their darkness, a guide who can lead them along the right path in life, point out the pitfalls and snares, and take them to the high places where they can look out over the beautiful vistas and appreciate the good in life and the best qualities of mankind.

As clarification: Be patient. You need to spend time on your own. Once you have found your inner wisdom there will be more than enough time to return to the world of emotional bonding and physical commitment.

As a third party/obstacles: Any opposition to you making a commitment is necessary. Now is not the time to rush in. You would be making a mistake. A social life might take priority over your commitment to one person. Many partners rather than one?

Or perhaps the person who is stopping you from getting together with the person you desire has very good reasons – maybe they would be a better match for you or know someone else who would?

You would be foolish to rush in. Stand back and take a proper look around.

X – The Wheel Of Fortune

As the querent: Life: the merry-go-round. It's a rollercoaster ride and you know it. Up then down, then up again. Makes things exciting, and breeds passion. And if you can't live passionately, what's the point?

Depression is one possible down side. If you can learn to recognize that black spiral from the warning signs, you may be able to train yourself into positive behaviours and ways of thinking that stop it before it can start. Diet, exercise, and sunlight may all play a part in keeping you on an even keel. Do things that make you feel good.

Take up art, music, writing – something creative and positive that'll give you a focus for your energy. Leave your critical brain behind and just do for the sake of doing.

Karma is strongly in evidence in the workings of your life: if you give negative, you get negative; if you give positive, you get positive.

Take the ride, enjoy yourself, have fun. And if things go badly or you feel down, remind yourself that events will get better soon enough (especially if you help them along), and do things that make you feel happy. Get your positive head on.

As the love interest: This person's life seems to be up and down by turns. They could be quite fatalistic about it. They are likely to feel that fate or destiny has mapped their personality to be the way it is, and similarly draws people and events to them because of their Karma.

Cycles and rhythms are very important to them.

They may have had their bio-rhythm chart mapped. They could well be keeping track of the moon, or the astrological gyrations of the planets and the signs of the zodiac, in an attempt to find some underlying pattern or reason which guides their lives. And, chances are they may think they've found one. Either that or they'll boldly declare that life is a crap-shoot – things just happen is all.

This person may have a bi-polar disorder such as manic depression or adventurous cyclothymia – their emotions could be up and down like a yo-yo. You may think it's difficult to live with – how do you think they feel?

<u>As the querent's Higher Self/Influences/Themes</u>: What goes up must come down. What comes down must go up. Life is a cycle that keeps on turning.

Once you've picked up on the cyclic nature of events and phases in your life you may feel more secure, as this pattern at least has a recognizable form and there are certain triggers and signs that you are learning to spot for each part of the weave.

Fate and destiny definitely have their fingers plugged into your life. And you feel strongly that there is a direction and purpose to the events that mould your evolution. If only you could work out what that purpose is…Search your heart, something within you is calling, that something is linked to what you are supposed to be doing with your life in order to make the most of your current Karma and destiny.

<u>As the love interest's Higher Self/Influences/ Themes</u>: Fate has a strong part to play in this person's life, as does destiny. Chances are they realize this, and have a strong feeling of purpose or quest about their life course and choices. If not, give it time, they'll almost definitely develop this sense.

If you are trying to convert this person to your social beliefs, work ethic, or religion, probably best to forget it. This person gets enough regular proof of a guiding light, that they are likely to have a very deep and unshakable faith in whatever they deem to be "God", and will be set on their own unique path to self fulfilment.

This person will go through the same ups and

downs in life as others, but they find meaning in the process. As a result when things go wrong, they are more likely to shrug and look for the silver lining than other people who might crumble or despair. They sense the universal balance, and know events will come back to a position of benevolence and benefit soon enough, specially if they work towards it.

As the querent's link card: You spend your life searching for that perfect someone who is fated to sweep you off your feet and take you to the Eden of the Perfect Relationship. In your search you've encountered plenty of scoundrels and bounders; and several people you thought may have been normal turned out to be frogs once you kissed them. However, Karma is working in your favour, helping you get through your inner obstacles, so that when you do eventually meet that certain someone, you will have a realistic approach to what a relationship is and not be quite so upset when they fall off that slim pedestal you have tried to force them onto.

As the love interest's link card: This person may regard the quality of their relationships as being the luck of the draw – some are good, some are bad. However, what they really want is to find the person that they are destined to spend their lives with.

The mix of idealism and cynicism here provides a stark contrast between this person's desires and their experience of what desire has lead to in the past.

Helping them to find the middle road between blind idealism and cynical despair could be easier than you think, as this person is capable of being very realistic despite first appearances.

As clarification: Fate is playing a part here. You might get to control events, or you might have no control over events. Whatever happens, it will be a blessing in disguise. Karma is playing a part here, and you will find your life changing around you. Pay particular attention to your Higher Self card, it may shed some light.

As a third party/obstacles: Some things just aren't meant to be. If the universe doesn't want you to get together this time around it'll find a way of doing that. Your Higher Selves made that choice for you. Trust that your true self knows what is best for you. Being forced to walk away might be painful for you, perhaps for both of you, but you will be stronger for it, and ultimately something more rewarding will come into play at some point in your future. The way is being paved for it now. Hold on tight, things will get better.

XI – Justice

As the querent: You like to think of yourself as impartial and objective in all things. You probably like to weigh up all the facts and give everyone a fair hearing before you make any decisions. Honesty is important to you, and you know that you need to be honest with your innermost self if you are ever going to get a true view of how others see you.

You try to leave emotion out of your thought process and approach things with a fair and unbiased opinion – however, each of us has an emotional response based on past experiences and to deny that it is part of your rationale in decision-making would be to lie to yourself.

To try to apply this approach to love is probably

foolish, as love is an emotion. If you love someone you love them, and no amount of denial, or your mind telling your heart how it should feel, will change your feelings. Similarly, it would be a mistake to get involved with someone just because they are exceedingly eligible, and try to tell yourself that you will grow to love them, or that you should love them, when your heart has no intention of complying.

Relationships are about more than suitability or convenience.

As the love interest: This person may come across as quite mercenary; they approach love with a logical list of requirements, and if all the boxes get ticked they are likely to tell themselves that love will evolve within them – whether it does or not is another matter. The heart doesn't usually do what the head wants.

This person likes a balanced and objective approach to life and emotion, where decisions can be based on fact and logic and the correct decisions and responses made as a result of the unquestionable evidence. When life refuses to be tied down like that and things become messy and emotional, they may just try to close their eyes and look away – but life has a way of forcing the issues. As they value honesty they will eventually make themselves look, assess the situation and find a way forward.

Once they make a decision it is usually irrevocable, because they will have taken into account all the necessary information already. You won't change their mind unless you can show them a new piece of the jigsaw that they missed during their initial assessment.

<u>As the querent's Higher Self/Influences/Themes</u>: Perhaps you come from a legal background, or perhaps you are intimately involved with the law yourself? Somehow, though, justice is going to play an important part in your life over and over again.

There is a possible tendency here to see the world as black or white – without any of the shades of grey that dominate our lives. You know what's right, you know what's wrong – and that is how you see the world around you. It's a very 'us versus them' position to take.

Life can seem very unfair a lot of the time. The random chaos, tragedy and obstacles of our world do not usually depend upon justice to declare them necessary; they just happen.

It's how we cope with the injustices that happen to us that shows character; what we take from each experience, and use as we go forwards in our lives.

The more information we have, the better informed we are, the less likely we are to jump to erroneous conclusions. If you are going to take the position of judge over the activities of your friends and neighbours, then it is essential that you learn the full facts, before you announce your conclusions. Better yet, quit judging everyone – it takes away from the real process, which is to learn how to live well.

<u>As the love interest's Higher Self/Influences/Themes</u>: What you give is what you get.

This person is learning about the effects of Karma. The universe as well as their Higher Self is trying to teach them about justice in all its forms.

Being able to view people, events, the world from an unbiased perspective is the goal here. If this can be done, then fair decisions can be taken about how to respond. Weighing up the pros and cons becomes important.

This person may approach relationships the same way, determining the pros and cons before getting involved. As long as that original balance is maintained they are happy to abide by their initial decision. But life doesn't work like that. As people live together more evidence becomes available as to who the other person is and how well you interact with each other. Every new fact will alter the balance and thus affect their ongoing decision-making process.

This person wants life to be fair, they want rewards to be earned, and they want indiscretions to be punished. They are also likely to be tireless in the quest to uncover "the truth", so if you have any skeletons in the closet you'll get the best response from them if you are up front about it right from the start.

As the querent's link card: You are looking for someone with a level head and a keen mind, who will always be discrete, and can be counted on to take your views into account before making any decisions or taking any action that will affect you.

You probably don't like surprises. You hate to be treated unfairly. You need a balance between your social life, your home life, and your work life, and you want the person you are with to have the same outlook; giving the same level of commitment to everything they undertake.

You also want the person you love to be able to provide an unbiased and fair opinion, with rational arguments for and against, to help you decide how you really feel or think about things. Someone whose judgment you can trust in all things.

As the love interest's link card: This person is looking for equality and fair play in a relationship, and they will give the same in return.

This person's life is all about balance: reward based on merit, punishment based on guilt, and keep the status quo whenever possible.

This person probably has a first class analytical ability, and precise methods for determining the facts and details that they need in order to make their decisions.

This person will consider everyone's needs before taking any action that will affect them.

If you hurt this person by being unfaithful, they are the type of person who will calmly assess exactly how much pain they are feeling and then set about inflicting the same on you. Expect to get your wardrobe slashed, your car spray painted, and your love nest demolished. If they can justify it to themselves, they'll probably do it.

What goes around comes around. You've been warned.

As clarification: The decision as to whether to commit to another person can only be solved with logic and reason, not emotion and intuition – that alone should tell you everything you need to know. If the decision is not based on emotion, then I have to ask, "What on earth do you think you are doing?" – Is what you are doing right or wrong? If it's right, you might decide to go for it. It could be for the best, but be sure you know what you are getting into. For justice to be done, you have to have access to all the relevant information before you reach your verdict.

Positive Karma. A relationship or marriage that will stand the test of time.

If this relationship is an arranged marriage, and you are happy with that, then this card bodes very well for the future. It should be a happy and prosperous union, which you both find rewarding.

As a third party/obstacles: The person you are going up against is not someone to tangle with. They hold all the cards, they make all the decisions, and if they set out to damage you they will do you serious harm: physically, socially, emotionally, even mentally – whichever field they choose to contest in. Perhaps all of them.

Anyone you take into your confidence to help your cause is likely to betray you either by accident, on purpose, or because they have their own goals and you've just played right into their hands.

If I was you I'd retire from the field before this mess gets any worse. You will lose.

XII – The Hanged Man

As the querent: You are always searching for the truth of a thing, the hidden essence that other people have missed. Interestingly you seem to osmose some of the deepest truths from other peoples' fears, lies, and fantasies.

Love is the greatest fantasy, and the greatest truth of all. And you understand it far better than most people think, because you *know* it through experience which means that you are also far more realistic about romantic love than many people would think. You understand the lie and yet you search for the ideal.

You know of the hard work involved in a lifetime commitment, but you also grasp the rewards possible from such a work.

When you find what you think you want, you tend to bind yourself to it totally – to experience every last scrap of it. The problem with this approach is that many people either find it overly intrusive, or just plain overpowering.

In a relationship the other person frequently needs enough space to be able to breath. Try to let them have some free time to do their own exploring. You'd hate it if you were chained to a rock in a barren cave and were not allowed out to paddle in the waves and play games with the wind (Well, after the first century or two at any rate, once you'd thoroughly wrung every last drop of experience and information from your surroundings).

You love a good mystery, and that's what other people are – usually to themselves as well.

As the love interest: Guardian of the gateway to the otherworld; this person is going to have some unusual beliefs, and even stranger tastes. What initially attracts you about them might be what drives you away in the long run. And it will be difficult to escape, because the bonds are strong.

This person is wrapped up in their own world. Enraptured by the very strangeness of their own existence. But, if this Black Narcissus deigns to notice you, you'll find yourself on the edge of a precipice looking out over a landscape as alien as the bottom of the sea. Prepare to have your mind opened; just check they haven't got a crowbar behind their back before you get too close.

This person could be lost in a world of drugs and addiction. If so, keep away from them. They will do more damage to you than to themselves. You aren't helping if you support their self-delusion, you'll only get caught in their web of self-destruction.

Magnetic, deep, hypnotic, and a raging storm when crossed. If they want to make you suffer, they know how.

As the querent's Higher Self/Influences/Themes: Most people can't even begin to understand how you cope with the stuff life throws at you. That will probably go for your lover too; so don't expect him or her to understand. They'll try if you explain, but chances are they'll end up confused – or worried about you. All you really need is someone to hold you in their arms and keep you safe until the next upheaval you have to deal with.

Sometimes life is easy, other times it throws everything it's got at you – including the kitchen sink. Things seem to work out well for you in the end though. And however bad life gets, you always learn something about yourself, which puts you ahead of the game.

Fantasy has the potential to become reality; love is what you make it – as long as neither party is fooling themselves. Check the love interest's cards carefully – they may not be viewing the querent with a clear eye. If they are deceiving themselves the relationship will eventually fail, causing the querent serious trauma.

As the love interest's Higher Self/Influences/Themes: They have a strange view of the world. An odd fish this one, driven by the tides – seemingly rudderless, and yet able to steer a course through the worst weather. This person will never give in to threats or blackmail; such things are meaningless to them. Life or death, that's all there is – and the contemplation of both that is only possible from the middle way, or knife edge. Seems to live in a dream most of the time – except when they look directly at you with those disturbing, magnetic eyes.

They know more about nightmares than you could ever understand. Don't even try.

Their life will be strange and eventful, constantly changing. But they live in the calm at the centre of the whirlpool, it all seems normal to them.

As the querent's link card: It looks like you have found what you need, at long last. Problem is, if they don't reciprocate you are just fooling yourself, yet again. There are plenty of other people out there who can make you feel the same way, and perhaps you should hold out for one of them?

If this person genuinely does love you then bliss is yours. And the heartache and tragedy that goes with bliss. How can you really appreciate one without the other? There is a middle way in this relationship, as long as the two of you keep talking. If you rely on emotion to communicate all your hopes and dreams you are going to wind up very disappointed. They are not psychic you know, you have to tell them what you want, what you need.

They may find you a little strange, but that's because you are unique. They will accommodate your wishes if they can. If not, then try to understand that the reason they can't give you the world is because they don't know what it looks like. Not everyone does. It's not because they hate you. Describe it to them, maybe they'll come up with something better? And if they don't, maybe you should set about getting it for yourself? They can't do everything for you. Breathing, for example, is down to you.

As the love interest's link card: Oooh, you lucky person, you are exactly what they need, and they probably know it. Doesn't mean it's going to be easy, they may hate you as much as they love you. But you are good for them and they won't be able to keep away. Bodes well for an affair. Perhaps even for a marriage – as long as you can cope with that depth of commitment...They are going to bind themselves to you, it could get messy and claustrophobic. They really need the stability of a solid emotional bond, if you are able and willing to give it you will both prosper.

As clarification: An uncomfortable union upon occasion, but extremely rewarding. Both parties will have as much to give as they get from the other person. And both will end up wiser and happier for it. Recommended.

As long as you remember to make up in the special way that they adore (they will do the same for you), this relationship can definitely last the distance. Take turns. And try to keep the discussion *healthy*. If either of you set out to hurt the other person the results are your own fault, you both know better.

As a third party/obstacles: This person is going to be a magnetic draw for the person they are attached to, however far apart the two of them are.

If this person does decide to do battle in order to retain the loved one, they are likely to resort to deceit and illusion, using the other person's emotions as their trump card.

They may appear to have accepted defeat and swum away to greener pastures, but chances are they'll return as the eye of the hurricane, at any time. Expect storms – and strange looks from other people who have listened to the lies.

Could be more trouble than it's worth.

And that emotional trump card they'll use, it's usually a winner. You're likely to be the one that gets strung up.

XIII – Death

As the querent: You understand the cycle of change: for something new to evolve, something old and outdated must pass.

Everything has its time, its moment.

Your life is about your constant quest for something new, and the process of rebirth. It's not just a case of changing your name as frequently as you change your socks, it's about a deep inner process of evolution which forces you into new situations and environments. You choose to take the path that will bring change into your life.

Your job may involve constant travel, and changes to where you live. Or perhaps you are the type of person who likes to experience as much of the world as they can, so you change your job on a regular basis.

Evolution is the only thing that really matters to you.

Life with one person may not hold any appeal for

you; unless they are a human chameleon, or someone whose company brings constant and radical change to your life?

Alternatively, you may work in a field that relates closely to change: such as real estate, or head hunting.

As one of the meanings of the card is death, I wouldn't be at all surprised if you worked or lived in close association with the grim reaper. So perhaps you work with death: as an undertaker, or in an area such as forensics, or crime fiction? Perhaps your ideal house is a converted church with its own cemetery?

Somehow death, or the afterlife, may play a big part in your life.

<u>*As the love interest*</u>: This person loves change, they force it upon themselves. They may subconsciously bring it into their life, even if they consciously say it's the last thing they want.

Their life is a cycle of evolution and rebirth, they revel in change. They are like a butterfly, and may alter in front of your eyes into someone you never even suspected they could become.

It is likely that this person will move house, or change jobs, or join new activities and social groups more frequently than anyone else you've ever met. And the same could well be true of their love life.

This person may be an enigma to their friends.

One aspect of this card is death, so it is possible that this person might be a Plague Mary: if this person is exceedingly active sexually, you may want to ensure that you take full precautions before engaging with them, as they may have a contagious and potentially life threatening disease? Or they may not. But I would suggest taking precautions.

It is possible that this person works, or lives, closely with death – perhaps they are a grief counsellor, or a morgue attendant. Or more unnerving, they could be fixated on death: vampirism, suicide, murder, necrophilia, etc – or perhaps they earn a living writing about it?

<u>As the querent's Higher Self/Influences/Themes</u>: You will evolve into a more truthful expression of your inner being, whether you want to or not. Life and your Higher Self don't give you a choice. Life's lessons will get harder and harder until you are forced to examine your motives, actions and reactions at the deepest level of your psyche.

Change surrounds you, and death is likely to be a big influence on your life throughout this relationship. Perhaps your partner works with death, maybe you do? Somehow it will be a feature.

Changes are going to be unstoppable, and will sweep you up into a new way of living and thinking. These changes may be painful when they occur, but they will be for the better in the long run. If you do try to prevent such evolution, the stagnation and feeling of being trapped in a rut will get to a point when they are no longer bearable, and you will have to change anyway – and the process is likely to hurt more the longer you delay.

Change can be difficult. Instead of taking it on the chin, roll with the punches. Adapt and survive.

<u>As the love interest's Higher Self/Influences/Themes</u>: Change surrounds this person, and it is possible that death might too – perhaps they are a psychic?

Nothing is set when this person is involved: life forces change upon them as much as they force it upon themselves.

Fate seems to have an interest in this person's life, and the demands placed upon them may be both unexpected and painful. Ultimately the result is rebirth, growth, and enlightenment. But at the time the changes are taking place the results may not seem worth it.

Fighting the process of evolution can result in a lot of distress; once the mechanics of change are understood, and worked with, life will be a lot easier for this person to handle on an emotional and physical level. For example, if you know you are going to be moving house every six months you can plan your lifestyle accordingly.

As the querent's link card: Love is about a radical change in your focus. What's important and how you view things alters utterly.

The person you love, just by the act of existence, will show you something deep and truthful about the highest expression of self – which you realize that you are able to attain as well. An "enlightenment" will be forced upon you because of their presence.

The person you need is someone who will have a dramatic effect on your approach to life, even the way you live your daily life. This person will break down anything limiting that imposes restraints on your being, and teach you that change can come from within as well as from outside.

Love for you is a process of birthing, and birth is painful and scary, and liberating. It will lead you to a new and more meaningful life, probably in new surroundings.

As the love interest's link card: This person needs some radical changes in their life – and they need it at the deepest level. They want someone who can guide them in the methods and process of change.

They need someone who can help open their eyes to the beauty of the universe, and alter their experience of life at a level they had never before glimpsed or suspected.

In short they need a rebirth, and that rebirth needs to occur as an effect of love and loving relationships.

Perhaps your job requires frequent changes of residence? Perhaps you constantly crave new experiences and new life choices? Somehow your way of living will radically affect their way of living.

The process of change required will be painful and sudden, but ultimately it will prove deeply rewarding, as it will force your lover into a more truthful experience of life in all its vagary.

As clarification: This relationship will have a profound impact on both your lives. Good or bad depends on how you view yourself and the world around you. It will lead to necessary growth, although this will probably be painful for you, and if you fear change it may be extremely distressing. Your lives are changing on a deep level and nothing will ever be the same. Loss of some kind is likely to be linked to your union.

As a third party/obstacles: Events are likely to prevent the two of you being together. Sweeping changes – a move to another place, a job that makes the relation-ship impossible or even a death could be the cause of the split.

If you are prepared to totally change your location, way of life, your attitude towards what a relationship is, then it is possible that you might end up with the other person, and stronger for it. But in all honesty, it is extremely unlikely the relationship would survive the events – in whatever form they come. It is likely to be very painful for you. In time you'll heal. Seek comfort in your friends.

XIV – Temperance

As the querent: Moderation in all things is a saying you may live your life by. You feel that as long as you maintain your balance and your inner calm you can find happiness and success inside yourself and outside yourself. At some point in your life you are likely to feel as though you have become a bridge between the realms of heaven and earth. You will probably feel the presence of a guardian angel or guardian spirit in your life. This feeling of being looked after is very comforting to you.

You are good at finding the middle ground in any argument, and make a good diplomat because you can see the viewpoint of each side and know what words or language to use to bring them together.

You enjoy cooperation and sharing, and you value your emotional relationships.

The interactions between people and the blending of thoughts and feelings that occurs between them is something that fascinates you and calls to you. You love to be at the centre of this dynamic, watching all sides, keeping the balance. Acting as ferryman and gatekeeper.

Your life is about people and about being with people. It is also about mediation, moderation and bridge building: restraining excesses and finding the best balance.

As the love interest: If there is a group of people, you will find this person at the centre absorbing the emotions, words and actions of the people around them like a sponge. If there is an argument, this person will be a mediator, trying to calm both sides and get the core issues resolved.

This person is almost a bridge between worlds: they will bring together the different sides and help them convey information, opinions, and feelings to one another. Whether this is in the physical world as a relationship guidance counsellor or politician; or acting as a medium allowing contact between the world of spirit and the world of man; or a dream interpreter who brings the subconscious into the realms of the conscious, whatever the case, this person will be the central point of union where the two sides meet and merge.

This person probably understands excess very well, they have had to go through some experience of it in order to be able to have gained such a deep understanding of the need for moderation and restraint.

This person has an inner light that guides them, and a sense of security and confidence about themselves that many people spend their whole lives searching for. This can be quite magnetic and make them appealing for others to be with and be around. It's also likely to attract a fair number of loons.

The sense of an inner light and a connectedness to

the other realms, may lead this person to take on a spiritual life, helping others to find their way to God or to their life path.

As the querent's Higher Self/Influences/Themes: A peaceful life. The universe provides you with opportunities to share your emotions with others, as it is only through the process of sharing that you can avoid stagnation and irrelevance. If your life feels as though it is stuck or halted somehow, then you need to check whether this relationship of sharing is being practised by you in your social and personal life – if not then you will need to take steps to realign yourself with this inner driving force.

Your purpose in life is to be a conduit for divine intelligence, and positive emotion. Your role is to be a bridge between two or more sides – conveying what they need for peace, prosperity and growth between them. They are too divided and too close to see this for themselves.

Your goal is to find contentment in being. The key to this lies in remaining balanced, the pivot point should be maintained, you are the axis upon which and from which all else descends.

You may want to take the life of a hermit for a while as you investigate your inner truth, however your inner truth can only shine brightest amongst others – you can only teach when you come down off the mountain and dwell in the valley.

As the love interest's Higher Self/Influences/Themes: Serenity is a part of this person's being at a deep level.

They are a people person, and thrive on negotiating

with others.

They need to share their emotions on a regular basis, and will expect you to be open and encouraging of this process. Such communication is a foundation stone for any intimate or close relationship so this need in them is a very positive thing which you should both desire. If this person does not talk about, or physically express, their feelings it is unhealthy for them.

And they will also appreciate a quiet cuddle on the sofa where nothing is required or wanted…just to be in each other's company.

This person could be a guidance counsellor, a medium, a negotiator, a politician, a translator – basically they are likely to be in a profession that facilitates communication and sharing between different peoples.

Their life experiences will teach them that moderation, negotiation and sharing are the keys to personal satisfaction and contentment. If they have not learnt this lesson yet, then conflict could well be a major part of their current environment.

As the querent's link card: You need someone who will share their feelings with you, and who takes a moderate, reconciliatory and negotiator's role in any conflict that occurs in your personal life. They will be your voice of reason and calm.

You desire a relationship where the other person makes you feel safe and looked after. And you want your home life to be quiet and serene, a place of nurture and contentment – free from the excesses and conflicts of daily life at work or in society.

You want your lover to be your buttress,

supporting you and protecting you – sharing the weight of your load.

As the love interest's link card: This person needs a calm and happy home life, where quiet contentment is the norm.

They are looking for a relationship where emotions are shared, and living together is a process of merging and unification.

Communication is very important to them, and they are looking for someone who can help to negotiate or translate for them in their interactions with the outside world.

They are looking for someone who is happy to take on the role of protector and emotional supporter. Who can act as a filter between them and the harshest aspects of life.

It is likely that this person is either very receptive or utterly stressed out, either way, the effect will be to make them in need of a quiet life and protected environment at home. More so than most people.

If you are an argumentative type, or someone whose natural disposition does not lend itself to calm and a gentle appreciation of the one you love, then there is a very good chance that this person is not for you – or rather, you are not for them.

As clarification: This will be a good relationship as long as you treat each other as equals. Discuss your feelings, and share your thoughts, spend 'special' time with one another, otherwise you risk allowing stagnation to stifle a good union. Moderation is a better course than wild abandon – meet each other half way.

As a third party/obstacles: The affair with this other person is needed by your love interest. The other person provides them with something that you cannot. If you try to take this out of their lives, they may go to someone else who will cause real damage to your relationship. If you try to get revenge you will only damage yourself and your cause. What ever actions you decide to take, it would be wise to pause and think through every possible angle before you do anything.

Perhaps it is a hobby, a job, or religion that takes up your love interests thoughts and time. Whatever it is, it helps them find their calm centre and is important to them. Jealousy or envy will not help you get what you want, or to reach a compromise.

XV – The Devil

As the querent: If you spend your life repressing your needs or living with oppression, there comes a time when the process of liberation can no longer be stopped. The harder you squash something down, the more violently it will erupt when it does go. Think of a volcano: when it is plugged up tight, the pressure builds, until at last the very rock can't resist, and the mountain blows its top, the pyroclastic flow devastates everything; but when a volcano is free to spew, the lava flows slowly – sure it eats up whatever is in its path, but it's relatively easy to get out of its way. Lava doesn't travel at 300 miles an hour.

Emotions are the same. If you let them out freely as they come they are nowhere near as damaging as a feeling that has been squashed and battered for decades that finally finds release in an overwhelming torrent.

Your life is about the need for freedom, for liberty,

for escape. Fear and sloth are really the only things that hold us back. Examining your inner process, your real desires, will help you to identify and remove your inhibitions. Look with a clear eye upon your inner demons, and then release them. They only remain a demon as long as they are shackled. Forgiven and raised high into the light, they can be transformed back into the angels they once were.

Find a healthy way to express yourself and your desires. You must keep your obligations in perspective – we all need some time out occasionally even from ourselves.

As the love interest: This could be a really interesting relationship; it depends on how this card is in aspect.

This person will either be a liberator or an oppressor. They are a powerful person who has a strong effect on the people around them, whether those people realize it or not.

This person tends to ask disturbing questions, or show disturbing traits, that cause others to think about what it means to shackle themselves to the grindstone of life, as opposed to using their minds and their personal driving force to liberate themselves and go their own way.

Difficult to live with? Perhaps. But someone whose gifts are bounteous, though frequently misinterpreted by others.

As the querent's Higher Self/Influences/Themes: Life is constantly testing you, your strength and your moral fortitude. Your inner self and the outer world are constantly presenting you with the issues of oppression and freedom. If you live under the yoke, and yearn to be free then you are on the cusp of learning what you need to learn in order to be successful and happy within yourself. Release your fears, never surrender to the paralysis of doubt or anxiety, and you will be able to forge ahead and create the life you know you were born to live.

Being honest with yourself about your motivation, core emotions and inner drive is vital while this card remains at the centre of your soul. Life is about liberation from the forces that oppress us, whether they come from within or without. And your lesson is to face your fear.

Anytime you feel disquiet, remember that that feeling is there to remind you to seek your own path, your own truth – not that which society presents as truth.

<u>As the love interest's Higher Self/Influences/ Themes</u>: This person seems to be all about tearing down the walls, and when they aren't doing that, life is doing it for them – or forcing them into situations where they have no choice but to face their fears and overcome them.

Liberation versus slavery is the life lesson the universe is teaching them, and until they can be their own person, standing on their own two feet, doing what they want to do – rather than what someone else has told them they should do – they will not be happy. This is not someone who will be able to go quietly to their grave, they are a liberator and reformer and the universe will ensure that they have to take up their destiny if they ever wish to find inner peace.

This person could be the prison warden, or the

prisoner – but somewhere along life's journey they will have the misfortune to experience both of these states of mind. Life will change them, make them a light bearer, force them to a greater understanding of both the light and the dark in the heart of each of us. And through those experiences they will become an agent of transformation themselves.

Their experience will be unique, and they can be an uneasy and difficult person to hang out with as a result.

As the querent's link card: Tie me up, tie me down.

What is it that you really want from a relationship? To find yourself, the real you.

Now either you know this, and you are looking for a liberal and free spirit to share your life with; or, you don't know this, you think I'm talking rubbish, and all you desire is someone who enjoys bondage. Kitchen sink or bedroom?

Do you want to be the slave, or do you want to be the master? This is the crux of your relationship issues.

Freedom to love, and be loved freely in return. If someone is playing a part rather than being themselves, then ultimately you will be unhappy. You would be better off with someone who is not willing to compromise – even if theirs isn't a quiet life, at least it's honest.

As the love interest's link card: This person is looking for someone independent and real, a free spirit and liberator. Someone who has the guts to stand up and go their own way, run their own show.

If you are a corporate lackey who is content with

the status quo and following the rules, taking the orders from higher up, to have someone else as your paymaster – if you are content to live your life this way, then you are not the firebrand of salvation that your love interest is looking for. You have to be able to shake off your assumptions, fight for your rights as a person, be the black sheep or the individual in any crowd if you want to gain the respect of the person you admire. They expect you to be as free as they are. And if they are not currently free, then they expect you to be the path finder who'll help them break out on their own adventure.

No one said love was easy. Fear and repression are anathema to love.

As clarification: Why do you want to chain yourself to a situation that is untenable? Any limitations or restrictions that you think are forcing you into this relationship only exist because you allow them to exist. You need to follow your own path, not one that has been arranged for you by other people. Walk away. Your personal happiness is more important than what other people say is the right thing to do, so leave.

As a third party/obstacles: This person will tie you up in knots. They have your love interest ham-strung and believing every word they say.

Perhaps your lover feels the bonds of matrimony, parenthood, and/or religion are too important and too strong, and puts those things ahead of their own personal welfare and happiness. It may be impossible for you to get them to change their mind.

XVI – The Tower

As the querent: Your life involves one upheaval followed by another – and for some people you are a raging force of anathema that they just can't cope with. The person you are currently interested in is one of them. He or she will get a lot of pain and despair from their contact with you. If you are toying with the idea of an affair, please consider their feelings before you recklessly step in and create havoc in their life.

If everything about the relationship seems to be fine, and this card makes no sense, then it is possible that in the future you will grow bored or disillusioned and leave, totally destroying the other person in the process.

There is no need to be vindictive or nasty during a break up, have a care.

If the other cards bode well, then it is possible that you are a life lesson waiting to happen to the person you have feelings for. I'm not saying don't get together, I'm just saying consider what you are doing and how you are doing it very carefully. Your life is one big drama. Try to be more moderate in your outlook and approach.

As the love interest: Forget it. This person will bring pain and destruction. It's a job for the Samaritans. The person is possibly even insane. Run. And don't look back.

As the querent's Higher Self/Influences/Themes: "The school of hard knocks" – you probably invented the term. When you are with this person life starts going wrong, more so than normal. They seem to be a bad influence on your peace of mind. They snarl up your Karma something rotten: lots of unfinished business.

Events are disruptive, emotionally hard going, possibly even devastating – for both of you – mainly because of the dramas that are taking place in your life.

If you can cope with the storms, then this relationship has the potential to leave you stronger, wiser and more compassionate. It could be the most rewarding thing you have ever done – in retrospect. Certainly a time of growth. But painful growth that you are not emotionally prepared for.

If Death is the other person's personal card, then maybe you hooked up with them too late? There are sweeping changes going on in their life that will tear you apart as a couple even if you are perfect for each other in all other respects.

If the other cards are favourable you might consider this union, even a marriage, but it won't be a cake walk. You've been warned.

As the love interest's Higher Self/Influences/Themes: It won't be an easy life together. Everything that can go wrong for this person, will. A string of disasters courts them, and will be emotionally devastating, or at the very least exhausting and debilitating. Sometimes they even seem to take joy in bringing disaster down on themselves.

The clarification card (and the link cards) will show whether you should consider embarking on this relationship. It will be very difficult for you, as you will need to support the person through their trauma.

However, the relationship could be an outstandingly rewarding experience for both of you –

but I'd think twice about any kind of commitment unless most of the other cards screamed "YES!"

As the querent's link card: Oh boy. This person is everything you detest. They are anathema to you. Why are you even considering this relationship?

Unless of course pain and destruction is everything you want in life – in which case this person can devastate you as no other. Enjoy your misery.

They will destroy your self-confidence and your self-image. This is not someone to spend time with, however much everyone else tells you that your new beau is perfect. They are wrong.

Leave now – this is one time to let the consequences go to hell. Seriously.

As the love interest's link card: For some reason this person is looking for destructive experiences in their life. If you want to be Kali to their sacrificial lamb, then please, remember some things are illegal for a very good reason. Either tone it down, or walk away. You are likely to get into serious trouble here, and this person will egg you on.

Alternatively, if you want to drive someone to anorexia (or some other potentially fatal condition) with your shallow carping, this person will believe everything you say. Stop being so horrid to them and get a life.

Nastiness, obsession, dominance, bullying, and over-bearing power plays have nothing to do with love. You are fooling yourself and hurting them.

As clarification: Avoid this relationship. Neither of you will benefit or prosper.

As a third party/obstacles: This other person is a third party you don't want to tangle with. They won't rest until you have been obliterated utterly. You will lose. Walk away.

XVII – The Star

As the querent: You are someone who walks the path of hope. Every mountain you climb leads you to new horizons which can lead to a brighter future. Every new vista holds its treasures – its secret Eden waiting to be discovered.

Life inspires you to keep going, there's just something so rewarding about living – life is about enjoyment and you are amazed that more people don't see the wonders around them and within them.

You are open to everything in an attempt to make your life a richer place. You don't hold back with your emotions, and you say it as you see it.

For you life is a constant process of renewal and rejuvenation. You are inspired and inspiring. Your hope draws you ever onwards to explore the boundaries of what is possible.

Sadly there are a lot of negative people in the world who never look to the horizon to see what might be, they couldn't even begin to imagine half of what's out there. They spend their time shuffling about, looking at their feet.

If you fall for the trap of believing them when they say "it can't be done" or "it must be done this way" you will stifle your own process and delay your evolution. If they want to spend their lives in a six foot hole, leave them to it. You have better things to be doing, like living and having fun.

As the love interest: This person inspires you. There is something about what they do, who they are, that just captivates you. They are passionate, hopeful, and open in all things – so much positive energy in one person. These traits that they have inspire the same traits in you. Being around them is a cleansing experience for you; they are a breath of fresh air enlivening your soul.

Whether you get to be with this person or not, having met them has taught you a lot about your own potential and how you can be in your life. They have guided you to see that place in yourself where you are capable of tuning in to the universal energy of life.

Perhaps for the first time, you are learning to see with the eyes of a child, the eyes of the heart.

Honesty and a positive attitude are important to this person. They greet life with open arms and an open heart, and they like it when those around them can do the same. Being around negative people has a tendency to squash their spark – and because they give of themselves freely and without limitation, they can become drained and debilitated if they do not remove themselves from such influences.

As the querent's Higher Self/Influences/Themes: Your life is about hope, about the energy of rejuvenation that allows all things to develop and grow, to stretch out and find their place in the world.

The world offers you the chance to go your own way, and find your own goals and inner drives. Such a journey can be challenging, at times scary or painful, but it is also very rewarding and worth any personal sacrifice needed to get where you have to go.

While you may feel strongly that the grass is

greener elsewhere, you also need to consider that from constant effort in one area real growth and achievement can be attained if you put in the time and effort, and have the vision and patience to see it through. Anything that is really worth doing will take about ten years to get to a level of maturity and skill where rewards can be reaped. If you plant an apple seed, do you expect a tree to burst forth and start bearing fruit immediately? It takes time and careful tending.

Spring is likely to be your favourite time of year, when you are most energized. All that life force bursting forth, bringing new growth in the early sun.

People work to different patterns; if you find yourself always coming up with ideas and starting projects, but never seeing them through, then either you need to find a finisher who shares your dreams, or you need to learn about stamina and commitment – harness your passion: learn how to renew it so that each phase of a project, each new day, has the same hope and open hearted desire that the first day held.

<u>As the love interest's Higher Self/Influences/Themes</u>: This person does not hold back, they don't know how. Both their inner being and the outer world is driving them to give their all – and this person can achieve a lot.

Maintaining their hope and levels of energy is going to be a lesson for them. Just as the earth moves in cycles, waking in the spring, sleeping during winter, this person also has an energy cycle and once they have learned to accept that and use it properly you'll start to see results from their ideas and work.

Constant giving can take its toll, especially if the

people around them do nothing but take. This person's optimism and belief in the good in everyone can lead them to hang out with those who would take advantage of them. If you are one of those selfish types, someone who thinks they are in love but does not love enough to put the other person's needs ahead of their own desires and wants then be warned – this person will not be walked on for ever. There comes a point when they have nothing more to give and they have to replenish their heart. When that time comes they'll leave.

Real love is about giving and nurturing. In its absence only a barren wasteland can exist. They know about love. Do you?

As the querent's link card: You are looking for hope and inspiration from your partner. You want an open and loving relationship where each of you accept the other for who they are – and not some so called social standard of who you should be, or how you should relate.

You don't have the time to waste on social neuroses or old fashioned notions such as etiquette; you want to be out there exploring new activities and horizons with the one you love.

You are looking for someone optimistic and encouraging, who appreciates life and explores all the options. You want them to help you find rejuvenation and inspiration, and to renew your hope and faith in mankind.

As the love interest's link card: This person needs a positive, bouncy, inspirational, hope-filled person in their lives. They want someone who can look to the distant horizon and see the possibilities that lie out there beyond the average social scope of things.

You want an adventurer who will set out with you to conquer the next goal, and make the journey fun.

You've had your fill of negative people who stay within normal social bounds, stuck in the rut of their job, their home, their negative friends, with their mantra of "It can't be done. Stay with the crowd. Vilify anything or anyone who doesn't comply with the norm." It's time to leave them behind and find a new life experience filled with hope, fun, and real potential.

If you are the type of person who likes safety and to conform, and to comply, then you probably won't be happy with this person. They are looking for someone a little more outlandish than that, and their behaviour is unlikely to meet with your approval. They do not know their place, and if they did, they would rebel against it.

As clarification: A new romance, openness, hope. This relationship will provide inspiration and a feeling of security for you both. Things may get difficult at times, but that's the cyclic nature of life. Problems will be solved. Your prospects will improve.

As a third party/obstacles: This person represents hope to the one you love. Hope is something that we all need, and hope is something that it is soul destroying to fight against.

Do you really want to be part of a love triangle? You won't be able to sway your love interest in their desires. Their heart is set on someone else.

Do yourself a favour and walk away. You won't be

happy here.

XVIII – The Moon

As the querent: You can never take anything or anyone for granted, and you certainly hate it when anyone does the same to you. You are also likely to dislike it when people try to pin you down to anything concrete such as a time, a place, a promise. You have your own way of doing things: one place is as good as another; you have your own way of measuring time; and as for promises, you'll honour the intention if not the fact – that's what promises are about after all, the underlying truth of what is required.

Like the sea you have your own tides of emotion and energy. Water is important in your life; its reflective depths mirror your own inner process – you can hold much yet reveal little, reflecting back what is cast at you, or you can be clear as crystal with you inner thoughts on full display.

The moon reflects the light of the sun, and can thus shine more kindly – concealing flaws and revealing beauty – or its play of light and shadow can reveal the disturbing creatures of dream and shadow that haunt the night forest of the subconscious, bringing forth our fears and phobias, playing on uncertainty. A trickster and two edged sword. You are capable of sharing these moonly qualities when you choose.

The subconscious and dreams are places you like to explore, and can tell you much more than conscious rational thought about the inner workings of the mind and emotion.

You want to be loved and looked after, surrounded and engulfed by the emotion of it, and yet you are not likely to be a constant lover. Whether because you are trying to find satisfaction in too many arms, or whether because you are so wrapped up in your inner processes and communicating at the deepest level, that you do not notice that the other person needs more than shadows and telepathy from their other half in their relationships.

<u>As the love interest</u>: This is not the most stable person, emotionally they are likely to be all over the place much of the time. They rely on their feelings and desires to guide them through life, so trying to apply logic to what they say and do may not work.

They dwell in the world of the subconscious and dream, emotion and psyche.

This person has a fantastic imagination, and the power to make their thoughts take the form of concrete reality. Art, music and literature are natural fields for this person, or indeed any activity that they can feel their way through as opposed to applying plain old dry logic.

Any time this person makes a quick decision, it is likely to have been rushed because they want to get away from feeling pressured, or uncertain and paranoid. This person needs to take their time to feel their way through any decision, all the facts are never available to them up front so their longer process means that they can gather all the evidence they need before committing. If you rush them and things go wrong as a result, that's your fault. If you want a quick decision make it yourself, and then explain your motivation for your plans to them – chances are they'll be perfectly happy, or come up with an imaginative alternative that would never have crossed your mind.

<u>As the querent's Higher Self/Influences/Themes</u>: The pull of the lunar tides flows through you. The draw of the sea may be strong in you, or perhaps you live near water. Alternatively the tides could be those of the subconscious and emotion. Perhaps even the psychic or occult ebb and flow has you in its grasp. Whichever of the lunar forces it is that moulds your life and shapes your destiny, it will be stronger while you are in contact with the person you are enquiring about.

I would not be surprised if paranormal or occult phenomena have a strong impact on your life currently. Dreams and omens are everywhere in your life.

Do not make any quick decisions, nothing is as it seems at first glance when this card is influencing your life on the higher and lower levels – as it is here. Take your time and develop a feel for the situation before you even consider opening your mouth to comment or commit. There are more facts here that are not apparent at the moment and you need to know them before you proceed.

Life has a quality of mystery and glamour about it that while fun can be deceiving. Follow your feelings and your gut instincts, and you should steer a straight course to your goals. Trust your inner light, not the outer shining.

<u>As the love interest's Higher Self/Influences/Themes</u>: This person's life can be utterly unfathomable at times. There are hidden things taking effect and guiding events, and you may never discover the truth of it.

It is possible that the life they live out in the open is

not the life they lead behind closed doors. They are likely to keep one aspect (or more) of their lives totally separate from other aspects of their lives. This is a person who keeps secrets.

This person's lifestyle, job, friends, mental state goals and dreams are directly opposed to allowing them to make a committed, and long-term relationship. They will not be able to be with you. They may want to be with you, you may even be together, but something is going on that is going to interfere and make lasting commitment impossible. Unless you are having an affair.

This card bodes well for clandestine activities, and secret liaisons. If you are happy to remain as a lover rather than take on the role of spouse, then you could have a great time palling around with this person in the mystery and glamour that they call life. Just don't let yourself pretend that the myth you share is true, it's all done with smoke and mirrors, you know that. And it will always be that way.

As the querent's link card: Perhaps I am wrong, but I think you are looking for an extra-marital affair. You have some unusual tastes and you are seeking an outlet for them.

You are probably looking for the dream of romance. You want a bit of myth and glamour in your love life.

You need secret time, that is yours alone, where no one knows what you are doing – it makes you feel special.

Perhaps you are a transvestite, or maybe bi-sexual? You definitely want and need something in your close relationships that you don't seem to be able to get by following the mainstream trend.

You are looking for someone who can help you add spice, mystery, and star-dust to your intimate moments and private life. An artist, a poet, a musician, an actor/actress, a writer, a psychic or medium – someone who deals with emotion, dream, the occult, or alternate realities – is the type of person you want your lover to be.

As the love interest's link card: This person is looking for someone emotional and passionate, who under-stands romance, and is not afraid to share their deepest darkest hot-chocolate self.

They need mystery and glamour in their relationships, and if they don't get it they are liable to seek out an affair in order to quench their thirst for clandestine passion.

If you are Mr. Darcy or Gypsy Rose Lee you could be just what this person is looking for. Otherwise get yourself a secret hobby and refuse to let them have the faintest sniff of an idea what it is you do when you're off on your own, ever – it'll drive them nuts and keep them interested. And brush up on romance and courtly love, if you don't surprise them with roses, a trip to London for the theatre, a kaleidoscope, etc, on an irregular basis they're going to start looking for their silk, satin and chocolates elsewhere.

Take your lover to dance classes, learn to waltz and tango and rumba, then hit the dance floor of the nearest swanky hotel or midnight ball. Trust me, they need it regularly the same way you need air in order to breath.

As clarification: Your uncertainty is there for a

reason. Do not leap into a relationship just to try to ease your feelings of discomfort.

You need to walk alone for the time being as you delve into your thoughts and feelings and try to unravel who you really are.

If you do start a relationship it won't last. It can't.

As a third party/obstacles: Nothing is what it seems. You do not know this person, they live in a disturbing world. It is a mystery why you are being kept apart – a mystery you probably don't want to know the answer to. Seriously.

If you do get together with your love interest it will not work out in the long run. There can be no commitment here.

Perhaps your love interest is insane?

XIX – The Sun

As the querent: You feel energized and confident much of the time. You are a happy person who enjoys life. You value emotional contentment and personal satisfaction, and seek these in everything you do.

You like clarity in your world, and want to be able to see things as they really are. You prefer truth to white lies. Truth may sometimes hurt, but you think that that is better than maintaining a falsehood, or a mistaken opinion. As a result some people may find you hard to take, as they prefer illusion and assumption to truth. Illusion and assumption take less work.

As the love interest: The joy and optimism of this person is positively contagious, their enthusiasm for everything is inspiring. They really know how to live.

They find the positive in everything. They can locate the true heart of any issue, cutting away the irrelevant in order to see what matters more clearly.

They hate waffle and flannel, and prefer a direct, open and honest approach in all their dealings. This can be a little unsettling at first. But refreshingly, you will always know where you stand with them, because they will flat out tell you exactly how they feel, or what they think about anything – no matter how tender or sensitive the subject.

This person has seemingly boundless energy, for they are like their power source – even on the darkest night the sun is shining brightly somewhere.

This person may seem distant from time to time when clouds cover the sky, but they'll be back on form just as soon as they've burned their way through whatever opposition it was that faced them.

This person displays their heart on their sleeve with utter relentlessness. It is very unlikely you would ever need to use a crowbar to winkle out how they feel.

As the querent's Higher Self/Influences/Themes:
You are entering a time when life's bounty becomes clear. You are capable of reaching emotional satisfaction as a result of the influences around you. A time of action, energy, and warmth.

Clarity of purpose drives you. Success in your goals can be attained because of the new energies penetrating your life's path.

Self-deceptions are banished. This can be a painful and searing process if you are not ready for it; but it will leave the way clear for a truer expression of self and an understanding of your life's purpose. A glimpse of the inner you, and what you can be if you work for it.

The positive energy surrounding you will aid in your process, giving you the energy, and access to a source for help, which you need. A new understanding of love could be a part of this.

As the love interest's Higher Self/Influences/ Themes: This person seems to be content and happy in their life, having found a truer way to express themselves. Perhaps they are self employed, doing a job they find great enjoyment in; or perhaps they have the friends, home, and life they desire?

Alternatively, life could be in the process of stripping away their illusions, making them face the reality of who they are and what they need to do in order to gain true happiness in their lives – this could be a painful series of events for them, but the energies involved will ensure the best outcome and a happy ending…that allows them to grasp true contentment.

An energy shines from this person, helping those around them see truth – which those affected may not like.

As the querent's link card: You are looking for someone confident and happy who can buoy you up when you're having a hard time. You want to be happy and contented in a relationship, and be able to trust your partner one hundred percent.

You are a 'can do' person, and you have no time for the negative and depressing in life. You need someone who has as much energy and enthusiasm as you, so that you can share activities and days out, and get the same level of joy from doing the things you love with each other. Shared interests are probably a must for you.

It is likely that the idea of family appeals to you; and having children as part of a permanent relationship may well be high on your list of things to do.

As the love interest's link card: This person is looking for a life partner who is happy and energetic, full of beans, high on life; someone who can throw themselves into any activity with the same level of enthusiasm and raw joy as they do.

An open and honest approach marks this person's character, and they want the same from their lover.

Sometimes they can be too honest, refusing to tell little white lies in order to smooth ruffled feathers, and they value this in others. If you are the slightest bit insecure you may well regard this person as your nemesis in short order, as you will not want to hear their blunt and undiluted opinion as frequently as they will give it. However if you can handle their tactless relentlessness, you can learn a lot from your association with this person, and they will enrich your life beyond anything you had previously imagined.

They want to share all their life with someone, so if you can't keep up with their level of energy, or even set a stronger pace, then they will probably grow disillusioned or bored, and if that happens they'll be off to conquer the next mountain on their own or with someone else.

As clarification: All your dreams will come true. A celebration; a successful marriage; romance; a child. It is time to take positive action.

As a third party/obstacles: The relationship your love interest has with this person is perfect. The love they share is deep and profound and you will not be able to come between them. Take a hike, there are other fish in the sea. Respect their union.

XX – Judgment

As the querent: Your life is about transformation, and it can be a real trial by fire. An intense passion for change and liberation makes you set a fast pace throughout your life, and drives you on to explore new facets of yourself that you would otherwise never uncover.

Karma is at the heart of every outcome of every event that you set in motion. If you do bad or evil, you will reap the whirlwind; if you do good, you will gain the just rewards either in this life or the next.

While life can be hectic, you do get the chance to take a step back and assess how things have progressed so far and use that information to judge where you want your life to take you next, and what personal changes you need to make in your approach and lifestyle.

As the love interest: This person can surprise and amaze you: the twists and turns that their life's path has taken to get them where they are now are virtually impossible to extrapolate going by the image they currently present. And there are definite phases to their life, marked be each new life-altering decision they take.

This person can quickly assess something's usefulness or validity, and then make use of that information to form a plan that will rebirth their original goal from the ashes of the wreck that resulted before.

This person makes their life: good and bad. They create new opportunities, and make dramatic changes. The far reaching implications of their actions are not lost on them, although they may not be conscious of the full effects and consequences until they have had time to stop and look around at the new landscape they have made around themselves.

Some of the transitions and transformations that this person goes through can be unbearably painful, but their abundant joy in the process of regeneration explains why they continue to pursue such change.

Because this person tends to go through radical change at all levels of life and personality, you might have a tough time making a permanent commitment to them. The person you start out a romance with will not be the same person that you end up living with ten years down the line. But then, we all change. Question is: will you change in compatible and complimentary ways? It's the same gamble we all take, but for some reason it's more obvious and dramatic with this fish.

As the querent's Higher Self/Influences/Themes: The pace of life can speed by as you get caught up in transformative events. And this process of evolution that the world and your inner being demand of you is not something you can resist. The best you can do is take a breather now and again to work out what just happened, whether it was good or bad, and how to proceed the best way from here.

If you resist transformation it can be brutally painful and traumatic, but the rewards of change can be great so the older you are the more you realize the process is beneficial, and embrace it. Of course, as you mature you will eventually want to settle down and relax – the universe may have other plans for you. The adaptability and internal strength that you have cultivated so far will help you survive and triumph.

Enjoy life, it may not always be easy, but it can be surprising and fun if you take a liberal approach.

<u>*As the love interest's Higher Self/Influences/Themes*</u>: Life will drag this person through some life altering circumstances, from which they will emerge changed on a deep level. What's more, the universe seems to put them through this trial by fire on a regular basis, forcing them to evolve continually.

They will either adapt like the phoenix, being reborn from the ashes of their old persona, or they will suffer harsher and harsher lessons until they either learn to adapt or succumb to the pressures around them.

The chances are that this person will enjoy the process of self-transformation and step blithely from one situation to the next with only a short period of reflection on what was before they forge ahead. Their seemingly easy acceptance of mind-blowing events could leave you shivering and pale the first time you witness it.

Life with this person will always be interesting, and will always be subject to dramatic change. Keeping up with them, and learning to evolve at the same pace they do is likely to be a big challenge in any relation-ship you have with them.

<u>*As the querent's link card*</u>: You are looking for a fast pace of life, with constant change and renewal

providing opportunities for personal growth and achievement.

You enjoy taking the time to pause and look over the past before you set out on your next endeavour. You may well enjoy photo albums, or any other method of cataloguing and assessing the past for its value, and the lessons and experience that you can take forwards from it.

You are looking for someone who will pull you with them through the adventure of their life, undergoing new experiences, or living in different cultures on a regular basis.

A normal – pre-planned – job for life, house, marriage, kids type relationship is likely to be anathema to you. You demand the extraordinary rather than the ordinary as your destiny.

The person you are with also needs to have a fine sense of judgment being able to discriminate between good and bad. Such things are always subjective, so if their taste is out of synch with yours it could spell trouble for the relationship. You like caviar, they like cane sugar; it's an uneasy mix – but who's to say it wouldn't work if the right people are involved?

<u>As the love interest's link card</u>: This person has a sense for what's what, and if you ain't it, they ain't interested. This sense is a bit like radar – it makes no sense except to the person watching it ping – and it has been honed by years of challenge and change to pick up on the slightest alert.

For this person love is like an asteroid smashing into them from out of the blue, and leaving them utterly changed, reeling in the devastation it has left in its wake. So when they fall victim to love yet again, they may be reticent to dive right in…depends on their previous experiences and level of wisdom.

This person judges every event, every feeling, on what has gone before; so if their reaction to something is over the top, or odd in any way, then you can be sure their history meter has just detected a hit. You'll need to ask them about what happened before if you want to make sense of their reaction. They may not even be consciously aware of why they are responding the way they do.

Your love interest needs someone who can bring sweeping and profound changes into their life, whether on a physical or personal level. Their quest is evolution and growth, and the only way they have to measure that is to judge with their mind and with their heart and with their soul. How that translates into real life choices is another matter.

As clarification: Karma will determine the results. Your approach, attitude, and quality of emotion will have a direct impact on the outcome. Change is on the way, this is a card of endings and new beginnings. You need to evolve and find your own answers.

As a third party/obstacles: If there is someone else, this person has you pegged and therefore can outmanoeuvre you. Massive changes are occurring.

It may well be that force of circumstance is what will keep the two of you apart, rather than another person. There will be far reaching implications in a change of circumstances, the dramatic events will take precedence over your personal wants. You cannot deny the inevitable. Accept what is happening and move on.

XXI – The World

As the querent: After much soul searching, and a period of learning, you are finally doing something with your life that you find very rewarding. Great success can be yours, both emotionally and in the realms of your work and physical environment.

Once you have achieved your goals, you will of course embark on your next project, goal, or quest – learn what is required, and set out to make a success of that too. You know of the hardship, lessons, dedication, and hard work required to make these things happen for you. Nothing is ever handed out on a silver platter. If you apply yourself well, you can succeed; for you, life is very much what you make of it.

If you are looking for a relationship, you are likely to find real love in short order.

As the love interest: This person acquires the expertise and puts in the hard work necessary to get the job done and achieve success in their goals. Never think that what they have came easy to them – if you don't respect the process, they'll spot it in an instant and know you for a faker.

Experience has its rewards, and this person is enjoying them.

It is likely that they are an entrepreneur, or self employed; always setting out for the new goal, the new project, the new horizon, and somehow managing to pull everything together and make it work. They are willing to endure a lot of hardship on the way to success, so don't make the mistake of thinking that because they are on top of the world right now they will be tomorrow. Sometimes they knock it all down, or throw it away just so they can start out from scratch and build it all up again. They enjoy the process. If you are with them during this you could find yourself destitute just as frequently as you are on easy street.

As the querent's Higher Self/Influences/Themes: The universe is constantly pushing for you to do more with your life; your Higher Self needs you to take on new journeys and new adventures – so just as you have found a level of success with one thing, something different will throw its glamour over you, and you'll find yourself overturning every stone in your path in order to achieve this next goal. And then the process starts again.

Both exterior and inner forces drive you onwards, and you relish the hard work and feeling of satisfaction involved in continuing on your life path.

If you try to pause in your journey, it is possible that everything you have built up will be taken away from you so that you are forced to go to it once again. While your life can be very demanding, you also find it to be a lot of fun.

As the love interest's Higher Self/Influences/Themes: This person seems to be driven by demons sometimes, other times it is outside events driving them on; either way this person is constantly on the go, taking on mountains and conquering them, then moving on to the next mammoth task.

You may think they work too hard, but as long as they enjoy it you are better off letting them keep on their merry way. Chances are they are doing what they love and if you attempt to stop them you may get left behind in a spoil heap.

As the querent's link card: You are looking for a superhero to love, an honest to goodness hero or heroine who will look after you and keep you safe from the vagaries of the world. Of course they will also be running their own empire, so they may not have as much free time to spend on you as you would like, even so you will love them utterly if they do match up to your dream.

As the love interest's link card: This person wants everything, and they need you to help them get it. They may even consider it your duty to give it to them.

They will expect you to be able to move mountains and conquer new worlds for them. If you can be their hero or heroine they will love you utterly, and you will never need to doubt that they are sincere.

If you aren't Hercules you might want to think carefully about getting involved with this person, as eventually they will find someone who fits the description, and then you'll be yesterday's news.

As clarification: You will get what you want, a perfect and fulfilling relationship. Just remember that once you have achieved something it takes work to maintain it, and more than that, after a moment of attainment will come the need to continue on your journey. Whether you continue together or apart is up to the both of you.

As a third party/obstacles: As the world turns, so must you. Your love interest will be kept apart from you, probably by their single-minded pursuit of their worldly goals.

If another person is involved, this other person has everything your love interest could possibly want.

Alternatively, your love interest will not feel the need for a relationship with you.

You would do better to find someone who cares about you, you will never find happiness in a loveless relationship.

Ace Wands

As the querent: You are an ideas person, and you have a great passion for starting projects. To bring anything to completion takes careful nurturing and hard work, which you understand. With discipline, then, you can bring your ideas to fruition. Just be aware that not all ideas are good ideas.

Being able to discern the difference between good and bad ideas can make the difference between whether a venture pays dividends or sends you into frustrated ruin. Do not allow your passion to cloud your judgment when you first embark on any venture.

You love to do new things, and working to create something unique excites you. You enjoy exploring your imagination, seeing how far you can take a novel idea, and what you can make from it.

You seem to be on a quest for that which is new: you are always starting new projects, trying new food, or falling in love with new people. This may not be too good a trait to have if you want to make a relationship that lasts. The trick is to learn to fall in love with the same person over and over again.

We never really know anyone except ourselves. Assuming that you know everything there is to know about someone (and are therefore bored) is pure foolishness. No one is boring, give them a new puzzle to solve and watch them set about solving it. People react differently with different people and in different situations. If you allow your relationships to get into a rut, what does that say about you?

As the love interest: This person is one of the energetic demons of the world – always starting new projects, creating things, having stuff to do, people to see, things to talk about. A real initiator.

I would not be surprised if this person is an entrepreneur or artist, someone who forges ahead and gets things done. It might take them a while to get a handle on finishing what they start, but once they do, look out!

What this person needs is support and a safe environment to work from. High fliers need firm foundations – after all if the runway is bust, how are you going to get up enough flight speed to take off?

Passion is this person's life blood; and the act of creation – bringing things into the world – is why they live and breathe. They are likely to be a monster of ego, but possibly incredibly insecure as well, this combination will make them somewhat exasperating to live with as they will want to be an utter control freak, and yet if the smallest thing goes wrong they may crumble into a whimpering heap – right before they jump up, deck whoever's closest, tell the world in general exactly how they feel, and storm off to start their next masterpiece.

A tiger in bed, but with a strong possibility of many, many children – bringing things into the world is what they do, remember?

If you want the long haul, and love the idea of bringing up kids yourself (they won't have time they'll be working on their next project), and you can give them a haven, and cope with their all or nothing approach to life, then this person could make your blood run very hot.

As the querent's Higher Self/Influences/Themes:
You are affected a lot by energy – if there is a lot of it around you are fairly bouncing off the ceiling, if there is little energy in the atmosphere and your surroundings then you feel all limp and unmotivated. You may be prone to S.A.D. and require plenty of sunlight in your life to thrive. Or you may have a sugar sensitivity and/or get hyperactive when you ingest certain chemicals that are present in food. Make notes, work out your rhythms and patterns; it'll help you make sense of why you get low or high at different times.

Lightning storms are likely to exhilarate you, and you love that fresh feeling after rain during a long, hot, unforgiving summer.

Like a daisy you are drawn to the sun, and to the moon, and to anything that you find energizing – if people do it for you, you'll be drawn to crowds and the nightlife; if certain colours do it for you, you should surround yourself with them; if blue skies and white sands frying under the heliosphere call to you, then go to them.

The universe surrounds you with opportunities for new adventures and experiences. The power of art can sway you, just as good music can make you pause and listen. You want to create new things, and give new experiences to the world.

Your mission is about bringing energy and physical form into the world; whether you are a midwife, or an artist, or a cinematographer – somehow your life involves bringing new things into form.

Bringing passion into other people's lives moves you and makes you feel complete.

As the love interest's Higher Self/Influences/ Themes: This person is surrounded by activity, or they make it themselves. They never stand still for long, there's just too much for them to do with their time.

This is one of those people who is always busy, either for themselves or helping other people. Their level of energy can rival that of Mercury at times. Dizzying, heroic and passionate.

This person loves the act of creation. Inventing things is their forte – whether they know it or not. Bringing things into reality – fact from theory, book from thought, art from impulse – it's what they do.

This person is an initiator, with boundless energy for discovery and invention. They may need help bringing their projects through to completion, but the last thing they need is someone who pours cold water on their ideas before they have even started to take form. If someone had told Da Vinci he should give up on his dreams and become an accountant, and he'd actually listened to them, the world would have been a poorer place.

My advice, if you aren't prepared to support this person even during their more far-fetched episodes then don't get involved with them in the first place; they won't appreciate your endless realism, and you won't be happy living with an impassioned dreamer – and no, you won't be able to change them.

As the querent's link card: You are looking for a

new level of passion in love and relationships. You need someone who expresses love through art and/or the artistry of being, someone who is passionate about life and living. This kind of person will inspire you to find a more involved way of living and loving, just through being themselves. You need someone enthusiastic and optimistic to be with.

As the love interest's link card: This person approaches life with passion and enterprise and they need someone who does the same. They are looking for an enthusiastic lover, who enjoys beauty, and who enjoys living to the full.

They are also looking for a spark, that can become a full grown fire – they need a connection that has the chance of becoming a long-term commitment. They want someone who can nurture and inspire them, who will share their passions.

If you are a realist, or the type of person who pours cold water all over fantastical or farfetched dreams, then you are not well matched for any kind of endeavour involving this person…even if the rest of the cards promise success, take care, as long term there could be problems around your conflicting attitudes.

As clarification: From small beginnings come great things, so take the initiative. Put in some careful, hard work and you'll get what you want. This card bodes well for a good relationship with excellent prospects. You energize each other and inspire each other. Make sure you keep things new, fresh and dynamic for each other and you won't go wrong. Gentle nurturing is the name of the game.

A child might be on the way.

As a third party/obstacles: Delays can be very frustrating. If you are too single-minded or tactless, you are just going to cause further delays and problems for yourself. Your love interest does like you, but the time isn't right for a commitment to each other yet. Try to be patient. If you can't be lovers, you can be friends. Sort your own life out and see what develops in the future.

Ace Cups

As the querent: You enjoy the start of love, that time when everything is new, when passion first ignites, the whole process of discovery. Any period where emotions are forming, or passions are rising, excites you.

You have a tendency to create emotional situations on purpose. One question you really should ask yourself next time you are upset, is whether the person actually did anything to merit your reaction, or whether you pulled the emotions up out of yourself on purpose and are feeling something for the sake of feeling something? Where did your current torrent of emotion come from, inside, or outside? Is anyone really to blame, or is it down to your personal response system?

Relationships of all kinds are vitally important to you, your interactions with other people give you a feeling of validation and are your gauge for how well you are doing with your life.

You should not pin your success and happiness on how other people respond to you, you need to find your own self worth and feel confident in who you are whether other people agree with you or not. You cannot be all things at all men without a lot of conflict, instead, try being yourself.

You are a happy person at heart, who feels things deeply. You like creating positive emotions in others, just don't damage yourself, or lose yourself in the process.

Writing, music, and art are all areas you might want to explore as ways of evoking emotion in other people.

As the love interest: This person is driven by their emotions, they have a need to feel, and can sometimes go out of their way to create new emotion where nothing has changed for a while: this may manifest in picking fights, or in getting romantic, or finding something to be sentimental about, etc. Don't take it personally, just think of them as being like the sea, they surge and swell and break and retreat, and then start over. Bear in mind, that they are likely to take it extremely personally though. Let them wash over you – you are the rock, they are the water; over time you may get ground into sand, but for them every time they break on your hard exterior it shatters them. If you help them to sit quietly in your arms instead of rage against you you'll both benefit.

If they are provided with new forms of stimulation, so that they have the chance to express new emotional responses on a regular basis they should remain interested and positive. It's when things fall into a rut that the negative side of their personality will come into play – then they are likely to either cause trouble on purpose in order to stir things up, or they'll go looking for emotional satisfaction somewhere else or with someone new.

This person loves people and will probably have a massive network of friends and acquaintances – it's part of their self validation system – having people to feel about and to feel for them.

If you are with them, you are probably stable, secure in yourself, and a saint. Either that or you are just as much of an emotional whirlpool as they are engaged in a harmonious dance of mutual response.

As the querent's Higher Self/Influences/Themes: You are always getting involved in situations that require an emotional response, or are filled with emotion from the start.

Whether you are rubbing people up the wrong way, or the right way, you find yourself swamped by feelings; either your own, or those of other people.

Sudden passions develop around you all the time. And it is likely that people tend to have a strong reaction to your looks or your personality.

You might want to consider the role of talk-show host for one of those high-strung shows, or perhaps political commentator, revolutionary journalist or writer, becoming an actor or actress might be your best career choice – whatever you do, if it is compatible with life's tendency to throw you in the thick of emotional situations that require an emotional response from you or those around you, it will make your personal life a little easier to handle.

As the love interest's Higher Self/Influences/ Themes: Emotional situations circle this person as if they are the eye of a storm. Either they are putting their foot in it, or life is smacking them upside the head, or cupid is their stalker – if this person isn't an actor or actress, they should really consider it as a career, as this might help take some of the pressure off their personal life.

If you can cope with the surging feelings that surround and engulf this person, you can be their rock. They need someone calm and level headed who doesn't explode with anger or passion every other second.

It is likely that this person creates as much of the emotional conflict in their lives as the universe inflicts on them. They may not have an easy time, or they may revel in it; but it's going to be a tough place to live – next to them – as you'll get to share in the tragedy, love, joy, pain, and ecstasy that pours into their life from all fronts. It will also be unbelievably rewarding, if you can cope with it.

As the querent's link card: You are looking for a deeper emotional commitment than you've had from another person before. You need strong feelings, and want to be able to see the same unquenchable desire in them.

It is possible that over time you may start looking for new people, new relationships, as that initial upsurge of romance and the myth of love are very important to you – be warned, many people are looking for monogamy or long-term commitment and won't appreciate it if you gallivant off with others.

Imagination, intuition and fantasy are all things you look for in love – you crave the myths, dreams and legends of love – role play might be an important aspect of your bedroom gymnastics, and you need someone who enjoys these games that add spice and romance to loving.

One problem you have is that you want to merge yourself fully with the other person or you want them to merge themselves fully with you. This kind of union can result in restriction and a dulling of passion – if you know someone too well, where is the room for fantasy? Each of you must have your own activities and commitments outside the relationship if you want to keep the freshness and commitment intact.

As the love interest's link card: This person is looking for love and commitment of a solid, real kind. They want that ring – once they've found the right person.

This person wants someone who is not afraid to show their feelings. They want someone who displays their passion, they are a sucker for romance, and they need rose petals in their love life like a duck needs water.

Your love interest has strong feelings in love, and wants to find the same in their lovers. If there is a strong upsurge of emotion and an undeniable initial attraction when you meet, this bodes well for a great relationship - as long as you can keep the romance side of things top notch. Fan those flames, keep the passion hot. If this person starts to cool off, it's over. Don't think that you can just lie back and everything will be fine, maintaining love takes work, you need to make an effort to keep it going.

As clarification: This could be love at first sight. You are both strongly attracted to each other right from the start. It could be a love/hate relationship, but it is more likely that everything will remain positive. Such a strong physical attraction could be a problem if either of you is already promised to someone else. As long as you are free to indulge, both of you will get supreme satisfaction from your union. Marriage is likely to follow.

As a third party/obstacles: The person you love is unavailable. You have strong feelings for them, so coping with not being a part of their life is going to be painful for you. Best advice I can give, is remind yourself that there will be someone else in your future who is even better for you than your current love interest. Keep that hope in mind and endure.

Ace Swords

As the querent: You have probably had to sacrifice a lot in your life in order to attain your goals.

The decisions you make tend to be of the 'life altering' type, that result in dramatic changes. It takes a lot of inner strength to make your own road in life, but that is definitely what you do.

You know that to focus your aim and fly to your mark, you need to leave behind all the ties and baggage that would otherwise hold you back. Sometimes that means leaving behind people and things you would rather keep close.

Other people may not understand it, but you know that you need to achieve your goals, and the only way to do that is make the decisions and take the actions necessary to obtain them. That's why you are forging ahead on your path through life, and they are still stuck doing the same old things they've always done, and wishing for more.

As the love interest: This person is someone who has a tendency to up sticks and move in order to get to somewhere else that they'd rather be. They do it with their house, their job, their friends, and also with their relationships.

This action can be seen as foolhardy, or brave, depending on your outlook. It certainly takes a lot of guts to live the way they do. They may not always burn all their bridges, but the constant and dramatic changes that they bring into their lives can effectively achieve the same effect.

Once this person is done with something, they are done with it. If they decide that they have taken the wrong path and the two of you are no longer destined to walk side by side, there's no point trying to cling on because they will have unscrewed all the handrails. When they say something is over they are usually right, it's just that they are good at spotting these things before most people – they have heightened senses when it comes to the collapse of relationships, or indeed empires, and they always get out in good time.

If you've spotted a leak in the ship's hull, this person is already fully packed and booked on another liner…look, see, they've just stepped across onto the tug boat, along with all the ship's rats – did you really want to waste time packing? The tug is about to leave.

As the querent's Higher Self/Influences/Themes: The universe, and even your inner nature, has a way of forcing you to leave your nice cosy new home – just as you're getting settled – and set out for pastures new. The new pastures are usually a lot better than the old ones, but it can be a real wrench leaving behind everything you've built up to date.

Sometimes the sweeping changes that life inflicts on you are to do with relationships, or family members, rather than moving house or job, or country, or lifestyle. These emotional upheavals can be far more traumatizing than the 'simple' act of moving your life to a new country. The sacrifices and pain you have to go through can be unbearable; but when something is done, it's time to move on and head for the new goals, new pastures, new people.

Good things can come from your enforced gypsy lifestyle. New experiences, new vistas, a wealth of life experience. Being able to adapt and survive is one of your strongest and best traits.

<u>*As the love interest's Higher Self/Influences/ Themes*</u>*:* This person acts upon your life like a whirlwind, uprooting everything, tossing you (your belongings, and your lifestyle) high into the air, seemingly careless of where or how you land, and then breezing on to their next victim – unless of course you are an exceptionally adaptable sailor and can throw up a sail, catch their wind, and get transported with them across the world on their endless journey.

This person's life is filled with constant and utterly disruptive change. Sometimes it is forced on them from the outside world, sometimes they force it on themselves from deep within their psyche; but upheaval and renewal is the theme of their life.

Fate stalks this person, hand in hand with tragedy and ecstasy, luck is another constant companion, sometimes wearing a face of good, sometimes a face of ill.

As long as you are aware of life's lesson for this person – when something is done it's done, and there is no going back – then you could be a valuable asset for them. They really need someone constant who they can rely on to be with them through the vagaries of their life, moving with them, accompanying them on their random, tornado-blown journey to wisdom and old age.

You would probably do better to fall in love with this person after they have passed their mid thirties, as by then they will have had plenty of time to come to understand the value of a compatible, good, and loyal lover. In their earlier years they are more likely to still be finding their feet, and throwing everything and everyone up in the air on the slightest whim, and leaving them behind in their wake. If they are still young you might want to keep them as a friend rather than a lover, and trust that things will evolve if you are still close later down the line? Then again, who has time for that these days?

As the querent's link card: You need someone who understands what love is, and can communicate their thoughts and feelings effectively. You want someone who has a new perspective, who can keep things interesting by innovating in the process of relating to each other – providing new ideas for things to do, or coming up with new topics of conversation.

Knowledge, understanding, and some conflict will keep things ticking over nicely for you. You enjoy a challenge. Just be aware, conflict can destroy love as easily as help to spice it up. Choose your battles carefully or you may end up alone. You need someone whose Personal or Higher Self card is compatible with your airy warlike nature.

As the love interest's link card: This person likes some conflict in their relationships, making up can be a lot of fun. Thing is, knowing how to balance it; ensuring that the duelling doesn't enter the grounds of the serious can be difficult – you can kill a relationship as easily as spice it up.

If you like a quiet life and hate conflict, stay well clear.

This person has lived with pain and heartbreak, they may even be a repeat love triangle addict, or unreciprocated love junky. When you get to the heart of the situation, what they really want is a cuddle and some serious down home loving, they just aren't sure they deserve it which is why they keep going after the impossible.

This person needs a knowledgeable lover, who has investigated technique and form. If you have a degree in massage you're off to a good start. While this person is looking for cerebral excitement, it is possible to stimulate all kinds of areas of the brain and body just by hitting the right points in the energy system – if you don't know about Shiatsu or Reflexology you might want to start taking lessons.

When this person falls in love, they fall in love with their mind first, then their heart follows. If you enjoy scrabble, and crosswords, and debating the news you've got a better than average chance of getting into their thoughts and into their heart.

As clarification: Dramatic changes are happening in your life. A situation that is difficult to handle is occurring, but the ultimate result of something you see as negative will turn out to be for the best.

You can cut through all obstacles, using the power of your mind to force what you want into existence. Question is, is this the right thing to do? The most important thing is to be honest with yourself about your intentions and the wisdom or stupidity of your actions. You will have to make a personal sacrifice. Even if everything seems to be starting well, walking away might actually be the most beneficial course of action for you to take?

As a third party/obstacles: Getting into a fight or argument is not the way to go. You're hurting enough as it is without causing yourself extra pain.

Your thinking is fuzzy at the moment and you are reacting to stimuli rather than thinking things through clearly. If you took some time out and applied your brain to the matter at hand, you would realize that things are not as bad as you think they are, and that you actually have a very good chance of winning out despite the current obstacles to your love. Bide your time and get clever.

Ace Pentacles

As the querent: You have reached a point in your life where you are prepared to knuckle down and put in the hard work necessary to achieve financial or material reward.

You are ready to lay a foundation stone – whether that be starting a new business, or finding the thing you want to do with your life, perhaps getting a home and a family, you are now at the place where you are able to start working towards it with serious intent.

You have the drive and energy required for starting

new projects, and you have the ability to find a source of investment, which could be from a gift, or perhaps your new partner has spare finances, maybe an inheritance or legacy is coming to you, perhaps a business loan can be arranged because you now have a sensible business plan in place?

You are making solid plans for putting something physical and real in place, and if you attend to the new structure, carefully nurturing it, there is the potential here for something strong and real and successful to grow. Hard work will be rewarded.

As the love interest: This person has plans for the future, and is putting in the work toward achieving their goals. Perhaps they have just started their own business? They are serious in their intent and motivated to achieve success. They also have been putting in the ground work needed to make their goal possible – this is not some idle dream or speculation. With hard work their vision will pay dividends.

There is an opportunity for them to achieve success and increased wealth, and they are willing to put in the hard work and careful research necessary to achieve it. If you are sensible you will support them rather than get in their way.

If you are looking for a person with a solid view of life and a realistic inner approach, who wants something lasting, meaningful, and visible from life, this is the person. They may be an architect or writer or entrepreneur or builder or artist – whatever their work, it will produce something physical and lasting that future generations can look to. They have the same approach in their personal life.

If you want a quick dalliance with no strings then

this may not be the one night stand for you. Make sure they know the score before you start making any moves on them; if you lie to them or lead them on, and this person does decide to go for revenge, it will leave a lasting scar.

As the querent's Higher Self/Influences/Themes: The world looks after those who look after themselves.

You are probably already aware that almost nothing is given for free, but that if you make opportunities, lay the foundations for things to evolve or happen, then the universe will help them come to pass. E.g. corn cannot grow if you do not plant corn seed.

If you do plant corn seed, tend it well, providing water if there's drought, shelter from the strong winds when needed, and weeding when needed, then come the summer you will have a strong crop ready to be harvested. The earth provided the corn with what it needed to grow, and you kept it safe, so it grew, fruited, and was abundant. This is a good metaphor for the way your life works. Do the foundation work, and the necessary things to keep the activity on track, and success will follow – sometimes seemingly from out of the blue.

In general you may feel that you are looked after by a higher power, and that if you tune in and put yourself in its way, then anything can be possible. Problem being that if you should go against the universal tune, put barricades in the path of the universal flow, you will get swept away and the damage that could be inflicted on you is likely to be tremendous. Lesson? Get out of your own way and let the universe get on with it.

As the love interest's Higher Self/Influences/Themes: Destiny seems to have a hand in this person's life. If they set out to achieve something and put in the ground work, help seems to materialize out of nowhere. Good things seem to just 'happen' for them.

However, I doubt this person will ever win the lottery, life's lesson for them is that work is required for achievements and success to follow. Because the universe does have a tendency to hand things to them on a plate when they are in desperate need, it may take them quite a while to learn this. If they, and you, pay attention to the windfalls life gives them, you'll note that they get given just what they need and no more. Not what they want, what they need.

Frugality and hard work will see them through to times of plenty.

They need a lover who will be their partner for a lifetime, they are not looking for a short term liaison or a fling. Their higher self and the universe will help them find that person, possibly when they are not expecting it. If they are with you when the universe moves in this way and you are not the one who is meant to be with them you will both need to find a way to come to terms with it and accept it…if you try to stand against *The Way* of life, destruction is the usual outcome.

This person's life is about growth and physical activity and being themselves. Until they find themselves their life will be subject to the laws of evolution, be warned.

As the querent's link card: What you want is

someone who manifests the vigour of youth – don't restrict yourself due to ageism though, you could miss out on something really special. The experience of love, the body's response to tangible affection, this whole physical aspect of love is important to you. You need someone who can keep this exploration of the body and the physical new and enticing.

You enjoy exploring new ways of living and methods of doing things. Perhaps you would be interested in someone who has an alternate view on how people should dwell in the world – a traveller, or a vegan, or a bohemian – someone who has a different approach to that of the rest of society.

Whilst you do enjoy exploring the new, taking a new lover every five minutes is not recommended. The level of STDs in the population may be one reason, but the main reason is that you would get real satisfaction from a love that turned into a permanent commitment, and if you keep dropping the old in favour of the new, you are not going to get to experience that reward. Exploring the old in new ways, or gaining depth and staying power through experience are likely to be far more satisfying for you, if you give it a chance.

Love and friendship can grow and transform over time. If you limit yourself you won't find what you really need.

As the love interest's link card: This person is very physical, and they want concrete satisfaction, for them love isn't just about two hearts uniting; it's about sex, money, a place to live, rings, ceremonies, children, etc. They value the physical manifestations of love, romance and passion.

This person is happy to put in the energy that creates the sparks that can get these things into potential, but they also want to commit to the work of bringing them into reality. In other words, they may be a tiger in bed, but they want a lot more than that.

If you want a permanent union, and you are prepared to put in the hard work necessary to get the rewards of partnership – in the true sense – then this person very likely wants what you've got to offer.

This person wants and needs stability. If all you are after is blistering sex, make sure they know that before the one night stand becomes two nights, becomes three nights…as they'll start thinking wedding rings.

As clarification: Wealth can be yours. Perhaps the person you like has money, or they can open up a business opportunity for you? The problem is that money in and of itself won't make you happy. Together you can be well-to-do; however it might be better to keep your relationship as a business arrangement rather than attempting romance.

As a third party/obstacles: Money will keep you apart. Perhaps you are in financial straights, perhaps they are? Maybe you have a gambling problem? Or maybe they are rich and see you as a gold-digger? Alternatively the person you like might be a gold-digger, or have a wealthy suitor who you just can't compete against? Whatever the case, it is financial issues (or attitudes) more than anything else that cause problems between you or prevent the relationship.

Two of Wands
As the querent: You are positively bursting with

energy and enthusiasm. You are quick to understand how to make something work, and you are good at balancing the desire to create with the planning required to actually make something real.

You naturally balance passion with planning – if you apply this to the area of love, you will be able to win the heart of any true romantic. Or at the very least, capture their attention. If you apply it to other areas of your life, you are capable of being very successful at doing whatever it is that ignites your passions whether it takes the form of work or a hobby.

Problems occur when your passion wanes, for then you want to move on to the next great thing that stirs your inner fires. Worse, if there is nothing you are able to find to excite you, you feel lifeless and dull; without inspiration, what's the point?

Luckily for you, you find it easy to inspire yourself about a whole multitude of different things – sometimes your biggest problem is knowing where to focus the bulk of your attention. If you allow your energies to be divided, the danger is that you will achieve nothing: starting many projects and finishing none of them. All plans and no follow through.

As the love interest: This person needs equilibrium in their life – a balance of loving and thinking, working and playing, sleeping and waking.

They have large reserves of energy for those things that inspire them, and can seem tireless at times. Other times, getting them to stir themselves from the sofa may be a Herculean feet. The trick is to get them to connect back to their inner passion again, for it is this that drives them and supplies them with energy.

This person is great at coming up with ideas, and

planning how to put them into practise. Where they may need help is actually doing it. This could come down to you. The problem is that there are so many exciting things to explore that they may lose interest after they have planned out what needs doing, as in their mind they have done it already, and they want to move on to the next task.

Alternatively this person will get inspired, put a plan into motion, and you won't see them for dust as they rush off to bring their plans to fruition – once they've conquered that adventure trail, invented that gadget, flown to the Moon, then you might be able to catch up to them, as they are taking in the sun lying on the beach thinking up their next venture.

This person is a forceful powerhouse, and will not be swayed once they are set on a particular path (unless it's by a better, more inspirational, idea). This can make them argumentative and tough to be around as they are very unlikely to compromise. Why should they, when they believe that they are right? Tact is also unlikely to be a strong point with them, they'll say what they think, when they think it. Direct and forthright.

At least you'll always know where you stand; as long as you ask them a direct question they'll give you a direct answer.

Either you'll love them or hate them. They are that kind of person.

<u>*As the querent's Higher Self/Influences/Themes*</u>: You seem to find yourself at the centre of things quite a lot of the time. People seem to value your opinion, and your company. You ignite passions and get plans set in motion – it's like you're a catalyst for other

people's ideas, desires and inspiration.

The universe seems to use you as a balancing point around which events, people, and relationships 'happen'; kind of like that saying "Always the bridesmaid, never the bride" except somehow you wind up being both.

Life happens to you, and you happen right back at it. It's definitely a two way thing. Much of what goes on around you is set in motion by you; after all, if you didn't encourage fate and destiny they'd go play with someone else, right?

You appreciate people who come into your life who don't have an agenda, or a platform they want you to endorse. You find people who can be themselves, and who are true to their inner calling, are refreshing to be around. Most folks are too busy running in circles to take the time to find out who they really are deep down inside.

You enjoy talking about things that people are passionate about, and love to know what others feel and think about things. Even if you have diametrically opposed viewpoints, you still prefer a blazing row to shallow small talk.

You like equality and get upset when you see inequality, or if things tip out of balance. Balance seems to be the way the universe works for you. Perhaps because of this, if life is going badly it doesn't overly concern you, as you know the universe will send good times of equal measure to you in the future to make up for it.

Karma is also one of those concepts that appeals to you, it acts as a check or balance.

<u>As the love interest's Higher Self/Influences/ Themes</u>: Life happens to this person, it's all you can really say about them. Destiny has them in her sights; the crosshairs of fate are centred on them. The universe spins around this person in its mighty swirling orbit, and as it spins it takes them with it. They have no choice in this.

This person is like a balancing point. They are likely to inspire passion and plans in others, either because of who they are, or because of their vision and enthusiasm.

This means that they could be a great advertiser or public speaker or creative film producer – a natural ringmaster for whichever circus happens to be in town at the time.

Strangely enough events, artwork, expeditions, religions and fashion tend to be inspired by and hinge on this person and their presence in the world. They are a muse of creation and their opinion seems to matter to all kinds of people. They are the poised quiet person at the centre of the party who exudes charm and a raw animal magnetism that works on an utterly subconscious level. Even when they are being noisy and uproarious, there is still something quiet, sparkling and calming at the back of their eyes, which pulls people to them.

Because of their personality, this person is capable of changing the world in their own unique way.

Being real is the only way to impact on their radar. If you come across as fake or sycophantic, shallow or presenting a face that isn't your true face, they'll spot it a mile off. Be yourself, that's who they want to talk to after all, the real you. They spend their life coping with mirrors, if that's all you hold up for them you'll get nowhere, fast.

As the querent's link card: The creative, passionate impulse held in balance. This could mean that you are looking for a relationship between equals – in which case the implication here is that you need someone who has the same level of libido as you, and someone who shares your understanding of and desire for romance.

You are looking for a relationship of give and take where each of you benefit equally.

You would not be content if one of you was dominant and the other submissive.

The alternative meaning is that you need someone who is balanced within themselves. Someone who holds the power and the mystery and the passion of love; and yet who balances those creative energies on the verge of becoming – like a cup that is full to the brim, and the tap is still flowing, and yet the emotions have not yet spilled out to splatter messily upon the foundations of your lives.

The person you need will be full of life and the power of living, and yet need you to help them unlock their potential, so that they can share their life enhancing energies and example with both you and the world. Teaching, perhaps?

As the love interest's link card: This person needs someone who is full of life and potential.

They are looking for an equal to share their lives with. They need someone who understands the power, mystery, and romance of love, and who shares their desires and needs.

The action of yin and yang held in the balance – the potential to spawn all of creation held in check by the constant dance of opposites – birthing, feeding and destroying one another, only to continue the spiral of birth and death, light and dark, creation and destruction in an immortal and eternal embrace.

This person wants someone powerful, or someone with the potential for power; they need a person who holds the subconscious wisdom and the conscious will that begets greatness – the creative essence combined with the creative drive that when focused is unstoppable and can bring things into being against any level of opposition. Whether this creative power is something that is recognized by the world, or just by them, is irrelevant, all they need is that it is there.

<u>As clarification</u>: You may be intrigued, but you prefer to continue the dance rather than commit. Friendship is more of a priority for you. You work well together, complimenting each other's strengths and weaknesses which makes you an unbeatable team. In time your relationship could develop into something more, but for now keep things simple.

<u>As a third party/obstacles</u>: You are your own obstacle to this relationship. You have realized that it is time to walk away, and while it might be sad that you cannot be together, you are actually ready to move on. You are no longer prepared to put up with all the little things that you ignored or glossed over when the two of you first met. The faults you see in the other person have outweighed their charms.

Two of Cups

As the querent: You are looking for a long-term commitment, and you want your lover to be your friend as much as your room mate. Partnership is where it's at.

You will not be happy in a relationship where the other person spends a lot of time away from home, as you want to spend as much time with them as possible. Hopefully this won't be a problem as you are a very loving and giving person – just be careful not to smother the person you are with. Many people need time to themselves and hate being interrupted when they are involved in their hobby or their favourite TV show.

When you do find the right person, your relationship will be one of the most rewarding things you could possibly imagine. I would suggest that you take up a hobby of your own, or find something that you can do with your friends that does not involve your lover, as you need to keep your independence and your own personality. The reason I say this is that you have a tendency to give all of yourself to a relationship, which is wonderful, but you may lose yourself and your identity in that person. Living your life vicariously through your lover's achievements, friends and work is not healthy; you need to have your own interests, friends and activities so that the two of you can have something fresh to talk about when you are together.

One of the great joys of a partnership is the differences, and other kinds of experience, that each person brings to it. Try it out. It might be a wrench at first, but you'll find it pays dividends in the long run.

As the love interest: This person values friendship and commitment. They are looking for a relationship that will last the distance. If marriage isn't on your mind, you should probably back off in a hurry, as this person is likely to be able to find a way to entangle you in a permanent kind of way.

It is quite probable that you may fall head over heels in love with this person. The connection here is likely to be more than just physical or mental. A long-term friendship, marriage or love affair is likely to result from your meeting.

This person wants to share every aspect of their lives with the person they love, so if you are a private person who needs their own space, there could be problems here. This person is unlikely to give you the space and territory that are essential to your peace of mind. It is possible that if other cards are favourable a compromise could be found – but ground rules are going to have to be laid down early if you want to have any time to yourself.

This person seeks emotional contentment and commitment. They are probably keen on having a family, and will look for romance in their love life despite the realities of having to cope with kids, a job, and keeping a roof over their head. Expect to have to go the extra mile, and be close and snugly if you want to keep this person happy. They need to know that you will be there for them no matter what.

This person could become a stalker if they are spurned – check the other cards, specially the love interest's link card, for personality traits that could lead to this type of behaviour.

As the querent's Higher Self/Influences/Themes: Other people play a very important part in your life – any time you need support you turn to your family and friends for a shoulder to lean on.

Because you value communication, commitment and sharing between people it is likely that you may place too much importance on your relationships with the wrong people. True friends are few and far between and can usually be counted on one hand, you know, the people who don't mind you spending 5 months living with them when you are homeless and out of work and desperately trying to hold it together.

Don't confuse close acquaintances with true friends. When you are in trouble, trying to lean on someone who doesn't want to be leaned on will only end in rejection and additional pain, at a time when you are already stressed out.

Luckily most of your life is happy and fortuitous, and you tend to meet nice folks easily.

The universe could well put you in the role of mediator a lot, when there's trouble you're the one who ends up bringing the warring parties together. Keep in mind that some people want to fight, they like to fight, and these people won't appreciate your help. Other times fighting can be a sign of irreconcilable differences; I know that you think that every conflict can be solved, but if you and the person you love are fighting the whole time, should you really be spending your entire time trying to patch things up? There comes a time in life when the pain is too much, at those times it's okay to protect yourself and say "Enough! No more!" and demand equal rights. No one should walk all over you and your needs just because you are nice. Lots of people will though. Sometimes they are the people closest to us and, if so, they need to be told what's what.

As the love interest's Higher Self/Influences/ Themes: This person's life seems to be about being a nice person. They share their lives, their passions, and their pain with everyone, and they won't necessarily understand if you don't feel the same way about living life as an open sponge.

They will provide a shoulder for everyone to lean on, and as a result they may frequently get taken advantage of.

When you talk they will listen, and feel for you, and sympathize and empathize – it will be as if what has happened to you has happened to them.

If you love this person and you want to find out how they feel about something, anything, everything, you will need to spend a lot of time being quiet and just listening. You'll need to be good at body language to pick up on their nuances, and *feel it* when they are upset. Learn the slight changes in their tone of voice, the subliminal messages and their use of words like "um" and "maybe".

The role the universe has picked out for this person is mediator and mender. They are likely to spend much of their time ensuring that everyone else is happy, and it is likely to frequently be at their own expense. Friendship, sharing and caring, at any cost.

If you love and nurture this person, and tend to their needs, and pick up on how they really feel, and listen to what they really think, then they can be the most loving person you have ever met. Take advantage of them or browbeat them and you deserve to burn in the hottest pit in Hell.

There is alternative reading for this card – it could be that on a psychic level this person is drawn to you, or you to them. There will be a sharing of minds or emotions which is likely to prove very magnetic for one or other of you, so that the person affected finds it difficult to back away no matter how inappropriate or unpleasant the other person is as an influence on their lives.

The love interest will find it difficult to maintain any kind of barrier between themselves and other people, or with the world in general. They are likely to feel everything. They may be very, very psychic. Or they may be classified as mentally ill. But the effect will be the same, an inability to differentiate clearly between themselves and other people, and/or between their emotions and other people's emotions.

<u>As the querent's link card</u>: You are looking for a husband or a wife, you are done wasting time. You want to settle down in a permanent, loving, committed relationship where the two of you will share your thoughts, hopes and dreams.

You need some romance and luxury in your love life – strawberries and champagne are one of those things you can always bring home yourself for those special occasions. Don't just wait on your partner to think of it.

You want someone who is sensitive to your needs – you may even be looking for someone who has an almost psychic connection with you. Not everyone is able to sense things as acutely as you do, so be prepared to tell people what you want. It may 'spoil' the moment, but once you've trained your lover to your needs, they should give you what you want without too much prompting.

As long as you are realistic about your lover – knowing that they are a different person from you, with different priorities, awareness, and needs – you should get on fine in a marriage. You tend to expect too much upon occasion, they won't always know, or understand, what you are thinking or feeling. Clue them in.

<u>As the love interest's link card</u>: This person is looking for a long-term partnership or marriage. They are not into wasting time on flings anymore – so if you are not after something long term, or if you don't love them and are just taking them for a ride, then I suggest you back off quick. This person is likely to be very involved mentally, emotionally and physically with the person they love, and will find it hard to let go – as a result it is possible that they may become a stalker, or act psychotically around any new paramour.

This person needs their lover to be able to read their moods and be almost psychic in their ability to read this person's mind. If you are good at picking up on the little things, the slightest subliminal hint, an expert at body language, then you could be what they are looking for.

They need someone committed, romantic, and willing to share their life in all things: mind, body and spirit. If you share the same religion, philosophy and hobbies, that's a good start.

If you enjoy cuddling on the sofa, picnics in the park, walks out under the full moon, bringing home little gifts, and have a perfect memory for anniversaries and special dates, then this person will be swept away by you in short order. They love harmony and will want to be friends as well as lovers.

This person is capable of great acts of kindness, and will do a lot to please the person they love. If the two of you get on well, then this person will help to make a relationship that is both amazing and joyful to be in. Your friends could well be jealous of the level of intimacy and fulfilment that you share.

If you have a hard time remembering your own birthday, let alone anyone else's, and you don't have a romantic bone in your body, then the two of you are likely to get right on each other's last nerve. Walk away and find someone less demanding who doesn't need constant attention and emotional support.

As clarification: A loving relationship where two people meet in harmony and contentment. The likely outcome is a happy and satisfying marriage.

As a third party/obstacles: Jealousy, infidelity or a divorce may be keeping you apart, however, it is likely that once the heat has worn off you'll get back together again. Check your Higher Self cards to see if this might be an option. Alternatively, another person has come into your lover's life and they are blissfully happy together. If this is the case you would probably do better to back off and leave them to it.

Two of Swords
As the querent: You have a lot of emotional baggage in your life, which probably manifests itself as a feeling of pain, or as a numbness to what is happening inside you and around you. It is likely that you have been deeply hurt in the past. The actions of a loved one have traumatized you in some way.

The consequence of this is that every time you encounter a similar situation, or one that subconsciously reminds you of the past hurt, or evokes the same sets of feelings, you are likely to over react.

You want to run away and hide from anything that threatens your equilibrium, and feelings of love could easily trigger this response, if the love is the same type of love that caused you to suffer previously.

Retreating isn't always going to be a viable option for you, so the sooner you learn to come to terms with your feelings, and track down the cause of any uncomfortable reaction you have to emotionally loaded situations, the sooner you will be able to regain your balance.

Your emotions get rocked out of shape a lot. The whole process of rocking is to accommodate something new and then regain the centre point. It's a bit like waves in water; the water wants to stay flat, but external forces act on it and tip it out of shape, so the water sloshes about grinding against whatever it touches until it is allowed to settle down to its calm, flat, even surface.

You have a need for harmony and you hate conflict and tension, to the extent that you are willing to roll over almost all the time in order to have a peaceful life. Some times things get too tense to be ignored like this, or the conflict is serious and unhealthy.

If you say something about your discomfort earlier in the day, find a way to tackle the emotions before they start billowing out of shape, then you are far more likely to be able to find a reasonable solution to the problem without too much strife. If you leave the stuff that gets on your nerves – eventually the last straw will break and the conflict could end up being out of all proportion. Deal with things as they come up, don't just leave it or try to run away.

As the love interest: However smooth this person may appear on the surface, underneath they are actually quite anxious, and have trouble making decisions. They look at their different options and experience internal conflict. To choose one thing is to deny another, and how would that be fair? Or worse, could it be the wrong choice, perhaps the other option is better? They seem to spend much of their time hamstringing themselves with these kinds of questions, or paralyzed by the worry that they might upset someone.

They are afraid of being seen as a bad person, and they desperately need harmony in their lives. As a result they can ignore the obvious, turn a blind eye to the truth, and will likely carry on in an untenable situation, just to preserve the status quo.

This person's fear of doing, or saying, or thinking, the wrong thing means that they can be extremely aggravating to be around if you are of a more self-critical and perspicacious temperament. If you like getting to the truth of your own emotional responses, and enjoy weeding out all the dark corners, shining light onto your demons, then you might want to run. You have the mental and emotional tools this person is lacking, so if you do click, great. You'll be able to teach them a lot. However, they are likely to drive you to distraction long before you can get them to start listening with unclosed ears, let alone teach them anything about self-analysis.

On the positive side, this person can easily see both sides of an argument, and empathize with both, so if you have a relationship problem, this is a good person to talk to about it. They will be able to explain events from the other person's perspective and give you a handle on where the miscommunication or trouble lies.

If you like a quiet life and want to spend it with someone even-tempered, then this person is likely to fit your bill.

<u>As the querent's Higher Self/Influences/Themes</u>: You have a tendency to allow fear to make you stalemate, stop you cold. What life is trying to teach you is to face your fear, find out what the root cause of it is and then deal with that. Until you honestly look at what lies behind your fear you are going to have a hard time coming to terms with the 'big freeze', overcoming it, and moving on to a better way of living.

"A life lived in fear is a life half lived." "Fear is the little death." When you remove fear from the equation, life can be a lot of fun, and a pleasure to experience. So what's stopping you? Apathy is just another symptom of fear. So, get on with it! Take a look into the darkness, shine some light on it, what do you really see in the depths and is it still relevant now? Life is about the differences that exist between us, as well as the similarities. The differences can sometimes be extreme, and any choice can seem like a route to disaster. But think about it a moment – if you do nothing, what do you achieve? Nothing.

Growth and evolution occur as a result of conflict. Conflict is created by having a difficulty or opposition acting upon you. You may not like conflict, you may not like opposition, but without them how will you learn, adapt, and grow? Sometimes in life you have no choice but to get on and deal with things – the penalty for doing nothing can be too severe. Like not handing in your tax return on time; have you seen the penalties they have in place for that?

First you need to identify whether a problem is your problem, or whether it is someone else's problem. If the problem stems from something you have to do, or your attitude, or your actions – then the answer is simple, do what you have to do, find the underlying belief that causes your attitude (are you being unreasonable?) and examine its validity, change or modify your actions to something less/more offensive. And the biggest question of all, is the perceived problem really a problem? Is there anything you can do about it or are you helpless before it. If there is nothing you can do to mitigate the circumstances, then why are you worrying about it? Adapt your plans to take that issue/problem into account and work around it.

Walking away, or ignoring a conflict or issue, is likely to give the problem the opportunity to escalate – instead turn and face it, deal with it, find a solution before it gets out of hand. Stop a snowball from rolling at the top of a mountain, and you've just got a fist full of snow. Try to stop it from rolling at the bottom of the mountain and you'll get flattened by the avalanche. So either stop it while it's small, or make plans to move house before the avalanche wipes out your house. Yes? Don't just stand there saying "But I didn't think it'd get this bad" as everything is wiped out around you.

Peel away the layers, look at the underlying cause honestly, and then find a strategy that will allow you to successfully deal with it. Other wise the universe is just going to keep rolling those snowballs at you.

<u>As the love interest's Higher Self/Influences/Themes</u>: The universe might appear to have it in for this person. Trouble will erupt around them, and seemingly they've done nothing to incite it. That's just it you see. They've done nothing. They couldn't decide what to do, they were afraid of getting it wrong, and as a result events that should have been nipped in the bud have spiralled out of control.

This person needs to learn to make decisions. They also need to learn to take action.

Fear and apathy (which is born from fear) are their lifetime enemies.

This person needs to learn to look honestly at the heart of any situation, heck they need to look honestly at their own emotions and what past traumas they stem from, if they want to make progress with taking control of their lives.

Frequently the universe will present this person with two options, one of which is the exact opposite or anathema of the other. To take up one opportunity will instantly eradicate any chance of taking up the other one. If you love them, watching them struggle to decide what to do will almost send you insane. To you the answer may be obvious, but to them it isn't. Before you leap in there with a fix, have you considered that it could be that they know something you don't?

If you take up the slack that this person is dropping, and don't give them the chance to learn from their mistakes, and to grow in confidence, then it is possible the universe will smite you with a doozy that even you can't handle. You can take on some of it, but make sure they get the practise at being honest with themselves, and in making decisions; it's for their own good.

As the querent's link card: You seem to be looking for someone who will put up with anything. Someone who wants to preserve harmony at all costs. Someone who hates to fight and backs away from conflict at the first sniff of trouble.

Which makes me ask: Why? What kind of monster are you?

Even if it's just a case of snobbery, and/or you want to be the prim and proper couple at all times – you are living about two hundred years past your sell by date.

I would hope that you take a long hard look at your motivations and sort yourself out. I don't think you're truly ready for a relationship with another person yet, you've still got some personal growing to do.

Sexually, it could be that you are a sadist and you are looking for a masochist to play with.

As the love interest's link card: This person is looking for someone who will let them get away with murder. They want a wet blanket that they can wring out, a doormat they can walk all over. If you are a masochist, and you want to team up with a sadist, then congratulations you have found your match!

If your personal quirks don't stretch to masochism, then I recommend that you avoid this person. However demure they may appear at first, they will try to wrap you around their little finger and are likely to treat you as if you were a slave to their slightest whim.

They are likely to be manipulative and a game player – the games will be at your expense.

If they claim to love you they are lying; they don't know what love is. They are looking for a possession, someone to own and control.

Run! Run away now!

As clarification: You are in a bad situation full of painful feelings and you want to ignore the truth. There's no way around it. If your love is unreciprocated a relationship is just not possible. Try to understand why you feel the way you do; admit the truth to yourself and face your inner fear honestly and openly, only then can you start to heal.

As a third party/obstacles: Face the facts, it's not working. Cracks are appearing in your or their façade, and it is only a matter of time before the dam bursts. Betrayal is present. Instead of clinging to a relationship that is past its sell by date get back out into the world and start living your life again.

Two of Pentacles

As the querent: You don't just want the potential for action, you want to see it working; you need to act in the world – to create your life.

When things hang in the balance there is a lot of power there as two opposing forces strain against each other, seeking liberation. If these equally strong energies can be liberated from their struggle and channelled to flow side by side, the resulting torrent can accomplish anything – and that's what your life is about: finding your inner direction, ceasing the internal conflicts that prevent you from making progress, and then powering forwards bringing your plans into the world, acting on them, and making your goals a concrete reality.

Study your inner process, remove your fear and your apathy, and work to make 'it' happen. Constant effort will bring your dreams into (a very successful) reality.

One note, money will always be in the balance, rich or poor, you are likely to have just enough to do the things you need to do, which will force you to prioritize – so conservation is as much a part of your life as liberation. Two lessons evolve from this: 1) prioritize, make sure you spend your resources on the thing that is needed next in order to achieve your current goal, 2) dare to dream, you need to consider money carefully, but when it comes down to the wire you are likely to be able to find the resources you need to make your goal a reality, however wild it is…if you are prepared to put in the patience, the sacrifice, and make the required savings at the required time.

Another thing you need to be aware of is that your penchant for the most exciting, fast moving game in town can be detrimental to you – if you spend your time mesmerized by the whirling patterns, you may miss the big events right behind them…kind of like being fascinated by the dancing rainbows in the splashing white water and thus not seeing the cresting tidal wave that the drops are falling from.

As the love interest: This person is good at juggling their finances, somehow they manage to find the cash they need to pursue their life in the way they want – because they are constantly juggling, they will not often have a surplus and if they do achieve this they'll need to save it for the lean times.

Don't expect this person to be able to pay for a luxury lifestyle, they can only afford the essentials for living and learning. They won't be likely to win the lottery either.

If you are looking for a wealthy person who will support you, I can confirm right now, that this person has learned to practise frugality. So you might want to move on and look for your sugar daddy, or generous widow, in another part of town.

This person is very versatile and is used to having to change their plans due to unforeseen obstacles. They may even like the challenge such adaptation entails.

This person likes action and movement; and having many things to do, or to attend to, sets their heart beating faster. However, like a kitten, they may miss the big picture and come a cropper because they were playing with the sparkly, moving, exciting things rather than paying attention to the important stuff.

This is a person of dualities, so expect them to be quite contrary and contradictory whenever they feel like it. Initially you may find this unpredictability exciting, but it can be really annoying when you have a specific goal in mind and they suddenly switch to 'alternate approach mode' – putting unnecessary spanners in the works when it is most inconvenient.

As the querent's Higher Self/Influences/Themes: Life is teaching you what it means to be resourceful. You seem to be forever juggling your stuff, finances in particular.

I hope you enjoy meeting a challenge, because the

universe will certainly give a lot of them to you – in spades.

Learning to be thrifty and to live within your budget is likely to be one of the first lessons you are faced with, and it's going to be a constant theme in your life. Obliterating wastefulness, and learning to be versatile will help you greatly. But you will also find it almost impossible to save, just make sure any spending you do is on things that will last and provide long-term pleasure as well as the frivolous things – then at least you'll have something to show for your efforts at work.

If you should ever win the lottery, or come into a windfall of some kind, chances are it will either be used to pay off your accumulated debts, or will be spent like water so that, in short order, there is nothing left.

Be warned – spend any financial surplus you get on land, property, premium bonds, or something else that can ultimately end up providing you with an income, or that can be sold at a later date if needed.

You'll spend much of your life breaking even. It's better to be rich and breaking even, than poor and breaking even.

As the love interest's Higher Self/Influences/ Themes: This person spends their whole time juggling money. They will likely have enough to live on, but they may never get more than that. Something will come along that eats up any spare capital they have – so do not expect them to be able to keep you in the lap of luxury.

This person is resourceful – they have to be – and versatile. The lesson life is teaching them is to be self-reliant, and to be frugal.

They are likely to develop a sensible approach to money and resources at a fairly early age – perhaps one of their parents has taught them well, but it is more likely that they have had to learn the hard way from life's lessons.

It doesn't seem to matter what level of wealth this person has, their outgoings will equal their income. If they do happen to be landed gentry, they will have to spend every penny on keeping their estate in working order. If they are downright rich, chances are their ex-wife is bleeding them dry. Don't expect this person to have any spare cash, no matter what image they project to the general public. If you want to save up any money for your old age, you'd better do it yourself in a separate bank account or investment vehicle that they don't know about – otherwise they'll probably help you spend it before the investment matures, or hex it somehow. Your nest egg is down to you.

<u>As the querent's link card</u>: Love is a dance of opposites as well as similarities, and for you the opposites are what makes things interesting. The differences between people provide the potential for all kinds of new experiences, and you need someone who understands the value of 'individuality in union' that this implies.

You like versatility and a multitude of options in everything you do, and you want the person you are with to have the same approach. There are a lot of people out there who may like a little bit of versatility and change, but when it comes right down to it what they really want is stability and predictability and you may not be ready or willing to hang out with someone like that, so check their goals and motives before you get involved. These people will be magnetized towards you because of the sense of freedom that you evoke in them, so take care to be sure the person in front of you is the person you want to be with.

You want someone who enjoys being challenged; games and adventures are part of the lifestyle you are looking for. You need someone who is willing to take the occasional risk.

<u>As the love interest's link card</u>: This person enjoys the variety and potential that exists when two people work, play, and love together. Their favourite dance is the dance of opposites – think of yin and yang in the constant dance of creation and destruction, spawning and devouring each other, the flow from one state to another and back again.

They enjoy excitement, movement and change. They are intrigued by anything active that will supply them with a challenge.

Chances are that they will enjoy sex and the process of discovering and stimulating their body and yours.

If you know massage you'll be leagues ahead of their previous partners. But be prepared to use massage in a non sexual context – just for the shear enjoyment of touching the other person's skin. If you expect sex to be the reward, forget it. They don't mind this kind of contact being part of sex, but sometimes they just want the closeness of touching and being touched without a need for anything more.

This person needs someone who will take risks and try something new. They want someone who will introduce them to new experiences.

If you are the type of person who gets lost in your job and pay little quality attention to your lover, then you will lose this person as they won't put up with having to make their own fun, or take holidays on their own. They expect you to share most of your off time with them; you won't get away with coming home and spending the evening logged onto the computer or doing additional work that you've had to bring home.

As clarification: Will you? Won't you? The two of you are seesawing back and forth like a feather falling to the ground. The two of you have got your timing so wrong that in hindsight you'll find it laughable. Walk away before the situation turns into a car wreck. What you think is perfect really isn't, part of you knows that.

As a third party/obstacles: You haven't got time for a relationship right now. If you don't focus and keep your eye on the ball, the whole house of cards is going to tumble down around you. And you still won't get to be with the person you love.

Put love relationships to one side, you can always pick up where you left off later on once the books have been balanced.

Three of Wands

As the querent: You have probably discovered early in life that every mountain you climb is just the foothill on the way to a higher peak. Some people might find this depressing, but if you allow yourself to revel in your achievements, you'll get a real feeling of satisfaction from each goal, or way station, that you achieve along the journey.

You are capable of getting a lot done, and doing it well. Each new achievement opens up more opportunities for you.

You like to have a cheering squad at your back when you start a new project. People are great motivators for you, and will help you greatly in the early stages of any endeavour – if you sweet-talk them the right way, and make sure they get a slice of the pie at the end.

You are likely to cut your own path through life, you are an individual. You may even be an entrepreneur; running your own business. That's where you are likely to shine, as you have a knack for getting things to happen the way you want them to happen.

Hard work, good communication, and people skills should help you find success in whatever you choose to apply yourself to.

Your motto is likely to be, "keep on keeping on".

As the love interest: This person is one of a kind. Independent, artistic, and passionate about what they do. This person likes to push the boundaries, and get right out on the edge of exploration. They put in a lot of hard work, and find their achievements satisfying.

Possibly an artist, possibly a comedian, whatever this person chooses to do with their life they will not be happy if they are towing the line nine-to-five in someone else's office with their nose to another person's grindstone. They are more likely to be self employed or working in partnership with a friend, finding an outlet for their inner muse; and if they aren't now, I bet they will be before they hit age forty.

This person's lifestyle may mean that they come across as a bit of a loner – but don't be fooled. They value deep partnerships and commitments, and as long as they keep communicating with the people around them they'll do well emotionally.

One thing about this person, they start projects, they reach their initial goal, and then discover that there is still a lot more to do before they are finished. This is a test of their character – if they knuckle down and keep at it, and manage to inspire themselves to continue, then they can be very successful. If, however, they reach their initial goal, look at everything else that there is yet to do, and give it up in favour of the next idea that hits them, then they may well go into a cycle of never really getting further than that first flush of success in each project.

This person may need help learning to weather the bad times, and may need to develop their stamina to a level they didn't think was possible. If you encourage them when they are feeling low and nurture their talent it should pay real dividends later on.

This is a person filled with potential, and they are going to get somewhere in their lives. It may take a while, but this is someone to believe in and stick by...If that's not what you are looking for in a spouse, or if you don't have that kind of patience, then you might want to go find someone different. Not everyone is willing to keep up the paying job and maintain a roof over another person's head while that person is finding their feet and discovering their forte.

Don't let them take advantage, push them to do their thing, but don't squash their spirit or their spark – give them the room they need to manoeuvre and it'll pay off in the long run.

As the querent's Higher Self/Influences/Themes: Life is a constant journey. You work hard and reach the place you were aiming for; you think you've achieved your goals, only to discover that your initial goal was not the end, just a way station.

But that's what keeps things exciting, isn't it? Broadening your horizons.

Generally the universe should allow you to prosper, and support you in achieving each step in your life. You will find your achievements along the way satisfying, even though you do have to make some sacrifices to get where you want to be.

Relationships with people, especially a significant other, should go well. It is through them and from them that the universe will provide its main support to you.

If you isolate yourself you will suffer, because your route through life is a people route. Socialize, gather a team, communicate. Family can be a source of strength for you.

As the love interest's Higher Self/Influences/Themes: The universe is teaching this person about stamina; they need to learn to stick with something after the initial flush of success, or the initial completion, and take it on to the next stage and the next and the next, until the potential of their initial idea has been fully achieved.

The universe is pushing this person to follow their inner fire, they are not someone who will be able to follow the herd or settle into the rat race. They need to have a dream and then live it. Any time they do try to go for the comfortable, socially acceptable and normal career choice the universe will mess it up for them somehow. This person is not destined to work for someone else, they need to realize that and take control of their lives. They will not be physically allowed to do what other people tell them they should do; they will be forced to follow their own very individual path.

If you love them and are willing to support them while they find their way, great. If you boss them into taking a job just because it's what society wants of them, then you only have yourself to blame for the consequences.

This person can succeed in a big way if they are nurtured and supported by the people around them, and they will get a lot of satisfaction from following their dreams and all the achievements along the way that go with that.

If they try to follow the usual path that many people take through life – of aimlessly wandering and never knowing what things they love to do, or having the guts to do what they really want to do – then they will crash and burn continuously, until they work out that they have a destiny and get on with achieving it.

<u>As the querent's link card</u>: You are looking for a non-conformist; an individual who is set on their own path, and who follows their inner light.

You need someone who is open and honest, who has a straight-forward, no-nonsense approach, and who will tell you exactly what they think and what they want. You don't want to spend your relationship time guessing and mind reading in order to satisfy the other person.

It is possible that you are looking for someone who will be your lover as well as your business partner.

In short, you want someone creative and self-possessed who has a good head on their shoulders and isn't afraid to call it as they see it. And you want them to be passionate about everything they do…otherwise, what's the point?

As the love interest's link card: This is a person who likes to know everything up front, they want the unadorned truth, and they want it now. They haven't got time for shilly-shallying around, because they are a very active, busy person, and prefer to get right to the heart of the matter as soon as possible.

If you um and ah, and act all indecisive around them, you'll drive them nuts. If you can't make a decision tell them you can't make a decision, and if it's about something insignificant ask them to decide for you. They'd prefer that than spend half the morning waiting for you to decide whether to go to a funfair or the park, as you are wasting good leisure time.

They like honesty, and don't mind being on the receiving end of it, so why not give it to them? After all they aren't going to stop to spare your feelings, they'll tell you exactly what they think.

This person knows about hard work, they play hard too. And it is very probable that they want to get married. When they find someone they want to commit to they are likely to jump into it with both feet at the first opportunity. They are one of life's pouncers. So if you get the 'click' vibe and you know you've found what you want, don't be shy or hesitate, take the chance! It's possible they may even beat you to the punch.

If you are someone who prefers to take their time, and skate around the edges of an issue – come at it from all sides so you can get a proper feel for it before you make any decisions – then you will probably have some problems getting comfortable with this person, and they with you. You'll regard them as too impulsive, and they'll regard you as too hesitant. That's not to say don't get together, it's just something that you should both be aware of.

If you are the type to sleep around and then lie about it (or omit to mention it), or the kind of person who will tell white lies in order to spare people's feelings, you'd be better off staying away from this person, as if they discover you have been less than fully honest with them, their temper is likely to go through the roof. They will then question and second guess everything you tell them, or have ever told them, or will ever tell them. That doesn't make for comfortable bedfellows.

As clarification: Okay, so you've made first contact, but there is still a lot more work for both of you to do on building the relationship. This card is a good omen for a long-term commitment or marriage.

As a third party/obstacles: You've found someone else. Swallow your pride, come clean, and head out after your new flame. You really weren't expecting this. Alternatively your best friend is taking advantage and you are the one left out in the cold. Some friend.

Three of Cups
As the querent: Life can be a struggle, but in

between there are moments of celebration. You are likely to find these joyous times which are shared with family and close friends to be a deeply rewarding part of your life.

Births of all kinds excite you, the birth of an idea, the birth of a project, the birth of a physical object like a book or piece of art, even more so the birth of a child. You love any kind of celebration, especially family celebrations such as a marriage or an anniversary party.

Your life is likely to be about accumulating these emotionally satisfying moments of achievement and celebration – perhaps your career involves bringing these moments of joy to other people?

You enjoy it when you are able to indulge in some carefree leisure, and are likely to do whatever it takes to make these times possible.

With this card in your personal life, it could be that you are quite fertile, as I would expect this card to indicate conception, alternatively it could point to adoption. I would be very surprised if you don't like children and actively want to have kids.

As the love interest: This person could have a very large family, if not then they probably would like to have a large family.

This person loves to achieve emotionally satisfying things, and craves celebrations and parties. They may spend a lot of time at weddings, christenings, births, or any other type of celebration – perhaps even as part of their job?

They find the emotional bonding of friendship and the deeper emotional bonding of love intoxicating, and will do a lot to keep the people they care about happy.

This person wants to share their carefree leisure time with other people; the one thing they find better than being happy themselves, is having a whole lot of people being happy and sharing the good times with them.

I would expect this person to have a whole slew of kids, lots of them. If you are a divorcee with children from a previous relationship, there's a good chance this person won't mind a bit and will embrace your kids as their own.

As the querent's Higher Self/Influences/Themes: This card is about shared celebration of emotional achievements which have lasting consequences. Now whether that achievement is about the conception and/or birth of children, or the creation of a book or piece of art, coming up with a useful invention, or the start of a business, the effect will be similar – a moment of emotional high, followed by the continuing work of everyday life.

What the universe is teaching you here is that the initial achievement, while a great thing that should and will be celebrated, is not the end of the matter. Work continues, as does life; so perhaps the message is don't expect all your eggs to hatch out at the same time. One book doesn't make a full on writing career, one piece of art doesn't make someone a successful artist – a body of work is required, and that involves continuous hard work and also the eternal process of learning about, and mastering your skills in, your chosen field.

Learn to share the good times with family and friends – anniversaries are there to be celebrated, not mourned. Live it up, have fun.

The other lesson here is that you can't spend your whole life with your nose to the grindstone, isolated from your family and friends, without some kind of emotional damage being done.

Wise up early and have fun whenever you can. Life is too short to waste it on seven days a week/twenty four hours a day in the office. Do stuff you enjoy, make the most of having a family, spend time with your kids, take time out to follow your heart. Allow yourself to be you!

Being a zombie tied to one daily routine doing what other people have said that you must do in order to be considered a success; that's not a life, that's a living death. Hedonism was invented for a reason you know. And being a little bit selfish isn't a sin. Get out and about and live!

<u>As the love interest's Higher Self/Influences/ Themes</u>: The universe is teaching this person to enjoy life and celebrate achievements and the good times with other people.

The three of cups is symbolic of the shared celebration of an emotional achievement which has lasting consequences.

Because this is a universal influence, or an influence that their Higher Self is bringing into their life, this influence is likely to have a long-term impact throughout their lifetime; in other words there will be a continuing series of achievements or events which are emotionally satisfying for them and require celebration with their family and close friends.

It could be that this person has spent most of their life to date living the way other people have told them they should, rather than living for themselves –

perhaps they spend all their waking hours at the office, seldom have holidays, and do what is expected of them, rather than being true to their inner passions and doing the things that they really want to do with their lives. The lesson then would be to take time out and do things with their family, see their kids, perhaps even to jack in their job and pursue their dreams. They need to learn to have some carefree fun in between their other obligations.

The alternative situation is that this person is pursuing their dreams, and they are having some initial success, but they need to learn to crack on with the hard work that will turn the initial success into lasting success. Sure they should celebrate what they have achieved, but the good times can't be wasted. If they sit too long on their laurels they might fail to strike while the iron is hot and thereby lose out on a rewarding career. They'd have to start over again from the beginning.

There are times to work, and times to party, this person needs to discover the balance between the two that will allow them to live a happy and fulfilled life.

<u>As the querent's link card</u>: You are looking for a happiness junkie, you want someone who will celebrate anything and everything – in particular you want to be with someone who enjoys emotionally satisfying gatherings such as engagements, weddings, births, baptisms, book launches, retirement parties, birthdays, any celebration that can be shared with family and close friends that marks an emotional achievement.

You need someone cuddly and tactile who will share a lot of quality togetherness time with you.

You probably long for a house full of people at all times. I expect you find it quite difficult, possibly even disturbing, to be alone. You won't be happy with a shy retiring type, you need a party host or hostess.

As the love interest's link card: This person wants to get engaged, they want to get married, and they want to have kids. They will throw parties at the slightest excuse. This person loves to celebrate the good times. And they want to celebrate them with other people.

Emotional highs, shared with friends, family, or their lover are very important to them. Cuddles and kisses and romantic evenings are all high on their agenda.

Expect the house to be full of people living it up almost all the time.

If you are a quiet type, or painfully shy, or just plain antisocial, then you are not likely to get on well living in the same place as this person. And the option of separate houses probably won't suit them in the slightest.

As clarification: If you haven't bought the ring already now's the time to go and get it. Heck, maybe your lover will beat you to it? It's time to celebrate, hurry up and get united.

As a third party/obstacles: Either, one of you is having an affair, or alternatively the emotion of love is not shared. Neither of these situations is conducive to a long-term commitment. Wise up and get out before this gets really messy.

Three of Swords

As the querent: You have suffered a great deal of pain in your life. It's possible that you may suffer from depression? Whatever the case, somewhere along the way you have been seriously damaged emotionally.

It is possible that you have just come out of a very nasty divorce, or maybe you spend you life falling for people who are already involved with someone else. Having affairs where the other person has no intention of leaving the partner they are with will damage your self-confidence. Maybe you have been suffering from unrequited love?

Your emotional cycle of pain is one that needs to be stopped and then healed.

First thing to do is to look at the source of your pain, and you don't need to do it alone – counsellors and therapists are there for a reason you know? There are thousands of books on depression, grief, abuse, heartbreak, etc that can help you realize that a) you are not alone in going through what you've been through, and b) that there is a light behind the clouds, that's how come you get that silver lining that everyone keeps on about.

Once you know why you are in such devastating pain, you can set about rooting out the core of it and exposing it to the light. Once you find a way of accepting what has happened to you and forgiving yourself and whoever else is involved, then you will be on the path to transcending the pain, and be able to heal yourself.

Forgiveness is a very powerful force. There are books about that too, look into it.

Now, while you might want to rush straight into

another relationship – I have to ask, is this person a repeat of the old patterns? Are you going to increase your burden of pain by trying to obtain them and/or live with them in a close relationship?

If the person you are interested in is not going to be a source of pain for you, then fine, go for it. But if your current desires/attachment are a repeat of the old patterns perhaps it is time for you to back off, get down the library and start looking into the particular psychology that is causing you to fall into this kind of situation again and again.

If the pain stems from your past, a recent divorce, perhaps childhood abuse, or having had a violent partner, then it might be that you are not ready for another relationship just yet. Your emotions are out of balance, they are being thrown off by your past experiences. It would be worthwhile finding your balance, your inner harmony, and your centre again before you start looking to be with anyone else. Even if that takes some serious therapy. It's something to consider? Break the cycle and start anew.

As the love interest: This person is damaged goods. They have gone through an awful lot of pain, an agony that is too much to bear, and this has skewed their perspective. They are out of balance, possibly out of control. Their self image is distorted. Their ability to relate honestly to others may have been compromised.

It could just be that they suffer from depression and a lack of self confidence, in which case, as long as you are aware of the problem and are happy to live with them while they are like this (could be the rest of their lives) and try to help them adjust their psychology to a more healthy self-image and outlook, then fine. Take up with them.

If the problem underlying their depression is more severe then it could be that they are not ready for a relationship right now. This is something that you can investigate. But, please take care.

If this person has just emerged from an acrimonious divorce, it could be that they are on the rebound. Perhaps you two are perfect for each other, but just be aware that their emotional equilibrium is out of kilter and they may not be seeing straight right now. They will be looking for comfort, and might mistake that for love. If so, there's a good chance they'll leave you later on once they realize their error in emotional judgment.

This is all just stuff to be aware of. The person has been in serious pain, their self image is shot, their emotional balance is off, and now you are putting yourself into the mix. Are you really ready for this? Is it what you really want? Can you handle it?

They really don't need you to be adding to their pain or being a cause of more of it. Be sure you can cope, and that you are after the long term, forever after version of the fairytale. Take account of their needs.

As the querent's Higher Self/Influences/Themes:
The universe is bringing events into your life that are painful and which have a lasting impact.

You have been going through a tense time, you have suspected something for a while now, and at last events are being pulled out into the open. You are unsure whether knowing or not knowing is worse.

Now that the worst has been confirmed it is time to accept what has happened and somehow find a way to get on with your life, to move on. It isn't as if the tragedy you are facing has struck from out of the blue, this event is something that has been expected for sometime, the revelation had the feeling of the inevitable about it.

Perhaps the 'love of your life' has been unfaithful or has said that they are going to leave you, or maybe there is going to be a death in your family. Grieving will be a part of the process of recovery, whether it's over the loss of a loved one or over the loss of a dearly held relationship.

Find your inner strength. You can get through this, take each day as it comes, one day at a time.

The main thing is to know that pain is only a part of the cycle, joy will become part of your life again in the future. Joy and pain are two sides of the same coin, and that coin will keep on spinning, it's only a matter of time before the good times return and you can feel the sun again.

Have hope.

As the love interest's Higher Self/Influences/ Themes: The universe is bringing some serious pain into this person's life – perhaps someone they love deeply will be diagnosed with a terminal illness. Or maybe their lover, someone they view as the love of their life, is leaving them, or has been having an affair and they're about to find out.

The tension of suspicion will be replaced with the pain of knowledge. Something has run its course, or someone's time has passed. Whatever the event or situation, it is something that has been suspected for a while, it isn't a bolt from out of the blue. But it is traumatic even if it is/was inevitable.

Harsh reality has to be faced, no matter how

painful the process. This is not a time when it is possible for them to look away, and it's going to take a lot of inner strength for this person to get though the trauma they are living with.

This person will find the good times again – life is cyclical, sometimes we have pain sometimes we have joy. It's an ongoing process.

If this person can learn to take what comes when it comes, and deal with it then, rather than spending the whole time worrying about things that are beyond their area of influence and cannot possibly be changed, then they will be able to at least enjoy the pleasant times.

The severe pain they feel won't last, support them while they get through it.

<u>*As the querent's link card:*</u> Are you looking for pain in a relationship? The feeling here is of someone who is purposefully looking for a partner who is involved with someone else, or who will leave them, or devastate them somehow.

The implication here is that your personal psychology is preventing you from finding a happy and/or permanent relationship to be involved with.

Find out what it is within yourself that is preventing you from allowing yourself to love, and give, and be free and joyful in partnership with another person.

Perhaps you are denying your true sexuality, and living the life that society says you should live? If so, why torment yourself like this? Living a lie isn't living. In addition, if you don't love your partner, you are damaging them and lying to them and that's no basis for a relationship.

Be true to your heart, be true to yourself, and be true to your soul.

If your religion is what's stopping you, I think you need to take time out to study other religions and realize that there is a whole lot of diversity in the world. If God is a God of love he/she/it/they would not want you to suffer like this. You were created the way you were created, and if your sexuality is leading you to same sex partners you should embrace that. If your religion prohibits it, then get a new religion.

Belief is just that, belief. It's not fact, it's a theory. There is more than one 'book' in the world.

As the love interest's link card: This person has their inner wires crossed. They are looking for something transient and then when they find it they are telling themselves that it's the real thing, a permanent love at long last. Then when it ends they torment themselves over it – but they chose a relationship that was doomed from the start.

If you are married and have no intention of leaving your spouse, you're just what they are looking for: someone who can rake them over the coals yet again.

If you are sensible you won't fall for it. Walk away because this person is going to make your life very messy. They are going to fight when they said they wouldn't. They will choose the millrace rather than the millpond. They'll create a huge fuss and say you promised them forever, when they were the one who said all they wanted was a bit of fun, and they'll believe their own propaganda too. They'll be very emotional and very upset.

If the relationship between you both does start to threaten to be permanent, if you start to get serious, they will find some way to force you to leave them, or they'll find a way to back out and then blame you for it.

If you are a serial bigamist, or someone who takes many lovers, then they'll blame your infidelity and any lies you tell on the eventual break up – and because they are looking for maximum pain for themselves they are probably going to proclaim your "villainy" to the world, even if you were honest with them from the start and made sure that they knew you were a sex addict, an unfaithful type, or earned a living as a prostitute.

This person is looking for a situation where the person that they are emotionally involved with will hurt them. It is not recommended to get involved with someone who has this card placement.

As clarification: An ending. What has been is gone, possibly before it even started. Heartache is inevitable here. All you can do is cope with the pain, or grief, and find a way forward on your own. Life deals you these cards for a reason; find a way to accept what has happened so that you can get back to your inner calm. All things heal in time.

As a third party/obstacles: Let's face it. The fact that this didn't work out is for the best. You feel as though a weight has been lifted from your shoulders. So stop pretending to cling on.

If you are still entangled in the relationship, this card indicates that you should leave in order that you can begin your own healing process. If there is a good reason for staying, you should realize that it is possible to fulfil your obligations from a distance, you don't need to put yourself through this pain.

Three of Pentacles

As the querent: You love starting new projects, getting them to a stage where the plans have been drawn up and signed off…but then you get frustrated by the amount of work that is required to bring the project through to completion. And at that point all you want to do is give up and go start the next project.

If you can develop the stamina to see things through to the end, then you will be able to get where you want to be in life. While you might find it a struggle to finish things, it is something that you are definitely motivated to do.

You are obsessed with success and are very driven to be seen to be the best.

You want your efforts to result in lasting success, your drive is to achieve something timeless that will never go out of fashion or end up on the rubbish heap of history.

Time and resources are important to you, and you dislike it when people chuck away opportunities by being lazy or uncommitted. You hate wastefulness, whether it's wasting time, wasting chances to achieve, or being wasteful and/or creating waste.

You need solid foundations in your life, which means that in terms of relationships you are looking for someone who will be with you for the long haul. When they say 'Until death do us part' you want them to mean it.

One night stands are likely to leave you feeling uneasy, and if a relationship fails you are likely to find it tough to let go. You wanted to be successful at it, and you can't help thinking you've failed somehow if you and your lover part ways.

You need to realize that sometimes two people just aren't right for each other. Salt and sugar in the same bowl really doesn't work most of the time; you are better off keeping them separate. And the same is true for certain types of people.

Take time out to enjoy your achievements, and make sure you spend quality time at home with your partner – as you are likely to bury yourself in work and never see them. If you are never with the people you love, you can grow apart, and then they leave and you get upset…Remember that relationships take work if they are to be a success, you can't just leave them on the backburner and expect them to be unspoiled when you take a look days, or even weeks, later.

Schedule time slots for romance into your hectic schedule. Live, love, have fun.

As the love interest: This person enjoys using all the available resources to make things, or achieve things in the world of the physical.

They are very tactile, and want to have things they can touch or point to, to show off their success to the world. They will have a trophy room somewhere where all their achievements are on display – they may use their whole house or business for this purpose. Their ostentation in this regard helps them to reinforce their self image of being 'someone', or someone worthwhile, someone successful. We each have our methods of making ourselves feel like we matter, this is theirs.

This person probably dislikes waste of any kind, being it wasting time, or creating 'garbage'. Economy and efficiency are important to them, although this may not hold true when it comes to supporting their self image. They'll want the frills that mark them out as a person to reckon with.

Because this person is great at making plans that actually have the real potential to develop into something concrete and workable, they are able to become very successful if they can develop the stamina to see things past the initial stages of completion on through to final completion. They are motivated to achieve success so this stamina is something they are likely to want to cultivate within themselves.

Less creative, dedicated, hardworking people may be jealous of what this person has – but if they put the same level of commitment and vision into their lives and work they could have success and happiness too.

This person knows that fear, apathy and laziness are the enemies of achievement and fulfilment. It's a lesson we could all do with taking to heart.

This person probably isn't very patient. If they see you wasting time or talent they are likely to get angry or annoyed. Therefore if you are the type of person who wants to sit at home eating your partner's chocolates, and getting fat off their effort, then I suggest you go find a different success story to sponge off, as this person could have you out on your ear in short order.

This person is likely to be looking for a long-term, fully committed relationship, that will not end until one or other of you is dead. They take their marriage vows very seriously.

If a relationship fails, this person feels as though *they* have failed and they will move mountains to try to avoid that feeling. So if this person is getting lost in work and you want them to be lost in you instead, then hold them up and tell them the problems, tell them how you feel. Use plain language, make your desires and needs clear. Tell them your fears. Explain what you need and I bet you they change their ways in short order.

<u>*As the querent's Higher Self/Influences/Themes*</u>: The universe wants you to discover your talents and appreciate them. Once you know who you are and what you are good at, you should use that information to carve a career for yourself in an area that will make the most of your natural strengths.

It is possible that you will be good at a lot of things, in which case you really need to find the one you like best and stick at it.

Trying a lot of different activities and getting some really good information about business studies and being self employed is pretty much vital for you. The earlier you do this in your life the better.

You are likely to have the makings of an entrepreneur, so getting the confidence and discipline to follow your dreams through from planning to the eventual finish is pretty important. It is likely that a lot of the lessons the universe throws at you are about finding yourself and learning will power and self discipline.

You enjoy taking time out to really celebrate your achievements in the world, and it could be that you aren't the only person celebrating. Once you get on your path, it could be that you will receive worldwide recognition for your work.

One thing you need to learn, if you don't already

know it, is that wasting time is wasting life. This is an important one so I'll say it again: wasting time is wasting life. Make the most of every moment, do what you want when you want. Don't put things off, tomorrow can stretch out into decades – if there is a tomorrow. Buses don't always get the chance to turn up in threes. Hear what I'm saying? Get on with it!

<u>As the love interest's Higher Self/Influences/ Themes</u>: The universe is teaching this person about what it takes to finish ahead of the game. The lessons that they are learning are about what it takes to be successful. Getting the first stages of any project planned and completed to a level that will allow them to be a foundation stone for the work that will follow is vital.

Once this person has worked out how to separate the wheat from the chaff in the ideas forum that is their brain, they need to learn about the discipline, willpower, and knowledge required to see something through from foundation to completed success.

Their main task in life is going to be about finding their true nature, the heart of their being that motivates them to lead in their chosen field, they need to explore every avenue until they find out what it is that they best like to do with their time – the thing they enjoy most – and then they need to take their dream, their confidence, their natural talents, and make that into a career.

If this person isn't self employed, they should be, they can go a lot further as the head of the ship, and they will be far more fulfilled in their quest for success.

This person can get what they want from life, even

worldwide acclaim, if they can learn the psychological skills and physical expertise required to get them where they want and need to be.

As the querent's link card: You are looking for someone who is accomplished and skilled in the arts of relationship and love. You need someone who knows exactly what they want in all areas of their physical life, but relatively inexperienced – so that they still need to learn about the give and take of relationships.

You want someone who you can look up to, but who can also still learn from you.

The three of pentacles is about initial success in matters of the world, or physical achievements, but where there remains a lot yet to do before real completion and ultimate success can be claimed.

It could be that you need someone who will propose to you. Once the engagement is in place, then the relationship can continue on a more intimate level, perhaps?

In terms of sex, you are very likely to want someone who has experience, but not too much, so that there are still a lot of techniques that you can teach them in their pursuit of mastery of the bedroom.

As the love interest's link card: This person needs someone who is willing to go for the long term in a relationship. They require a lover who is willing to make a solid foundation in love; the commitment of an engagement would be an example of what they are looking for.

This person also needs someone who has quite a lot yet to learn, but who has made some real progress in the first stages of their career or home life. The same is true of sex: they need someone who has a firm grounding in the techniques of satisfaction, but who is willing to learn a whole lot more! So would prefer it if you have some experience, but not too much.

This person will want you to cooperate in building something for the future, the purchase of a house, the commitment of a proposal, the ongoing growth of a business. There will be some icon, or concrete object, that they can point to and say 'you have committed to and achieved this', and while there will be a long way to go before the dividends are available to be reaped, the foundation will have been set in place by your actions. And the foundation will be for something that the two of you can celebrate together.

As clarification: You can successfully lay the foundations for something solid in the future. Obsession, attention to detail, and making sure the little things are just right will pave the way towards your goals. With hard work, you can both make a real go of this. Just remember, you have a lot more to accomplish before you can safely relax, and even then constant work will be required, as with all things, to keep the relationship tip top.

As a third party/obstacles: You are the one that threw this away. You handled the situation incompetently and threw opportunities away. Bowing to social pressure was not the way to go. You are possibly too late to try again; the damage may have been done.

If you do want to have another go you are going to have to be honest with yourself and with the person you like in order to make any headway. Even so you are unlikely to succeed.

Four of Wands

As the querent: There's a good chance here that you have had a pleasant experience growing up, that your family have looked after, and nurtured you. You are at your best when you are allowed to be creative, and when you are in the company of others where all of you are working towards the same goal. So you're an 'artistic' team player.

You are passionate about your loves and hates, you feel things strongly and have no inhibitions about wearing your heart on your sleeve; you will tell people exactly how you feel about things when asked.

The meaning of this card is success, reaping rewards, and taking the time out to enjoy those rewards. The implication is that you really don't have to try that hard – but people who don't put in the effort, don't get anywhere, so maybe it's all on tap already?

You may have a lesson to learn about the hard work required before success can follow, but it's possible the people that you surround yourself with – friends, work colleagues, family – will help you and cushion you from some of the harsher realities that you might otherwise have been faced with in life.

No one can expect to be able to sit back on their laurels and make something of their life that way, but it's possible that you don't have anything to prove. You could also be one of those lucky people whose Mummy and Daddy keep them safe and provided for, for their entire lives.

Alternatively it's possible you are the hardest

worker on the block, it's just that what you do doesn't seem like work to you. You enjoy what you do so thoroughly that you may as well be indulging in your hobby or hobbies all day long?

When the sun shines, make hay. But remember to keep something aside, for the hard times and rainy days, to tide you over between festivals.

You like to have a positive, happy time through your life and you see no point in moping around about spilled milk or any other calamity. Therefore, it is likely that you won't be too keen on anyone who spends the whole time being gloomy and shouting about the disasters that are either on the horizon or all around them…You'll feel better with people who are full of sunshine, and warmth.

As the love interest: This person seems to be having a ball most of the time in their life. They are passionate about what they love to do, and do it to the best of their ability. If they are sensible they have surrounded themselves with a group of hard working positive people who will help them achieve their aims and success in life.

Creativity and play is important to this person.

It is possible that they might be rich, either because their family keeps them well looked after, or they have inherited or won their fortune. They may even have struck it rich at a young age from one of their early projects.

This person may need a friend who knows how to keep the sharks at bay – but then again it's probable that they already have a couple of people in their lives who fulfil this function for them. Also, if you are someone who understands the need for putting something aside for a rainy day until the good times come again, then you may be able to help them in that respect.

This person needs nurturers around them, not doom and gloom mongers, nor do they need opportunists. Chances are that they are pretty savvy and will be able to tell the difference between a gold-digger and a genuine lover.

Should this person trust you when you do not have their best intentions at heart, then shame on you. I hope you get your comeuppance.

If this person isn't well off, it may just be that their work is also their hobby, and they thoroughly enjoy every moment of every day. Certainly they seem to be all set to get the most happiness out of their life that they can. Good on them.

This person could make a good business partner in an industry where art or invention are the key to success, specially if they handle the creative and personnel aspects and you handle the money. They are a creative team player, who enjoys and works best in a relaxed atmosphere. Give them that, and you'll get the best from them.

<u>*As the querent's Higher Self/Influences/Themes*</u>: Fours can be seen as the brief lull after the action of the three, a well earned rest or even a retreat from what has gone before. But they can also be seen as the calm before the storm of change that is forced by the obstacles that come with the five. In terms of Karma, I guess you could view this life as a well earned rest, a timeout, before you go back into the hurly burly of cause and effect.

The rewards associated with this card, are those

rewards that follow hard work. The implication is that if you apply yourself to your career and work hard, you will reap the rewards of your labours. Perhaps your job has great bonuses, involves long holidays, and/or pays very well? The rewards could be about shear enjoyment, loving your job, as wands cards are about passion and creativity, and bringing things into the world.

Because this card is about being rewarded for your activities, if your effort is directed towards the positive, and applied in a positive way, you should get positive rewards, however if your effort is directed in a negative way, and you apply yourself to negative activities, you will get a negative reward. In other words, instant Karma might have a big part to play in your current life – if you are nice, nice things will return to you; but if you are nasty, nasty things will return to you.

Have you ever had that situation where you think nasty things about someone then next thing you know you smack into a wall or stub your toe? That's an example of what I'm talking about – instant Karma in action.

If you put in the creativity and effort, your life is likely to be enjoyable for the most part. We all have tragedies and life lessons to cope with, but your life is likely to see a lot less of them than many people.

As the love interest's Higher Self/Influences/ Themes: This person is probably going to have a great time throughout their life, loving the work they do, and getting plenty of opportunity to kick back and relax in favourable surroundings.

Don't get me wrong, they are going to have to

work hard in order to reap the rewards. But the creativity and positive approach that they put into every aspect of their life will see some very beneficial results.

One warning, if this person's approach is negative, the rewards they receive will be negative rewards. Probably every bad thought they have will result in something bad happening to them. If they are nasty to the people around them, and negative in the expression of their passion and life force, then they are likely to be one of the world's most miserable and reviled people.

Instant Karma will play a massive part in this person's life, so if they are having a really bad time, it's because they've got their mind set in the wrong way. If they reprogram themselves to the positive, their life will improve immeasurably.

In terms of Karma, this life can be viewed as a timeout between the hard work and achievements of their last life, and the struggles and oppositions that will force psychological, emotional and spiritual growth in the next life. As a result of this timeout that they've earned, they are less likely to experience as much tragedy and pain as many people do. For them, this life is about calm, and rest, and enjoying what they have.

It is possible that their lifestyle is fairly unique, so if you want to hang out with them you will need to be fairly adaptable, and be able to amuse yourself on your own when necessary. When this person goes into work mode, you will need to be able to leave them too it and support them in their efforts. They are likely to be quite Herculean in their work ethic. If you get under their feet the whole time they will be unlikely to thank you for it.

As the querent's link card: You need a relationship to be a place of sanctuary that you can escape to when things get tough. You want to come home to peace and quiet, and a truly nurturing love.

You are looking for someone who will give you breathing space, and who will allow you some rest and respite from the stark realities of life.

You crave someone who is creative and passionate who knows how to make the most of their leisure time with you; who can help you totally forget about your working stresses and problems, and get you into a much nicer headspace.

The person you need will be someone who has a calm and caring temperament, who has found their centre and knows how to create and live in a relaxed and happy atmosphere.

Someone who has a working knowledge of relaxation techniques would be perfect: if they practise meditation, or yoga, perhaps even hypnotherapy all the better, they can teach you how to reach the stress free place that you so obviously need to find.

As the love interest's link card: This person is looking for someone calm and relaxed, who will be happy to make their dwelling place a sanctuary from the stresses of their working life. They need someone caring and nurturing who finds fighting and arguing anathema. Woolly jumpers, snuggling in front of the fire, and a gentle and kind approach to sharing your lives together, is what is required.

If you like a good blow-up to clear the air, or just enjoy picking arguments or having aggressive discussions for the fun of it, then they will not find their time with you pleasant or conducive to continuing a relationship to the next level.

If you love meditating regularly and are in tune with the cosmic heartbeat, then you could be just what they are looking for.

Quiet please, they need to de-stress.

As clarification: Things are coming to fruition, but while early success is nice, don't rest on your laurels too long. Continued work is required to make a relationship work. It is time to consider settling down, making a home, ensuring the nest is well lined and comfy. These things are important, even in an 'open' relationship. Security and knowing the boundaries really will help.

Feeling secure will help to make you both happy. Don't underestimate the need for this.

As a third party/obstacles: Feelings of restriction and limitation are behind what is driving you apart. If you try to force someone to live a life they are not suited too, you should not be surprised when they protest or throw a fit and walk out. Whether you are to blame or whether they are not living their life honestly, it will result in the same thing – separation.

Alternatively someone else is already in the mix. This person has property, wealth, and has been working hard to make a connection with the person you love. Their persistence and effort has paid off. Safe to say, you missed the boat. Chalk it up to experience.

Do you really want to pursue someone who is enamoured of another? If they don't love you, they don't love you. Loveless interaction is no basis for a satisfying relationship.

Four of Cups

As the querent: You hate the boredom of the everyday grind. Working to earn money so you can survive just seems to sap the life and joy from you. Here's a question, if your normal daily routine instils such apathy in you, why do you continue to do what you do? Why don't you change the routine, change the job, change where you live.

You enjoy the shake up and movement and adaptation involved in new situations, new places, meeting new people, so why not aim for a lifestyle and/or working environment that can help provide you with the variety and spice you crave?

If you remain passive and inactive, then things will remain in the same old rut. If you want something different out of life, you have to make it for yourself, and it's not that difficult, you just have to be willing to say "I am going to do *this*!" and then actually get off your bottom and do it!

Adjust your attitude. *I can't* will get you nowhere. *I can* will take you places.

Once you realize that you are the one who has the power to control your life and to make the changes that you want, then you give yourself the permission and freedom to do whatever you want to do with your life.

Remember, you can try anything once. If it doesn't work first time, then plan better, change your approach, try something else. But don't stop just because you meet a few tiny little obstacles in your path.

Because you have this massive need for change burning underneath all that apathy, you probably aren't in the right place to start a relationship right now. You need to sort yourself out first.

The opportunities for what you want are staring you right in the face, you just need to change your attitude, get your head out of the sand, and take a look around you.

<u>As the love interest</u>: This person has hit a rut in their life, and they feel they are powerless to do anything about it. They have a desperate and burning need to regain the passion for living that they once had, or that they know is possible, and the way they can do this is through change. But something is stopping them. Their apathy or lack of ability to make a decision and act on it, is probably the result of fear.

Okay, so it takes guts to pick up your family and move somewhere else, or to change your career midstream, or to do something most people would only ever dream about – but this is probably what they need to do.

If you can help them to find the courage to step out of their normal routine, they'll probably be very happy about it in the long run. However, their mindset at the moment is such that they may see change as a threat or something to avoid for a whole list of reasons. In fact they may well be actively ignoring the opportunities to do the things they want that are being presented to them.

This person's attitude could well be one where they currently feel that the grass is greener elsewhere, and they may dabble with infidelity in an effort to relieve the boredom.

Any relationship that this person does get involved with right now, any commitments that they make, are likely to get thrown by the wayside in due course. Some time soon they will find the guts to actually set out to make the changes that they need to make, in order to feel fulfilled in their lives. When that happens, any romance or affair that was in progress may end abruptly.

As the querent's Higher Self/Influences/Themes: You've entered a period in your life where you feel discontented, possibly even jaded. Everything you have experienced so far, everything that you are experiencing now, somehow it all just seems like you've wasted the time away. What after all have you achieved?

You are actually being overly hard on yourself; you've achieved a lot even if you don't always feel that way. All your experiences so far are preparing you for the future. Your unease with life as is, is your inner drive getting you ready to move you forwards into a new section of your life. The help and support you need are available if you look for them.

The information you require that will allow you to make dreams into solid reality is at your fingertips, you just have to notice it and see it for what it is.

It's time for you to cast off the chains that you have made for yourself – any prison that you are in is of your own making, probably as a result of your attitude rather than any other cause.

Change how you view the world, change how you approach your work and your home life and your hobbies. The answers to your needs are there, all you have got to do is make a ninety degree turn and things will come into focus. Other people can help, they have probably even offered.

The universe is trying to get you to find your own pace and carve out a destiny under your own steam. Instead of following the herd you need to follow your heart. Realize that, and you'll be taking a big step forward towards getting what you need from life.

<u>*As the love interest's Higher Self/Influences/Themes*</u>*:* The universe is teaching this person a lesson about emotions, passion for life, personal motivation and the importance of their attitude in the process of enjoying and making the most of their lives.

This person is being confronted by their lack of passion for even the most basic joys of life – they spend their life searching for the perfect flower instead of really looking at what is in front of them and appreciating it for what it is. Heck, they may not even be searching, they could be so lost that all they can see is the negativity they are creating for themselves – like wearing sunglasses under the full moon, everything is black.

If they take the time to appreciate a sunrise, or get back to the greenery of the natural world, it would probably really help them. They need to get back in tune with the positive wellspring of unconditional love that is the source of life; that all pervading and penetrating essence of being that is the love of God, the creative principle in action.

They will likely need help to change. They need to be taken out of their normal environment and experience new, positive things. Six months exploring the countryside of New Zealand should help. By that I mean that they need to be in a place where they are away from any of their old "friends" (the negative people who are helping to keep them trapped), their old job, their old relationships (how they interact with their family), they need to be in a totally different environment involved in totally different activities, and learning an appreciation for life, and learning that they are the ones who are responsible for making things happen in their life, they are the ones who can see things in a negative light, or find the positive instead.

They need to take ownership of who they are and how they relate to the world; and regain access to their inner drive, rediscover their source of true power – the ability to look honestly at themselves, and to be themselves.

It is something that they can only come to themselves, such a deep inner realization cannot be donated by someone else, but other people can help them get into an environment where everything around them demands that they take a really good look at what is.

At the moment any pleasure that they do gain does not last, and they have a tendency to think that what they really want is just around the corner, or just beyond their reach. As a result they don't concentrate on where they are now or how to actually solve their problems, because they are living in a world of what if, instead of the world of what is.

As the querent's link card: You have a deep yearning for something, you're not sure what, but you think it might be provided by another person, or by love. You are trying to get the excitement and spark back into your life – apathy and boredom have replaced passion – you don't know exactly when things changed from fun to dull, but they have. So here you are looking for greener grass.

Thing is, another person can't give you what you are looking for, because what you want is something that only you can give yourself. Your inspiration, your lust for life, your drive; how to get it back? Change your circumstances – and I'm not talking about your romantic circumstances, there's a good chance here that what you have with a certain someone is actually very good if you bothered to pay attention and quit taking them for granted. Change your life circumstances: pursue your dreams, move house, change jobs, take up a hobby or sport, get out of the house and do new and different things.

Take up communication, talk about your needs and desires with your lover. Voice your inner conflict. They aren't psychic, you need to tell them what you really want.

You can be very needy and it's possible that you fear being left alone, and yet you refuse to shake things up, or to reach out and take the love that is on offer in your life. You want excitement, but you won't risk getting out there and actually having some.

Looking for a new lover, one night stands, and/or an affair is displacement activity from the real problem. Sort yourself out.

As the love interest's link card: This person has a deep need for some excitement and romance in love. They are likely to dig themselves into a rut and then listlessly drag their heels, making the rut deeper, instead of leaping out of it and making the changes they want happen.

The reason this person is unwilling to put forth ideas and suggestions for change, is that they have a deep emotional insecurity, and they use their boredom as a mask for these complex internal issues.

What they really want is someone who will make them feel safe and secure, and who will make decisions and be the more aggressive partner in the relationship. But, and this is important, they also need someone who will help them feel relaxed and happy about any changes that take place – they love to have stepping stones, and crash mats, and security blankets around them.

It will probably take a lot of very clever winkling to find out what this person really feels and thinks about the choices of activity that you are putting on offer.

Don't be too impulsive and rash, you are going to have to have the patience of a saint, because this person must be made to clearly state what it is that they like and that they want to do. If you say these are the options, they'll say "you choose", so you choose, and they hate it. They didn't want to make a choice because they didn't like any of the options on offer – they were being discontent and apathetic, but didn't want to offend you.

When they come bouncing up and say joyfully "Let's do something! What do you want to do?" they really mean, *I have an idea for doing something, but you have to winkle it out of me – lets sit down together (maybe on the lawn with a picnic) and make a long list of all the possibilities and eventually you might find the one I'm thinking of! But I ain't gonna tell ya. Prove you love me by spending this time with me helping me to get you to decide to do the thing that I want to do.* Buy in some nice food, romantic candles, have a close and cuddly day of deciding what to do today, and then go out the following day…because, by the time you've finally guessed what it is they want to do: a, you're already doing it, and b, the day will be at least half gone and there won't be time to put the other day-out plan into action today.

If you can't cope with this kind of emotionally insecure, manipulative, find-the-lady type of game-playing you might want to run from this person. They might be cuddly and calming and excellent at their work and at their home life, and good looking to boot, but they could just drive you insane…unless you love guessing games and your whole idea of romance is paying constant and devoted attention to the person you love at all times – in which case you are perfect for them.

<u>As clarification</u>: Looking to pastures greener isn't the answer. You aren't in the right place to start a relationship right now. Concentrate on sorting yourself out. Other people don't hold the answer.

What do you need to change in your life or in yourself in order to feel right?

Only you can make yourself happy. Opportunities do exist in your current situation, if only you'd stop hoping for someone else to wave a magic wand. You have to find the answers yourself.

<u>As a third party/obstacles</u>: The problem isn't someone else, it's your attitude. If you get off your arse and stop moping around you might actually be able to achieve something here. Seeking your pleasures elsewhere or running away because you are

afraid, is not going to help you obtain that which you find meaningful. So, are you going to sulk, or are you going to find a way of making it work? Any action will be an improvement – either away from or towards. Just make the decision and act on it already.

Four of Swords

As the querent: You are on the solo path of self-discovery at the moment. You need to find your centre, and recover your equilibrium – or even find it in the first place – and the best way you can do this is to retreat from the normal pressures and hurly-burly of life.

You are in hermit mode. You need a place to rest in utter tranquillity. Somewhere where you can contemplate the spiritual, the religious, and the philosophical without interruption.

You need to distance yourself from the world in order to find the answers to the questions that concern you right now.

It could be that you need some time for recovery and recuperation after an illness or emotional tragedy. Perhaps there has been a lot of fighting in your close personal family and you need time away to gather your energy and resources.

Getting involved in a close relationship, making a commitment to anyone right now, could be a mistake. Without this time on your own you will find it hard to get the energy and perspective you need to attend to personal matters that need to be resolved effectively. Make some space around yourself.

As the love interest: This person needs time away from relationships and the stresses and pressures of everyday working life. They are trying to find a place of retreat where they can regain their strength and equilibrium.

They probably have a strong need to examine the religious and philosophical aspects of their life.

Even if this person is in the middle of a crowd they are likely to feel alone, or the need to be alone.

The feeling with this card is a need to retreat and recuperate, the need to gather their inner resources and inner strength after expending too much of themselves.

There's a good chance that this person just wants to be left alone by everyone, including you. You cannot expect anything from them, not even friendship, as they have nothing to give – even if they wanted to – they are exhausted and are physically, mentally and emotionally unable to cope with any demands that you might place on them.

You can see to their needs as long as you do not harbour any expectation of a return, or place any kind of obligation on them. But respect their wishes. If they don't want to know, leave them be and go pursue love elsewhere.

As the querent's Higher Self/Influences/Themes: The universe and your Higher Self are very active in your life, driving you towards a retreat from the affairs of man in order to recover your inner strength and find your centre.

Your life is likely to be heavily influenced by a quest for philosophy or religion, or perhaps you are taking the path of the hermit – whichever is the case, you are probably going to be on a retreat from normal society and the rat race.

The universe will find a way to drive you away from other people and force you to look at your innermost self, who you are, what makes you tick, why you are here. You need to find your inner peace and happiness. Once you are comfortable with you as you, then you will find the strength to take what you have learned back into the world, but not before.

If you are pursuing a solitary life, you are probably on the right path. If you are lost in the crowd, then the universe may well hit you with illness, tragedy, or some other method of confining you to your own company until such time as you can make sense of who you are and what your purpose is.

Don't be alarmed – you will face nothing that you cannot handle, though you may need to dig deep to get through it. And it is possible to be alone in a crowd, so perhaps that is the route your Higher Self will choose for you. Whatever the case, you need some time to yourself to gather your strength and make sense of things.

<u>As the love interest's Higher Self/Influences/ Themes</u>: This person is being asked to retreat from the world, in order to follow a solo path of self discovery. They are being prompted to find their centre and their inner strength. They are likely to be being asked to examine philosophy or religion or their inner motives in order to understand themselves and their place in the world.

The path they tread is very much a solo path: as you should already be aware, each of us has our own *way* and that way can only be trod by us – no one else can take the journey for us.

As this person's journey is about retreat and

possibly recuperation, they need to be free from the pressures of the world and the stresses of normal life in the rat race, to accomplish their goals. They need to take time out, and if you dog them because of your desire for them, you are only likely to achieve the opposite effect from that craved. You will drive them away further.

There is a good chance that they have neither the mental, emotional or physical strength available to cope with other people right now. It could be that they are very, very psychic, and contact with the chaotic energy of others causes them pain.

I doubt you'll be able to achieve more than friendship with this person, and if you should find them receptive to your advances, there is a good chance that the universe will drive you apart sooner rather than later. That doesn't mean you shouldn't enjoy each other's company, it might be that you turn out to be the only and perfect person for them, but be aware that if they tell you to back off, they mean it.

Respect their words and respect their choices.

As the querent's link card: You are actually in need of a timeout from relationships. If there is any relationship you want to pursue at the moment it is your relationship to the divine and to yourself. Now is a time for philosophy or religion, a time for retreat and self-examination.

If you are interested in a relationship with another person that person is going to have to be a source of relaxation for you in your life, demanding nothing, wanting nothing, just being with you to share what they have. It's a very hippy-style situation that you are after. No pressure, just a calm life. A timeout from any and all kinds of stress.

In truth, you are being a bit of a hermit right now. You need time for yourself more than anything else.

As the love interest's link card: This person needs a timeout from the stresses and struggles of relationships at the moment. They are in hermit mode, seeking calm and a retreat from pressures of any kind. That includes the pressures of being wanted or needed by another person.

They need to look to their spiritual and philosophical peace of mind right now, in order to find their centre and their source. Another person in their life would probably get in the way of that. Right now they need space and quiet and to be left alone in peace.

If you are interested in this person, and you love them: then to give without thought of receiving, to love without thought of being loved, to provide without any kind of obligation, to have unconditional love without any requirement or expectation of it being returned – if you can do this then you might find a place in this person's life. But even the simple act of cosying up to them because you want company could drive them away.

This person cannot physically, emotionally or mentally deal with your wants and needs right now. They are going through a very deep process that requires their entire attention and resources, they have nothing to spare and nothing to give.

If you are sensible you will leave them to it and find another person to lust after and desire.

As clarification: You need to take time out and

recover. You are not going to get the rest and quiet you need if you head out on a love quest. Things will sort themselves out on their own if you let them. Sit back and find your centre of balance. Withdraw from the fray.

As a third party/obstacles: Events are occurring that you can do nothing about. Your lover is gone. Try to remain open and positive, concentrate on the good things in life. Seek out your friends and confidents – there are people out there who will help you through your emotional pain if you let them.

Four of Pentacles

As the querent: You really aren't in the right place to start a relationship right now.

You are overly concerned with the need to have money; whether it represents safety and security to you, or you measure your self-worth by how much you have, or maybe you want to be able to live in the lap of luxury – perhaps even with someone else paying the bills – whatever the case, any relationship that you get involved with now will result in the emotional wealth being put aside in favour of financial wealth.

The dangers inherent here are, if you are starting a business and a family, that you will spend your whole time at work and never see your spouse and children. They only grow up once, and if you miss out on it now because you haven't got your priorities set to 'family first', you won't get to see it.

Very worst case scenario is that you miss out on family, but that's okay because you'll get to see them later when the finances are secure, except just as the business starts finding its feet, the spouse divorces you because they've had enough of not being a part of your life, and takes the kids away with them. Then the divorce settlement takes half your finances and you end up back in the cycle of having to break your back at work in order to keep afloat and pay the bills.

If on the other hand, you are searching for someone rich so you can feel secure, I can assure you that going after someone because they are rich is not the answer.

Money won't make you happy, it helps because it means you can have the material things you want in life. But it won't fulfil your emotional needs, and the rich person you end up with could turn out to be a right monster. If you are prepared to live a hollow life, empty of love, in exchange for having a live in masseur then that's your decision. But if it was me, I wouldn't be happy living like that. At the very least make sure your rich lover is someone that you can be friends with.

Okay, so you have a hang up about cash and material possessions. It is possible, probable even, that you are an obsessive type personality as well as possessive. I suspect you may have very deep emotions for the people you care about, and a jealous streak a mile wide. I would expect you to be very territorial as well, possibly suffering anxiety if a stranger picks up or moves something you own. You would do well to try to get help calming down and becoming more at ease with sharing, as these traits are likely to be detrimental in any serious relationship you might become involved in.

You are a very able person, easily capable of acquiring the finances you need to replace any object that is damaged or taken from you, so your fear of loss on this front seems a bit silly if you think about it rationally.

Your jealousy and fear of the loss of people you love is likely to stem from abandonment issues that link back to your childhood. These will be less easy to solve, but at least if you put a bit of personal work into analyzing and coming to terms with your past, you'll be able to get a handle on your responses in the present and the future. Once they are no longer subconscious, but consciously recognized, emotional reactions then you are a good way along the road to sorting yourself out.

Learn how to quiet the anxiety and stress that underlie your drive to succeed and you'll have a much happier life.

As the love interest: This person has a very strong need for financial security, and a feeling of security and stability in their life. There's a good chance they have emotional abandonment issues from somewhere in their past, which are the source of their need to hang on to everything they have, whether that be people or things.

They are driven to be successful themselves, or to be with successful people. This could make them quite a headache to live with as they'll always be after the next 'hit', the next emotional high based on a feeling of accomplishment or achievement which they measure in terms of cold hard cash. Who has what. Possibly it's a case of keeping up with the Jones's. That or they'll be trying to carve out an empire for themselves, or marry into one.

There are a few things you need to be aware of about this person: they may have their priority scale set to cash rather than family, they may equate having with being, and they may mistake wealth with love.

In other words, they may spend their whole time at work rather than with the family. This will be because they are convinced that they need to put a roof over your head and feed you in order to have your love. You'll need to talk to them about what is important to you, and be aware that they are making sacrifices in order to please you – working themselves to death is not something they prefer to do, they would prefer to be with you, they just have their priorities a little twisted.

If they are a clutter monkey – they can't throw anything away – and collect all kinds of things to them (probably stuff that you would consider to be rubbish), it is either because they need to be able to look at what they have achieved physically around them, and probably they were deprived – could be physical, more likely emotional – at a very early age. If you can wean them off quantity in favour of quality that might work, but the real trick would be to teach them that what they need is the physical closeness of another person, you, rather than stuff – but they'll be worried you'll leave, which is why they want the stuff that won't leave.

If you are wealthy and they are coming on to you, it could be that they believe they love you – and they will probably be utterly genuine about it – but what they are in love with is the lovely crinkly, chinky cash in your bank account. They could believe that the receiving and giving of gifts is actually love…if you are in emotional pain they'll give you some object (possibly instead of a hug) because they think that that is what you need, conversely when they are in emotional pain they will want you to show your love with a valuable gift – you can always teach them about hugging, cuddling, and what love is really about at the same time and wean them off gifts of stuff in favour of the gift of closeness.

This person fears loss and abandonment, so they are unlikely to be interested in a short term fling or one night stand. They may be very standoffish until they are certain of your intentions and commitment because of their fear of losing that which they become emotionally attached to.

They are a very capable, loving person whose emotions run uncommonly deep – so your time with them could be very rewarding indeed. If you ever want to split up with them it could be another matter entirely, so if you are sensible and kind you won't play games with their emotions.

<u>*As the querent's Higher Self/Influences/Themes*</u>: There is quite a lot of internal conflict resulting from the influences on you. What it appears to boil down to is that you feel the need to hang on to things in order to feel safe, but the universe is trying to teach you about the freedom and joys of travelling light.

Things are taken from you, in order to free you up to experience news ways of acting and being in the world. But instead of putting the material to one side and taking the universe up on the lessons it is making available to you, you are trying to cling harder and harder to the old ways, the old stuff, the old methods of living, you cleave to the material things that are weighing you down and keeping you stuck in a rut.

One hint you might want to pay attention to, is that if you have the skills and craftsmanship to do a good job of whatever career you put your mind and talents to – those skills are a part of you, they will come with you wherever you go and whatever you do. As long as you are prepared to update yourself with the latest knowledge and techniques, your skills are likely to remain a source of income for the rest of your life – as long as you enjoy indulging in them. If not, find a thing you like and get skilled at that instead.

Another lesson here is about personal growth – particularly in terms of business – if you are skilled and you make a product or artwork that you like, you need to be able to let go of it, to sell it, in order to earn money from it. Otherwise you are like an artist or writer or inventor who lets no one see their work – they won't make an impact on the world until after their death.

Once something leaves your hands and enters the world of another person, anything can happen to it, it could get mangled or broken, or it could be put on display and admired. You will be unable to control what happens to it once it is no longer with you. You need to let go of that desire to control.

It's one of the first lessons of screenwriting – the script is only the beginning. Films are a collaborative art, and very few films are ever made that follow the writer's words, let alone their imagination, to the letter. Screenwriters have to be tough to survive; and once sold, they need to be strong enough to walk away when someone starts mutilating their baby, their screenplay. If they remained unwilling to allow their screenplay to be altered, they would never sell it, and they would never have a career in screenwriting as a result.

Learn to travel light – if things are being taken out

of your life it is because you are not allowing your adventurous spirit to soar, for fear of losing...what? Try something new once in a while, be prepared to travel, be willing to give up your creations to other people, learn to let go of that iron control, overcome your fear.

Stay safe, but be willing to give the new, unusual, and untried a chance. You might find one of these new things is a perfect fit for you and gives you a fulfilment you have never found anywhere else before.

<u>*As the love interest's Higher Self/Influences/ Themes*</u>*:* I suspect that the universe is trying to teach this person to be more adaptable, and more flexible in their life. It is likely that they will fear loss, or fear losing control, maybe both.

There is a good chance that this person is living in a rut and has built up a wall of belongings around themselves in order to feel worthy or secure. They need to realize that they don't require any of these things to be the free and happy person that they desperately want to be. As a result the universe will take things away from them in order to try to get them to see this.

The process is likely to be exceedingly painful for the person as they will not want to let go. Once they have learned that it is okay to let go, it's okay to branch out and try new things, it's alright to tell other people to get knotted and go live your own life rather than constantly trying to meet their approval and expectations; once they have learned this, life should get a lot easier for them.

They need to gain skills and knowledge, to perfect their hobbies to a level where the hobby can become a career. And to set aside their fear and pursue their dreams. They need to find the freedom of their inner heart and soul.

If you are a free spirit who knows the importance, the necessity, of following a dream then you have a lot that you can teach this person. They may find your confidence and daring a little scary at first but if you can help teach them how to fly, they will love you for it later.

If you are another type of person, someone who is happy with the lot they have been given by others and who doesn't want to make waves, and you just want someone sensible and dependable to share your life with – you probably think you've found your perfect match in this person, but you would be wrong. This person is going to break out big time, and do something rash, unpredictable and unnerving, the kind of thing the neighbours will talk about for decades. The universe and their Higher Self will force them into it. If you want dependable, search elsewhere.

This person may not know it yet but their life is going to be pretty wild, they will be physically unable to be dependable or predictable because they won't be given the chance. All those castle walls they keep building up are going to get flattened at some point.

<u>As the querent's link card</u>: You have a tendency to cling to that which you have. And you are desperate to keep any material or financial security that you have achieved. This combination may result in you going after someone who is wealthy, but who isn't necessarily right for you, or even nice to you.

You need stability, and to know that you are financially safe. Some fly-by-night seat-of-the-pants type person would make you quail and quiver. You need someone dependable and reliable, like a solicitor or farmer – someone who has their feet on the ground, their head on their shoulders, and who is predictable and loving. Someone who keeps their word, and who won't abandon you.

As long as you feel safe with your other half, you will be fine – but if you start to feel insecure the less pleasant side of you may well emerge, the side that is clinging, jealous, grasping, perhaps even some stalker tendencies may exist. This dark side of your nature, the negative side, is extremely unpleasant. If you let it rule your common sense that part of your personality could well drive your loved one away faster and more surely than any other influence in your lives.

If you source your own finances and squirrel them away, rather than relying totally on a partner it will take some of the pressure off the relationship. Try it, it could help.

As the love interest's link card: This person is insecure, and terrified of being left alone to fend for themselves. On the surface they may well come across as a lovely, attentive, bright personality who has your best interests genuinely at heart – and they do. It's just that they also have these deeper, darker waters where their insecurity lives, and it could manifest as clinging, or as jealousy, or the possessive nature of a stalker – if it gets extreme. Give them no reason to fear losing you, and you may never notice this side of your love interest, but there is a strong chance that it is there.

This person is probably an obsessive personality. They will be concerned with your welfare and happiness. They'll be nurturing and probably bend over backwards to accommodate you when they want to. But they are also consumed by the need to know that there will be a pay check coming through to the bank account each month.

Lack of money will be a very big source of stress for them.

Another way to stress them out is to rearrange the furniture, or sell your old rubbish down at the market. Don't even try to nag them into selling their old junk (of which there could be a lot), they probably would never speak to you again!

If you are a creative type who is happy to live day-to-day, and work out where the next meal is coming from when you get to it, then you are exceedingly unlikely to be able to maintain a long-term relationship with this person. They need everything planned. Possibly months in advance.

While they may like positive surprises they absolutely hate negative ones, with a vehemence you may never have witnessed before.

If you are dependable, have a good track record for earning money, and are looking for permanence, then this person could be just right for you. However if you are the type who likes to take risks, gamble, play the field and look appreciatively at other people, you'd probably be better off finding love with someone else.

As clarification: You want a relationship, but you feel that earning a living is more important. So, where do your priorities lie? Only you can work this out. Go with your inner voice.

If someone is a gold digger, or insincere, there are ways of determining this. Hire a P.I., or take a very close look at their friends. Are we talking shallow or deep?

As a third party/obstacles: An attraction for material and financial wellbeing has taken priority, and the person you love is pursuing this all-out. There isn't a whole lot you can do about this; they have to come to terms with what they want themselves before they will be ready for a committed relationship.

If a divorce is in the offing, it is because the person you love is more concerned with physical wealth than love, and has been for some time now.

Five of Wands

As the querent: A desire to achieve your aims no matter what, can mean that you get frustrated and/or angry when you are thwarted. You are the type of person who is capable of moving mountains and can do it with flair – as long as everything goes according to plan.

You almost never take no for an answer. And you really are not afraid of hard work. Which is good, because sometimes the work can be very hard. However, you feel aggrieved when other people aren't prepared to put in the same level of backbreaking effort as you.

All of the above can make you a very difficult, or shall we say challenging, person to live or work with.

Once you have learned to count to ten and hold your temper, you will be a much easier person to be around. Constant arguing, backbiting, and belittling of others is far from pretty, and if you do go in for that type of behaviour other people will see you as ugly, no matter how well coiffed you are.

When you do find yourself in conflict the most

productive way forward for you is to find a creative solution to the disruption of your plans. It is through conflict that we learn to be adaptable and flexible, it encourages our creative and puzzle-solving abilities, and it helps us to discover that charm and tact can be more effective than bullying or aggression. In short, when faced with opposition – instead of being a stubborn mule who refuses to budge an inch, and then turns into a ravening monster when the opposition also stands their/its ground – try to find a positive way to resolve the issue, see it from the other person's point of view as well as your own, be prepared to compromise when necessary.

In a relationship you need to calm down and take a milder approach when your lover disagrees with you. Encourage them to explain their opinions, so that you can come to understand why they feel the way they do. If you can grasp the root of the problem, and the importance of the issue in their eyes, then you will be able to come up with a solution which suits both of you. Always check that you are on the right track before putting things into action. Respect your partner, and be aware that they may be an expert where you are a novice; take the time to listen to what they have to say.

<u>*As the love interest*</u>: This person has very strong opinions and probably a very strong self-belief to go with them. This is great, it means you'll usually know what they want right away – specially if you ask them. The down side is that they can become bloody-minded, obstinate, difficult, and generally very argumentative and unpleasant to be around when they feel frustrated or that they are being opposed in any

way.

This person needs to learn to count to ten, and reassess the situation in the light of calm and rational thought before they embark on their usual tantrum.

If you can calmly explain why you feel the way you do, or what it is about their plan that is flawed and why, etc., and get them to understand your point of view they will probably calm down and apologize right away. But always remember this person is very arrogant in their self-confidence, so it doesn't hurt to open your arguments with "I love your idea," followed by your concerns. A little bit of careful flattery (nothing obvious) doesn't hurt with this person. Be positive rather than negative in your criticism if you want a quieter life.

This person can be both Herculean and fragile at the same time, and they tend to take things personally – the good and the bad. These qualities can be very attractive, but they may be the qualities that cause the most problems in the relationship if this person is unable to understand your viewpoint or opinions.

As long as this person respects you and sees you as someone worthy of trust and consultation you should have few problems with them.

They will try to throw their weight around, so you need to be someone who isn't afraid of saying no if this person is being unreasonable. They really want someone who will stand their ground and tell them what's what and why. They are looking for strength in their partner, another Hercules who will protect them and help them out when the going gets rough. They would also do well with a negotiator or peacemaker who is skilled in the arts of persuasion.

If you have a real argumentative streak and a

temper problem, you might want to back off and find someone else, as this person isn't the type to back down or back off from a fight when they get riled.

As the querent's Higher Self/Influences/Themes: Your life is likely to be very much about growth and lessons learned through a process of changes, these changes are forced on you by the obstacles and inner conflicts that are imposed by passion.

Artistic expression through words and/or pictures is likely to be important to you. As these are the medium through which we experience most of life, flavoured or driven by emotion, there will be particular resonance here for you – perhaps you should consider following your passions in order to find your career, rather than doing something dry and lifeless that holds no life force or inspiration for you.

The pressures of daily life, the minutiae of earning a living and paying tax and finding food, etc could be an exhausting chore for you. If you adapt your behaviour and learn the information that will allow you to proceed smoothly and efficiently in these areas, life will become a lot easier for you. A stitch in time saves nine, is a good motto for you.

Conflicting and difficult emotions are likely to be a feature of your life. If you can learn patience and objectivity in the face of the howling inner storm, apply some logic to the irrational, and calm down a bit you'll find things a lot easier to deal with. Stuff you thought was life-threatening when all you could see was the wave coming down on you, will likely turn out to be phantasms – insubstantial ghosts – when you look at them with a clear eye. And if when you look with a clear eye, the wave is still there racing towards you, advance preparation should nullify the assault: we're back to a stitch in time.

Life isn't easy for anyone that I've ever met, people hide their turbulence and pain from each other so it isn't usually on show. This isn't always healthy, and can lead many to think that they are on their own in any given situation. You are never alone in your emotion, someone else – usually many someones – has gone through, or is going through, what you feel. They learn to cope, they take the time to see it through, and they come out the other side wiser, stronger, and more compassionate towards others.

Take each day as it comes, deal with the conflicts presented, and have the confidence to follow your heart. When it comes down to it, life is about trying/doing and about having fun; winning and losing is a false set of guidelines that are set up by those who have something to prove.

<u>*As the love interest's Higher Self/Influences/ Themes*</u>*:* Love changes everything for this person. Their process of learning and growing has its main taproot in adapting their psychology and way of living and being through the conflicts that emerge from their pursuit of desire.

This person has some harsh lessons to learn that will affect them on a very deep and life altering level. It is possible that they could get quite irrational when they are in the throws of passion, their first set of lessons are going to be those of perspective and objectivity.

Depending on how far along their evolutionary path they are, this person could be ready for marriage and be searching for a spouse, or they could still be working through the process of falling in love without thought of the future or the long-term consequences.

This person lives and grows through the conflicts of passion.

This person is likely to be extremely creative, and harsh reality can tire them out and wear them down. If you are ready with a box of Belgian chocolates and a cool flannel for the times when the stress gets to them, you could well become their favourite intimate friend. If you also happen to be a solicitor or accountant who can take their troubles away and sort them out for them (get permission first), you'll be even more favourite. Just be aware that some of the life lessons they are faced with they have to handle themselves in order to learn self sufficiency.

You will need to be patient, a good communicator, and have a calm temperament. If you are prone to explosions or a short fuse, the arguments between you could be legendary – and that's not a good thing for long-term happiness.

<u>*As the querent's link card*</u>: At some level you have a need for change, change that is rooted in passion and driven by conflict and obstacles. Perhaps you like to have someone in your life who will stand on their own two feet and tell you what's what as far as they're concerned?

No wilting wallflowers for you, thank you.

Positive conflict, like positive stress can be good for us, helping us to break out of old patterns and discover new more rewarding methods of behaviour and ways of doing things.

A little bit of a shake up now and again keeps things moving along, maybe you feel it adds spice.

Whatever the reason for it, you are looking for someone who is happy to scrap now and again. Or perhaps it is just that the person you love drives you up the wall?

As long as neither of you get nasty about it, it could lead to a very rewarding and positive growing experience for both of you. Just try to grow together rather than apart.

The danger here is that one or both of you treat it as winning and losing – as soon as arrogance enters this equation the arguments cease to be healthy and become damaging. In such a case, if you are unable to find a way to discuss your feelings in a healthy atmosphere and change the way you relate, then you might want to leave and find someone less fractious to be with.

You want to be able to speak your own mind, and be respected for who you are, but you have a desperate need for love, and you fear abandonment. This combination is what is behind your argumentative streak. Positive communication is key here.

As the love interest's link card: This person is looking for someone who will speak their mind and hold their own in an argument. It is possible that they may even try to pick fights as they test the boundaries of the relationship.

Because they want someone strong to be with, and they are also strong, they may well get quite argumentative when they feel frustrated, ignored, or that you are talking rubbish.

They need someone loving and giving who will treat them like a princess, or a conquering hero, but who won't take any rubbish, and who can't be easily manipulated or overpowered.

Gift-giving and a lot of quality personal together time are likely to be required in a relationship with this person; if you can find a way to make them really feel special and loved they'll be content. In return you'll be given the freedom to be you, and they'll want the same respect in turn.

They need to know that they are safe and that they won't be abandoned just because they speak their mind.

The implication is that they are looking for a long-term love and probably marriage. If you are someone who doesn't mind the occasional spat, and is prepared to allow your lover to be themselves without demanding they change to fit around you, then this person could be that certain someone that you've been searching for.

Life with them won't necessarily be quiet, but it will be very rewarding if you can both learn to take account of each other's feelings and to communicate how you feel in a positive way.

As clarification: Boy, are you frustrated right now. You don't seem to be able to get anywhere.

Focus on the situation at hand. There is a creative, active and passionate solution to this. Don't let your shyness or self-consciousness get the better of you. If you take the initiative you can succeed, but it will be an act of major courage on your part. The likelihood of romantic success is higher than the chance of failure.

As a third party/obstacles: So the person you love is with someone else. If you allow your anger or feelings of betrayal to control you, you will just make things worse.

Retire from the scene gracefully, and at least you may come out of it with a better divorce settlement. You are in pain, but that is no reason to be nasty in return. Karma will be in action here, you would do better to allow it to do its long-term thing.

Five of Cups

As the querent: Spending your life worrying about your regrets for what is past is no way to live. So things may not have gone the best way possible, the trick is to learn from your mistakes or errors. You can use the experience you have gained to move forwards without making the exact same mistakes again.

If you keep looking backwards instead of thinking about the future and enjoying where you are now, you will trip yourself up because you don't see the rough track under your feet.

What's gone is gone, learn from it and move on. Don't waste your time thinking about the time you've wasted, do something about it instead.

If you dwell in the past, if you dwell in regret, if you dwell in the darkness – that's not really living is it? It's just existing, and probably existing in pain if you're honest with yourself. There's more than enough pain in the world, you don't need to add to it from your stagnant pond. There's a wellspring out there – *well*spring – and it's a lot closer to home than you imagine. Take a look at the stones under your feet and start moving forwards.

This card is about irrevocable loss, and wallowing in pain and emotion rather than noticing the positive new opportunity which has come into your life. A divorce, a death, the breakdown of a friendship, these are the type of events from your past which could prey on your mind. Because of the trauma you felt at the time you may be reticent to trust or love again, in pushing away anyone who gets close you could potentially be pushing away the future love of your life.

Quit holding grudges and focus on the nice things.

As the love interest: It is possible that this person is emotionally stuck in their past. They have been through the loss of a loved one. Whether that loss takes the form of a broken friendship, or a divorce, perhaps even a death – that loss caused them a lot of distress possibly even anger. They need to acknowledge that they had a part to play in the conflict, and take ownership of their responsibility for their actions and reactions to the situation. They should not overload themselves with guilt for something that may not have been their fault, but nor should they shift the blame away from themselves if they are partly responsible for what went down.

Until this person accepts what has happened and their role in it, they won't be in the right place to start a healthy long-term relationship. They need to forgive the other person and/or themselves, let go of the emotions that keep them trapped, and move on. If they haven't done this it is possible that the pattern could repeat itself – unfinished business usually comes back around to bite people in the arse.

So, basically you are dealing with a damaged person here who has some healing to go through before they are ready to set out on the love and relationships trail again. If you do go with them now you could well end up in a rebound situation where the relationship could fall apart as soon as they regain their emotional equilibrium.

You might want to consider keeping your contact with them strictly on a friendship level until you have a better idea of what you are getting into with this person. A friendship would also help you to find out whether they are even receptive to the idea of becoming involved in an intimate relationship of any kind at the moment.

Be sensitive to their needs. Also protect yourself. Sit back, take your time, scout out the terrain properly before making any move.

As the querent's Higher Self/Influences/Themes: The universe is teaching you to make the most of what you've got, and to seize the moment or live in the now. You are likely to experience enforced growth as the result of conflict and obstacles in the emotional arena of your life.

Life is too short to spend your time moping around over what might have been.

If you spend your whole life dwelling on the past you'll never appreciate what you have now, or work towards what you might otherwise dream of achieving in the future.

The pain you have been through distressed you greatly, you have probably suffered from irrevocable loss, but what's gone is gone and however much you strive to get it back, while you can set up similar relationships and events to those lost they will only ever mirror what was. Appreciate the differences, understand that unique is good.

Forgiveness is a great healer, so is laughter.

Also, you might want to try think about it this way: a break with the past is an opportunity for you to make changes that will improve your life. So while, for example, a divorce might seem like the worst thing that could happen to you, if a relationship was unhappy, or your partner was unfaithful, surely you are better off being able to make a new life for yourself where you now have the freedom to do all the things you really wanted to do, and make the choices that lead to a positive way of living away from all the old mistakes.

Take a chance, love yourself for being the person that you are, have some fun for a change.

<u>As the love interest's Higher Self/Influences/ Themes</u>: This person's life is about growth through emotional loss. They have caused themselves pain, or had pain caused to them, by lovers, friends or family.

As a result they may find it difficult to trust that they will not be abandoned or traumatized by the people they love most, or new people who they come to love.

The growth comes from seeing the positive lessons and opportunities available. One person's tragedy is another person's bliss, it's all a matter of perspective. And even in the worst circumstances there is usually something of benefit that can be taken from the situation. Knowledge and inner strength count for much.

Another lesson here is that they can rely on no one but themselves, so this person could be very self-sufficient and independent by the time you meet them.

Once they do eventually start to trust someone they may manifest a tendency to cling, or perhaps be overly possessive of that person, this will likely be due to a fear of abandonment. As long as you give them no reason to fear, and you ensure that they know and feel that they are loved, and understand that you won't blow away with the wind or disappear with the turning tide, then their insecurity should subside and they'll be happy to let you pursue your own hobbies and activities without constant interruption.

They need to learn to focus on what they have, and what they can bring into their life, rather than on what they have lost or left behind. If they dwell in the now rather than in yesterday, or what could have been, they'll be a lot happier.

You will probably need to be quite patient and compassionate in order to fit into this person's life. You may well be needed as a shoulder to cry on, or as a shelter from the inequalities and iniquities of modern life.

As the querent's link card: Your past relationships have been blighted in some way – when they ended the finality caused you a lot of pain and/or anger, perhaps?

If you allow the past to blinker you to what is standing in front of you in the present, you only have yourself to blame. This relationship may be difficult, but it could also be quite magical.

You need to get honest with yourself about your part in causing or solving any problems that exist between you…are you really to blame? Are you really free of all blame? It takes two to tango, but then, dancing usually works best with a loving couple.

You spend a lot of time going over what went wrong previously, it's time to forgive yourself, and the other person, and move on into a new, more positive, way of relating.

Ask yourself what kind of person you want to be with and why, then look at the person you are interested in and ask yourself whether they tick any of the boxes, or whether you are falling back into the same old pattern of setting yourself up for a fall. Seriously. Be honest with yourself.

As the love interest's link card: This person is looking for a relationship that is doomed to failure – on a subconscious level they are trying to find someone who will justify their feelings of inadequacy, or bitterness about love.

If they are drawn to you it's because they've picked up on enough of your personality to know that the two of you won't mix well in the long run.

However, there is also the hint of a positive element underlying all of this psychological mess – each of you has the potential to gain from this relationship, perhaps you could be the one person to put them straight and sort them out, so that they can cope with the long term? Perhaps you are both looking for something short term?

If you allow them to use you as an excuse for wallowing in pain, then you only have yourself to blame for the results.

As clarification: Okay, you may have made mistakes in the past, but if you concentrate on what you have lost rather than on what you might gain, you are shooting yourself in the foot. You have the chance to focus on the positive here, and there is always hope. With endings come new beginnings.

If everything has fallen apart, take this opportunity for new found freedom, and use it to do things you enjoy for a change. Be yourself, find out who you are.

As a third party/obstacles: The person you love has gone off with someone else? Quit being so self-absorbed. If you bothered to take note of the situation you would realize that this was for the best. You have the opportunity to start again and inject some real happiness into your life. You are likely to come out of this relationship the winner – even if you can't see it yet. Stop with the melodrama and look for the positive angle.

Five of Swords

As the querent: Conflicts and opposition in the mental arena – thoughts, strategy, and planning are likely to be most affected.

You are likely to be very motivated towards winning, and any perception of losing could make you react with anger or bitterness. You may even have a tendency to pick fights or create obstacles for other people in order to feel as if you are doing, or achieving, something.

If you feel as though you have lost out, or that you are a loser in a situation, then you allow your emotions to get skewed out of shape. When you take things badly to heart like this, it is likely that you may damage your self-image, which may allow depression or shame to gain sway over you.

When you are able to assess your chances of success realistically, and allow yourself to back out gracefully or ask for help; if you realize that you have taken on more than you can handle, you will find life proceeds a bit more smoothly. Battling to the end in an unwinnable situation, or getting obstinate and digging your feet in when the odds are stacked against you, is likely to result in causing you far more traumatic pain than you need to put yourself through. Knowing when to walk away is a very important part of mental, emotional and physical survival.

As long as you approach life in a positive way, using conflict to bring about necessary and positive growth or change, then you can be a very helpful influence to those around you. Perhaps a career as a barrister or lobbyist would be an appropriate use of your natural talents.

If you approach life in a negative way, then you could be a very damaging and unpleasant person for other people to be around. Or you could do a lot of damage to yourself. If you can find some objectivity and perspective, it should help.

If you can learn to see an argument from both sides, and feel compassion for the weak and for those who lose, including yourself, (whether that is loss of face, losing a fight, losing possessions, losing a legal battle, etc.) then you are likely to maintain a far better social life and not arouse so much hostility from those who you come into conflict with.

You will note that loving relationships are not about winning and losing, they are about an equality of enjoyment and experience in whatever activities you are undertaking together. If you win, win as a couple; if you lose, lose as a couple; and for goodness sake leave the concept of blame out of your home life – what a promoter of negativity and waste of energy the blame game is.

As the love interest: This person may be suffering from low self esteem, and/or depression because they have allowed themselves to wallow in the belief of being a loser and in the despair that accompanies that notion.

They are likely to feel insecure and that they are unable to be strong or to win – for whatever reason. Their sense of self-image has become skewed and tainted by the emotions that they allow to engulf them.

This person's emotions are very much based on their thought processes and beliefs, rather than on reality.

This person is likely to be obstinate, combative, frustrated and angry.

Alternatively this person may have managed to regain their self-confidence, in which case they may be feisty and argumentative…but as long as they have a healthy attitude towards winning and losing this shouldn't be a problem.

Objectivity and a sense of perspective are important to this person's mental and emotional welfare, as they can have a tendency to feel helpless and let events control them rather than to take control themselves, or they could be somewhat paranoid and see ill-will or conspiracy where there is none. They may also feel isolated, which won't help their paranoia or objectivity.

A compassionate and considerate lover could be this person's route to a sense of self-worth and happiness. An inconsiderate or bullying lover could drive them to extremes of behaviour and negative emotion.

Until this person realizes that they are worthy in and of themselves, and finds a lifestyle, hobby or job that brings them satisfaction and self-confidence, the danger is that they will place their sense of self and of self worth in the hands of others.

As the querent's Higher Self/Influences/Themes: You need to learn to turn the other cheek. The lessons here are about being able to find perspective, being able to forgive, and fully grasping why you should avoid escalating a conflict at any cost.

Perhaps you should take up Buddhism, or any other religion that believes in pacifism and the preservation of life; meditation and calming techniques are likely to be something you desperately need to practise in order to find the middle way.

Life isn't about winning or losing, it's about being. The Holy Grail is attainable if you look in the right place.

Your relationships, this life, are likely to be all about your relationship with yourself and your relationship with your environment. Love is a huge part of that, but it may not be the conventional idea of love and marriage between a man and a woman.

As the love interest's Higher Self/Influences/Themes: It could be that this person views the world as black and white, in which case they need to learn about grey and its value. Or it could be that they are very self-centred and thus are drowning in the paranoia which accompanies that world view, in which case they need to learn about objectivity and perspective.

Viewing everything in terms of justice versus injustice is a harsh way of seeing the world, and a difficult way to live as it would tend to promote anger.

Forgiveness is a much more positive and healing approach to normal everyday wear and tear.

If this person can learn about unconditional love, it'll do them good.

This person may be prone to depression, anger, jealousy – a whole host of negative emotions – because they are unbalanced. Once they find their centre they will be a lot easier to live with and it will be a lot easier for them to progress with their life. Encourage them to take up yoga, tai chi, meditation, or some other form of centring activity. Massage, aromatherapy, and other time-out activities should help.

Attempt to draw them away from aggressive activities in order to help them break their cycle of violence. Note: any sports, especially those such as fencing, kick boxing, or soft martial arts would all be suitable channels for centring, relaxing and controlling their emotions for a more constructive and positive way of living. Control and channelling of aggression are vital to success in such hobbies, so anything of this nature should help.

<u>As the querent's link card</u>: You seem to spend a lot of time fighting and picking fights. The other person knows just how to drive you nuts, either on purpose or by accident, and you can't stop yourself from reacting. Perhaps you just want to provoke a reaction?

You may win, or you may lose the arguments. The important thing to remember is to be humble and merciful in victory – if you allow arrogance, or an "I told you so" attitude to rule, you are likely to damage the friendship you share. If you lose, be graceful about it – sulks and tantrums won't help.

If you both react positively, then the making up can be a lot of fun.

If you hurt each other needlessly you are both likely to regret it.

It is possible that you have a tendency to sabotage the relationship, talking yourself out of a romance where a way forward might otherwise be found. Then again, if you have cause for dissatisfaction, perhaps moving on is the best course of action.

As the love interest's link card: Your love interest is feisty, that's for sure. They like arguments and may even provoke such fights with you. Perhaps they like the process of making up?

It could be that you rub them up the wrong way, either by accident or on purpose. Or perhaps they feel insecure and provoking a fight is the only way they know to get your attention?

As long as the arguments remain on a harmless level and you both make up well, everything should be fine – even if you do have a tempestuous relationship. The problem comes if you purposely set out to hurt each other, then the resulting pain and warfare can drive you apart.

This person likes storms, they view them as a sign of passion. If you can't cope with that, then you had better find a way to deflate them, or else exit the relationship quickly in search of calmer shores.

It may be possible that they have very different goals or attitudes from you, and this might be the reason why they spend a lot of time finding faults or questioning whether the relationship will work. If you have a fundamental conflict, e.g. one of you wants children and marriage now and the other doesn't, then it is probable that the relationship will be unable to continue. If you are willing to live the way they want to live, then the rift might be healed, but if you're not sincere about it a split will likely occur over time.

<u>As clarification</u>: Love should never be a battlefield. Walk away. Neither of you will win in this situation, it is not healthy for either of you.

Constant arguments and strife will take their toll on your psyche and your health, so be wise and leave before any of this starts. Even if you feel like the victor, are you? Really?

<u>As a third party/obstacles</u>: You really want to stand up for yourself and fight, hold your ground. But engaging in combat will not achieve the victory you want.

Any move towards reconciliation will be misread as weakness and be scorned. The best way to get out of the conflict is to leave and not look back. The people involved may try to provoke a fight, if so you should not rise to the bait, it will only cause you more pain. A dignified withdrawal is the best move here. Change your phone number.

Five of Pentacles

<u>As the querent</u>: Finances are a worry. Money is spent like water, it floods away from you.

Perhaps you have a gambling problem, or have somehow got yourself into a very large amount of debt?

You never seem to be able to hang onto your cash, as soon as you get money in your pocket it starts burning a hole there.

Investments don't pan out and conmen target you.

Other people who have been through, or are currently going through, the same experiences of hardship as you can be a source of help. If nothing else, talking to them will let you know that you are not alone, and may even provide information on new avenues of help which you had not thought of before.

You need to get control of your spending. Every time you allow your outgoings to exceed your income you are digging yourself deeper.

<u>*As the love interest*</u>: This person isn't going to make you rich. They are beset by financial difficulties, and have trouble hanging on to any money they do make. If you want the finer things in life you are going to have to look elsewhere.

If you don't mind being the proverbial 'church mouse' and think that love can sustain you through it all, then good for you. This person could be exactly what you are looking for.

If you are sensible though, you'll keep separate bank accounts, or one day you could check on your savings only to discover that they have been spent.

This person's financial problems are likely to make them feel depressed, or to lose all sense of perspective. They really need to change their whole attitude to money and to spending. It is possible that they may have a gambling habit, or very large debts where the interest payments are crippling. The sooner they cut up their credit cards the better.

<u>*As the querent's Higher Self/Influences/Themes*</u>: In terms of interpretation, this card isn't the easiest to follow: it is about loss in the physical world. What

form that loss takes, and which aspect of the physical world is affected is going to be a very individual thing for each person.

Because the sequence of loss is something that is being brought into your life, either by your own activities, or by fate, there is a wide range of cause, effect and outcome.

The purpose of this physical loss is likely to be to make you look at how you live and act in the world, and how you affect others and even the planet itself with your actions, and indeed how you affect yourself through what you do – or do not do.

By the end of the process you are likely to have radically changed your outlook on living, and towards yourself and others. Hopefully you will have gained a set of positive values, care and compassion for the people for whom life is a struggle, and will have determined the difference between want and need. There are many lessons here.

Perhaps it is time that you leave your material belongings behind and go walkabout; to take some time out to discover the true nature of self and your place in the world?

If all of that sounds a little too otherworldly for you, I guess what it boils down to is that you are likely to suffer from overspending – *if* you cannot learn to budget and to live within your means. Situations and people seem to draw your wallet out of its hiding place in your pocket and before you know it you've spent every penny you have, and possibly more.

Cut up your credit cards, cancel all your bank accounts except for your savings account (the one that won't let you go into debt), pay back your loans, and start to think very carefully about the underlying cause of your spending: is it to gain the love of others? Is it depression? Do you have an addiction to buying things?

Go to the library and find some self-help books – that's right, the library, not the bookshop. The library is free. Or get your National Health doctor to sign you up for some free therapy in your problem area.

It's bucket of cold water time. Sort your life out!

<u>*As the love interest's Higher Self/Influences/ Themes*</u>*:* This person never has any cash, and they are likely to start trying to spend yours if you give them half a chance. They may appear rich on the surface, but if you got to see the level of debt on their overdraft and loans you'd soon realize that they are living well beyond their means and cannot sustain their current lifestyle for any length of time.

Even if this person doesn't have gambling, purchasing, or drug addiction sapping their resources, and they manage their money well, I can virtually guarantee you that people and situations will keep cropping up in their lives that make them feel as though they are required to open up their wallet.

Physical loss of one kind or another will plague this person. It is likely to centre around their financial life, but it could also manifest as the loss of loved ones, friends, family, or even the use of their own body. Material reality for them will be a source of difficulty and will test their character fully.

The good news is that this person is likely to be a classic example of the old adage: "Unlucky in cards, lucky in love." So while they may not have 'a pot to piss in', they are likely to know the value of a good relationship, and be loving and sensitive to their lover's needs. If that happens to be you, just don't let them buy you gifts or spend money on you. They can't afford it.

As the querent's link card: Money is an issue for you in this relationship. For some reason the feeling here is the loss of wealth or loss of self-belief on your part, probably as a result of failing finances. Perhaps you want someone who will demand that you spend more money on them than you can afford?

The high maintenance partner that you seek is too high maintenance for your budget. Also, the love interest is someone who will not be willing to learn to live within your budget, so don't make the mistake of thinking you can persuade them to change.

Perhaps you are attracted to a person who is only interested in the divorce settlement they'll be able to get a little while down the line?

You feel the need to spend more money than you can afford in order to keep this person interested in you. Whether the cash trickles out or floods out, financial problems loom.

As the love interest's link card: This person cannot afford to lavish you with gifts, or pay for your lifestyle, but they do not appear to be able to say no. Their finances are a mess and going downhill fast. They may even be hiding any unpleasant financial truths from you.

If you care for this person the best thing you can do is find a way to reduce their spending. Cut up their credit cards. Teach them how to show affection with their thoughts, words and touch, rather than with their wallet.

Money problems abound. This may damage their self confidence and make them worry far more than they would normally, which in turn could damage the relationship.

As clarification: If you aren't already suffering from financial setbacks, then a relationship could seriously damage your wallet. You are likely to feel isolated. But people who are in the same situation as you may be able to lend a hand.

Romance might be a possibility, but keep an eye on your expenditure – you don't need to lay the world at the other person's feet for love to blossom.

As a third party/obstacles: Financial stresses have taken their toll. You need to change your attitude to money if you don't want future relationships to suffer in the same way. For a lot of people money equals security, and if they are scraping together the pennies to buy lentils and then see you splashing out on things they perceive as extravagances they are going to get upset.

Alternatively, if someone loves money to the exclusion of all else they are very messed up. You are better off without someone like this.

Six of Wands

As the querent: You have an abundance of self confidence; you know what you are capable of, and you are not afraid to try new and inventive avenues to get where you want to be. Your self-confidence allows your passion to be freely expressed, and as a result your creativity and productivity is running high.

The things you do in the world are likely to get

noticed by others, lending you fame of a kind. You are high profile in your specialist field and people laud you for your achievements.

However, because you have been noticed, any misadventures or failures that you suffer will also be noticed, and fame can become infamy at the drop of a pin. Despite that, people are still likely to flock to your banner as your confidence is infectious and they hope some of your fame will rub off on them.

Attracting the people you desire into your life is a matter of taking the right approach. Like a peacock you can strut your stuff and put on a wonderful show. If they don't find you alluring it could be that they are not a peahen, in which case cut your loses and find a more appropriate partner.

Go do your thing, and have fun!

<u>As the love interest</u>: It is possible that this person is famous, certainly they are someone who gets noticed for their achievements. People pay attention to this person, so is it any wonder that you are also attracted to them?

The competition for their affections is likely to be fierce, but if you are sensible you won't play that game, or fall into that trap. Be yourself, you have no need to show off and nothing to prove. This is the most effective way to capture your love interest's attention. They are used to other people being sycophantic around them. Avoid that and you'll likely earn major points.

Fame and infamy go hand in hand. As long as this person excels people will love them, just be prepared to hold their hand and pick up the pieces if one of their dauntless schemes goes horribly wrong and the pack of wolves that used to call them a friend turns to devour them.

This person is likely to be passionate and creative, with an artist's temperament. They have the fire of life burning within them, and can achieve the incredible – perhaps without realizing it – just by going after their goal with every inch of themselves. Everyone is capable of this if they set out to achieve something with that same level of single minded, undiluted passion. It's just likely that they do that all the time.

Self confidence can be their strength and their weakness. It can appear as arrogance, or if something goes wrong, they may turn on themselves and lose all sense of perspective.

A level head and an unprejudiced eye will help you to be this person's rock and/or rudder. Hold their hand when they need you, and let them fly free when they need to. Never try to contain them, they are uncontainable. Caged they would wilt away and die like a picked flower.

<u>As the querent's Higher Self/Influences/Themes</u>: You have the confidence, optimism and passion to achieve success, if you put your mind to it.

The universe and your Higher Self are setting up the conditions necessary for you to achieve recognition for you work/hobbies/abilities from the very beginning of your life. Limelight? You love it.

You find yourself put in situations where you are the centre of attention, with all eyes on you. It is likely that when you do well you will be lauded, but when you do badly you may be vilified. If you tread water, keeping to the same standards as before, people are likely to want to know what is wrong, as chances are they have come to expect you to perform and entertain them with your skills, antics, and coups to a greater level of proficiency and glamour with each event or project you undertake.

Fame and infamy will follow you around.

It may be impossible for you to have secrets as every action you take is likely to be scrutinized by someone.

On the whole this should be a positive influence on your life, helping you to obtain that which you want through diligence and hard work. Your lucky breaks will come in the form of other people who are ready and willing to help a person with the vision and skills that you possess.

Just be aware that if you are surrounded by investors, they will not like a flop. Always have a back up plan, in case you need to dig yourself out of a mountain of bad press.

Any jobs which allow you to gain the public eye, whether it be acting, writing, reporting, athletics, marketing, the priesthood, teaching, etc. will likely be where you will shine. The more publicity, coverage and exposure you receive, the better you are likely to be at the job, as you respond proportionately to the challenges you face.

<u>As the love interest's Higher Self/Influences/ Themes</u>: This person is likely to court attention from others, if not, then they will constantly be thrust into situations where they receive it.

This person's achievements are likely to be a matter of public record somehow, and it could well be that they are famous – if not on a worldwide scale, certainly in their area of expertise and within their field of work.

This person's activities are constantly scrutinized by others; when they succeed, people clap, when they fail, people boo and hiss. It's not fair really, but that's the way the cookie crumbles in this person's life.

This person has optimism, vision and passion, and can achieve pretty much anything they set their mind to, because their confidence will see them past the most daunting obstacles that would prevent other people from even considering taking the path they tread.

Chances are, when they fail they will do so spectacularly, and they will need someone in their corner to jolly them up and shield them from the harsher criticisms that are aimed at them by the crowds that were waiting to be wowed by the spectacle that never happened.

Life with this person should be fun, and for the most part very positive – if you allow them to do their thing. Tie them down, hinder them, or pour cold water on their dreams, and you will either find yourself out in the cold on your own, or you may damage their self confidence to a level where they stop trying and all the life drains out of them. Don't be a meany; support them, believe in them, cherish them, make them happy and the two of you should share a lot of good times together.

As the querent's link card: You seem to be looking for a partner who will bring you recognition in the public eye; someone who will be approved of, and their love will be proof to others of your success. Now you may think "trophy wife/husband", but it's more than that. You want someone you can be proud of.

Someone who will show you to others in your best light. Someone who will, by dint of being themselves, mark you out as someone to be reckoned with.

Now this could be perfectly healthy; everyone wants the best partner possible.

However, placing this kind of emphasis on love – and your lover – could be a sign of a less than healthy approach to self, as it implies that your own self esteem is based on how others see you rather than on your personal inner beauty.

If you value yourself dependant upon how others value you, you are likely to spend your life as a shadow, or automaton, living to please, rather than having the confidence to get out there, do the things that you want to do, and leave your mark on the world.

If you find yourself relying on other people to tell you who you are, how to live, what to do, what to say, if you need other people's approval in order to be 'happy' – then there's a darned good chance that what you perceive as happiness isn't happiness at all. Think about it. Is this you?

What do you really want to do with your life? Who are you underneath all the clothes, the perfect make-up, the public appearance?

Maybe you are happy and healthy and just enjoy the frills, the pampering, and the trappings of success?

Live how you want to live.

Ultimately what you make of your life is your choice. It's your decision. Just remember that if you allow others to decide for you, that is also your personal decision.

<u>As the love interest's link card</u>: This person is looking for a lover who will do them proud. They

want someone who will be approved of by mummy and daddy, and the neighbours, and the paparazzi, and their pet goldfish.

Winning public success and approval is important to this person, and you, my dear, are one of their methods for achieving that. If you scratch your bottom in public, or throw a tantrum in the street, don't expect a nice cosy romantic evening at home that night. You'll be in the dog house.

Now, the very fact that this person is interested in you says a lot. They believe that you are a desirable partner...it's possible that other people have told them this and they are basing their decision to court you on that...but hopefully it's just that they know a good thing when they see it.

They want you to recognize their potential, and glorify their name, devote yourself to their cause, believe in them one hundred percent, and talk them up all over town. If someone as fabulous as you is endorsing them, that's all they really want.

If you ever wanted to end the relationship, one way to do it would be to embarrass them. Develop foot-in-mouth syndrome. Hang your paint spattered, moth-eaten undies on the washing line in full view of the neighbours. Serve bad wine at a dinner party. Any of these could be a mortal enough sin to have them handing you your walking papers.

Okay, so I'm being a little flippant here, but shallow is a danger with this person. They may not be like this. But if they burn your favourite jumper – the one dear departed Auntie Beatrice knitted for you twenty years ago from mismatch ends – there's a good bet you just entered the neighbourhood watch zone.

As clarification: Despite the odds you can be successful. This card indicates that the choices you make and the actions you take will be approved of by those who see you fulfilling your promises. Continued success is likely, however be aware that fame can become infamy in the blink of an eye; so pay attention to what you do or say, and how you go about doing or saying it. Obstacles can be overcome.

As a third party/obstacles: What you are up against is making you doubt your abilities. Take a break from the struggle and reassess your own position, motives, and how you will achieve your goals. Once you have had time to catch your breath you can leap back into the game with new ideas and new strategies that should pay off. Don't try to force anything through, as any results will be slow in coming, but keep at it and you should find the light at the end of the tunnel. Be honest and have patience.

Six of Cups

As the querent: You value the wisdom and lessons that people from previous generations can hand down to you. You may have close links with Grandpa and Grandma, or perhaps you have a lot of older friends, maybe you work with the aged?

When you find yourself facing a conundrum, the answers will likely be found in either a previous experience that you have had, or in a similar event that happened in your family many years ago. A method of successfully dealing with the problem is there if you look for it; do not be afraid to ask for help from older and wiser heads than yours.

In practical terms, if you are trying to build or fix

something, it is likely that the skills you need can be found in someone from an older generation.

You value the tried and tested methods of doing things that have been proven to work over the years. Experimenting with new ideas and techniques that are untried in order to achieve a goal probably makes you feel anxious – gambling like this is unlikely to be something that you enjoy.

If you want to discover what other people think about relationships and love, don't be afraid to milk the information from your Great Aunts and Great Uncles. A lifetime's perspective can be helpful to the young in avoiding some of the relationship mistakes that have happened to other people before.

Aside from the lessons that are available to you from the past, do take care not to dwell in nostalgia, wearing rose tinted spectacles; you can waste today by not paying attention to it – then you wake up one day and wonder what happened to all your yesterdays. They vanished in a haze of dreaming.

If you want to accomplish something you can't just wait for it to happen, you have to set about making it a concrete reality. If you have held a cherished dream since youth, perhaps now is the time to set about putting it into practise?

As the love interest: This person may have a tendency to dwell in the past, or view things through a haze of nostalgia, thereby colouring the present and perhaps failing to make the most of what is in front of them.

They tend to stick to tried and tested patterns of behaviour, work, and general living, which means that they are prone to getting stuck in a rut. They may dislike experimentation, or it could just be that they are afraid of change or of getting the new techniques wrong?

The mix of sentimentality and bullheadedness in this person's character could lead to someone who can be quite unreasonable when they are emotionally invested in a person or issue and feel that they are being challenged in some way.

While you may think this person is a dreamer, stuck in the past, or that they place too much emphasis on the way things used to be, this type of thinking can be useful. Because they like to understand where things come from, how they work, etc. they probably know their field of expertise inside out, and will likely have a much broader knowledge and understanding of this area than other people – they may surprise you, if you get them talking. Also they are likely to be great at research, and may feel right at home in an archive or library, unless they are a social type in which case they'll probably prefer to canvass people for information; either way they are likely to do a great job of obtaining the knowledge/information that you want.

If this person can loosen up, and try out new things once in a while, they may find life a lot more fun. They would probably appreciate someone with a gentle approach leading them into the present day, and help them get a glimpse of the future.

If you enjoy radical and spontaneous behavior you are likely to be the type who will rub this person up the wrong way much of the time, and they are unlikely to be the kind who enjoys sparks or making up after a fight. They're liable to hold grudges and dwell on every aspect of what has happened to them at your hands – so avoid provoking them, or you may wake up one morning and discover a (metaphorical) landslide falling on your head.

This person's childhood is likely to be very important to them, and their upbringing will have had a major influence on them. They will likely hold a great affection for their older relatives. They will be interested in their ancestors, and knowing about their family roots is likely to give them a cosy warm safe feeling.

<u>As the querent's Higher Self/Influences/Themes</u>:
Your spiritual beliefs, your connection to your Higher Self, your abilities to perceive the paranormal, are all likely to be very strong and are a source of comfort in your life.

The immortality and continuity of your spirit are likely to be an important part of your understanding of your inner processes and of who you are. This personal knowledge that you have – or feel – of what was, what is, and what will be, provides you with a feeling of rootedness and confidence in your identity and your place in the physical world.

Perhaps you have memories of past lives, or perhaps you have an ancestral guide in the higher realms that you can talk with, perhaps you are able to access the akashic records, or perhaps you can divine the future? Whatever the case, your link with the occult, or other worlds, provides you with a level of security that other, less tuned in people, do not feel and have a hard time understanding.

The problem with focusing on the realms beyond the physical, is that you can live your life in a dream and thus miss out on what is happening around you and to you. The idea of the Hermit on the mountain, lost in spiritual contemplation, dwelling apart from the rest of the world is the feeling here – and the danger. The age-old questions occur: what good is wisdom that is not shared? And, if you do not live in your body in the here and now, how can you experience the fullest expression of Self? "To be, or not to be…"

While other people may not understand your beliefs and approach to life through the world of spirit – your use of the occult to answer questions and to find solutions to the problems that face you – this may well intrigue or fascinate them to a level where they want to find out a lot more about who you are and what you do.

You are likely to attract your fair share of nutballs if you talk about your beliefs or about your other-worldly experience of reality, but there are many people who are likely to gain a lot from consulting you. Your sensitive and caring approach to the people who share their wisdom with you or who seek wisdom from you will likely guarantee that you are in demand if you choose to use and publicize your gifts.

Your real guru is your own Higher Self, do not allow others to cloud your link to heaven.

A relationship with someone who is dismissive and negative towards your spiritual beliefs is not really an option. You can happily co-habit with someone who does not share your beliefs or goals, just so long as they are willing to allow you to be yourself, and so long as you are willing to show them the same respect and allow them to be themselves. Someone grounded who is fully involved in daily life may well be an asset to you, acting in part as your anchor, and keeping you in touch with what's under your nose. Ultimately, a balanced relationship with your Higher Self is the most important relationship in your life for maintaining your personal feeling of wellbeing.

<u>As the love interest's Higher Self/Influences/ Themes</u>: Are you willing to allow this person to be true to themselves? If not, take a hike.

This person is likely to have experience with, and knowledge of, the occult. They may have had paranormal events occur to them, and they are likely to have extremely strong spiritual beliefs. It is possible that they are earning their living through sharing the occult or spiritual knowledge they have with others…and if they aren't now, it is more than possible that they will in the future.

If this person gets a hunch about something, you should listen. They are tuned into a psychic frequency that is capable of providing really useful information, from the past, for the future, and for events as they occur now. If you ignore any warning they give, you do so at your own risk. Just be aware that it can take a while to fine-tune their abilities so that they get a clear picture of the right station. This takes experience, and experience takes time.

Do not be offended if this person holds back from having an intimate relationship with you, it could be that your energies do not work well together, or it could be that they have received a glimpse of the future which reveals that the relationship is doomed. Can you blame them if they don't want to waste their time and yours, possibly years of it, on a union that will bear no fruit? However, it could just be that they aren't looking at what's in front of them, namely you, so sit them down and lay your cards on the table in plain language. This takes courage. But if you want a lasting relationship with this person you are likely to need courage, as unusual and disturbing things may happen to them, or around them, a lot.

If you dislike the occult, or find belief in the world of spirit offensive, or if you just plain don't like things that go bump in the night, then there is every likelihood that this person is not for you.

<u>As the querent's link card</u>: The past alive in the present. Perhaps you are looking for someone with old fashioned values; or maybe someone who has similar personality or skills to one of your parents, or even to those of an ancestor; or perhaps an old flame has rekindled the spark and you are looking to repeat the old, comfortable relationship patterns with them?

Another option is that you are in a relationship where the age gap is considerable – that's fine, you can each give and receive a lot from each other.

Somehow knowledge or events from the past are going to have an effect on the present, and the lessons you can bring forward into the present are valuable ones.

This is no time to listen to the naysayers, or your peers – unless they embody ancient wisdom – take the lessons and information you need from those who have gone before. You are looking for experience, wisdom and knowledge from your partner; someone who can teach you everything they have learned in their life.

A little old-fashioned romance, and attention to family tradition, will likely be of benefit to both of you.

As the love interest's link card: This person is probably looking for someone older and more experienced than they are who can teach them about life, love and the universe in general. They want a confident lover who will guide them in areas they know nothing, or little, about. If there is a large age gap between you and you are the older person, then this age gap won't be a problem for them. (Their friends and family may not be so understanding…)

This person may have a strong attachment to someone from their past, perhaps a relative, or family friend. They need this bond, so do not try to sever it. There is a slight possibility that they have an aged relative that comes with them as part of a package deal: live with them, expect Granny to move in too – style of thing.

This person is looking for a real gentleman or lady, someone who has old fashioned values, who understands honour and etiquette, and who is perhaps a born romantic?

If you like roses in the vase on the dining table, and a gentle promenade on Sunday afternoons, then this person should be happy to accommodate you.

As clarification: The past is affecting what is happening in the present. That certain someone might be returning to your life, or a long-held love is beginning to find a solid footing. Your previous experience will enable you to find a way to o'er leap any obstacles you may encounter. Age gaps or social gaps don't matter here. If your hearts and minds are in accord a relationship will follow.

As a third party/obstacles: If this is a person, don't

mess with them. They know how to hurt you to your core and will leave you feeling vulnerable and in a lot of pain.

If this is an obstacle to a loving relationship, it is the tendency you or your lover has to tint everything in rose, and to compare current events with a fantasized past or imagined future – and come up wanting more than there is 'right here, right now'. However much things may have been perceived to be perfect once, that is not the case. Your inability to deal with 'what is real' is holding you back. You need to make an honest appraisal of the situation, strip away your illusions, and come to terms with the truth.

Without this change in attitude you will be unable to make progress in future relationships.

Six of Swords

As the querent: Meditation is likely to be a very useful technique that can help you clear your mind of troubling thoughts, and allow you the mental space you need to slowly process and tick over the issues so that you can find a calm solution to the problems at hand.

Any method of putting some distance between you and any difficulties you encounter will help you to gain perspective in emotional situations; whether you travel, or take time out in the local library, or just head off into the countryside or park for a long walk.

You have a knack for seeing how disparate things fit together, which means that you can be great at coming up with new ideas, or with problem solving.

A solo profession may suit you well, however you always need to keep a balance between work and home life, sociability and solitude, so try not to cut yourself off from others – they can be very helpful in shining new light on things that you just can't quite grasp. Other people also have different skills and knowledge that may be helpful to you in achieving your task, or completing your work.

You probably enjoy the company of others, as you are likely to be someone who loves to communicate. Perhaps the theatre, radio, or cabaret would allow you to gratify this need for communication and feedback? Writing, philosophy, design, architecture, engineering; these are all areas where you might find yourself a comfortable profession.

Ideally you are looking for a calm home life, with a partner and family who will provide a caring and harmonious environment.

You can be quite unconventional in your approach to life, love and the universe, so you would do best with someone who is open minded and flexible. Same goes for your boss – if you have one.

Some of your ideas and thoughts can be quite off the wall, or extremely creative, as a result not everyone will want to hear what you have to say. If you can learn the art of keeping your mouth shut in the company of intolerant people, and learn to pause before blurting out your first thought in order to mull over how it might be received by the people you are talking to, you may find yourself attracting fewer disapproving looks, arguments, or straight-jackets.

If you happen to be involved in a relationship that has turned sour, events are in progress which should allow you to leave the unpleasant situation easily and you now have the opportunity to move on to better things.

<u>As the love interest</u>: This person is a unique individual who can be extremely creative and inventive when they are allowed the emotional, mental and physical space that they need.

They are likely to enjoy travelling in the company of others, because the stimulation of new environments and different opinions will relax them and allow them to discuss new concepts and ideas that they may not otherwise be exposed to.

This person is a natural philosopher, and great at problem solving – although the thoughts and solutions they come up with may be quite radical and/or unconventional.

If you want to upset this person, all you need to do is drown them in emotion, cut them off from all stimulation (especially human contact), or subject them to constant storms. To keep a peaceful and happy life together try to be rational and calm, help them find a simple path when they are caught up in minutiae, and be prepared for the new and unusual.

If you are extremely formal, and have to plan everything you do to the last millimetre, you may initially think this person is right for you, as they can come across as very orderly; but trust me, they are unconventional, whacky, and generally strange. They have a tendency to conduct the life-spark, they may be prone to genius, and they are very likely to vanish without a word and only come back when they are ready. If you don't like surprises, change, or a constant barrage of communication, this person is not for you.

<u>As the querent's Higher Self/Influences/Themes</u>: Balancing the mind; order from chaos; the dynamic

balance of yin and yang. Rocky starts can lead to peace and harmony if you apply yourself to making the changes that are required.

If your childhood has been unpleasant, then your adult life is likely to be fulfilling and satisfying, as you will be motivated to create a beneficial environment that will allow you to live the life you want to live, as opposed to the life other people have told you previously that you should be living. Similarly, in new situations, or initial meetings with others, things may not go smoothly, but you are likely to be willing to make the necessary moves and resolve any misunderstandings so that ongoing contact with the situation or person will become easier, and even beneficial. Hence it is possible that you may find yourself in a harmonious marriage with someone you absolutely hated, or who absolutely hated you, at first sight.

Finding the silver lining on any cloud is a speciality of yours, and you should already know that for every bad situation a positive lesson can be learned from it…even though upon occasion a lot of time and perspective are required to get there.

Working with the occult is likely to be of interest to you, as you have an innate ability to communicate with the higher realms. However you should be careful to avoid losing yourself in one mental state, or fixating on one level of reality – when if you want real communication, and unclouded knowledge, all you have to do is open your eyes a little wider. Avoid the use of drugs as they will block the communication channels and make information received murky; remember a white lie is still a lie, however you dress it up, and lies of omission can be worse than an outright fiction. So take care with interpreting what you receive.

<u>As the love interest's Higher Self/Influences/ Themes</u>: This person is likely to be very in touch with their spiritual side, and they are likely to be psychic in some way. An innate ability to communicate with the higher realms, and an interest in the occult, means that they could spout a lot of wisdom, or a lot of rubbish – depending on how clear their lines of communication with the other side are, and on how wise they are in regard to interpreting what they have been given.

If this person is not interested in fortune telling, or reading auras, or contacting the angels in some form, I would be very surprised.

This person may have had a hard time during their childhood. It is also likely that new situations bring with them strife, or a feeling of disquiet, for this person – but any such problems are likely to be resolved in the long term, as they will probably work hard to iron out any issues or misunderstandings.

This person really desires a balanced and harmonious life, and if an obstacle seems insurmountable, or a relationship appears to be unsalvageable, they will quietly disengage themselves and vanish from the scene.

Expect the unexpected while you are with this person. Religion or the occult, and universal law, will likely have a very strong effect upon this person's way of being in the world.

<u>As the querent's link card</u>: You are looking for a relationship that will help you to leave your current troubles behind. You want home to be a place of rest,

peace and safety. Do what it takes to get away, and find some place where you can have the time you need to recover your sense of balance, and think things through without fraught emotion getting in the way.

You probably want to have a partner who will let you have the freedom to travel, and to try new things, with or without them.

Time to yourself, or in the company of friends, away from home life is also important to you:- so you need a partner who is very understanding, rational and calm; or you need a partner whose job or hobbies keeps them away from the house a lot. A long distance relationship might be exactly what you are after?

A possessive or jealous partner won't let you be yourself, so try to work out how controlling your loved one is early on in the relationship, before things turn serious.

You are the type of person who is likely to run for the hills when faced with complex or difficult situations in a relationship. Instead of abandoning your commitments at the first sign of trouble, you might want to employ your brain to find an answer to the issues that face you both as a couple. Using reason, and being reasonable, are probably your best way forward to a mutually agreeable solution.

It is easy for you to get lost in the small details, and in emotion. Try to keep things simple, think things through clearly, and if you find yourself swamped by emotion try to use logic to calm yourself down.

<u>*As the love interest's link card*</u>: This person is looking for someone who can give them a sense of calm and safety. They need harmony in their home life. If you are someone who can help them to relax

and find their centre after a long, hard, stressful day at work, you might just be perfect for this person.

Bear in mind that this person can get over emotional and fraught if they feel under pressure. They need plenty of space to be themselves, and may need time away from your togetherness on a regular basis, just to unwind. If you are happy to be left behind while they go on holiday with their mates, so much the better.

If you need to know what your lover is up to every second of the day, then you are not right for this person. They will hate any attempt to control them or keep tabs on them. If you are the jealous type, forget it, you will only bring yourself and this person strife by attempting to make this free spirit into the person you want them to be. You won't be able to change them and they'll resent you for trying.

This person is able to separate their thoughts from their emotions, and thus might come across as a cold fish while you are in the heart of tragedy or ecstasy – it's not a reflection on you, it's just that they are trying to see a clear path through to a balanced perspective. The thoughts they come up with while in the throws of passion, or the far away look in their eye as they get seriously intimate, may seem inappropriate but don't let it put you off; it's just that you are their muse and they feel inspired. Gently tell them that you expect them to concentrate on the here and now, and on you – after all it takes two to tango, n'est-ce pas?

<u>As clarification</u>: You need to separate your thoughts from your emotions in order to get some clarity and perspective on your situation.

This is your opportunity to get out of a difficult,

repressive or tumultuous relationship. Follow the North Star in pursuit of that job offer, go on an extended holiday, do whatever it takes to get out of Dodge. Just be discrete about it – if you want to leave the storms behind.

As a third party/obstacles: Problems have been coming to light. Either you have been separated physically by the demands of life, such as a long-distance job, or for some reason you are being kept apart. If this is why your relationship isn't working you are going to have to find some way to reunite, or call it a day. Continuing like this will not do either of you any good. Sit down together and have an honest discussion about your needs and options.

Alternatively, if it has all gone wrong and you just need some time to recover, then distance and travel – possibly with your friends – is the best course of action right now.

Six of Pentacles
As the querent: Easy come, easy go: well maybe not, but to the outside world it could look that way. Somehow you seem to be able to get the help you need, whether it is emotional support from family and friends, or financial beneficence. You never seem to have a surfeit, only enough to see to your needs, and sometimes you have to fight damned hard to get that. However, when you are in trouble, a helping hand eventually turns up, and likewise, because you've been through the tough times, when you see someone else struggling and you have a little spare, you are liable to give them what little extra you have.

You should know by now that you can't rely on

other people to help, sometimes the helping hand you receive is your own – planning for a rainy day, paving the way for a particular outcome by doing the required work in advance.

Balance is what this card is all about. Give a little, you get a little. Take advantage of someone, have advantage taken of you.

Life is very much what you make of it, so it can be heaven or hell accordingly.

If you've got away with take, take, take throughout your early years, be prepared for poverty and give, give, give in your later years.

Yours is a see-saw Karma of needs met, and the sooner you get the hang of working within that the better off you'll be, and the better able to cope with the downturns and upswings of fate.

<u>As the love interest</u>: This person has quite a lot of supportive people around them, and believe you me, they need them. Finances are frequently thin on the ground, and emotional distress can be a feature. Friends and family gather around to help this person. That'll be your job too, as long as you are with them.

When there is a time of plenty, this person won't want to go overboard, they'll want to save for the inevitable rainy day, so don't expect them to lavish you with gifts; also they'll give away their time, energy, money and support to some of the worst vagabonds you've ever set eyes on. You will not think of this person as prudent.

However, do not try to prevent them from giving selflessly, it will only create tension and probably a fight.

This person's life is about having their needs met,

it's not about excess. That doesn't mean they won't be rich, it just means that all their funds will be tied up and unavailable. Outgoings = Income. They could well be an entrepreneur, rolling in it one day and bankrupt the next.

If you need someone with a secure attitude to money, this person is not for you. They don't value money. They value the things that money can get for them, but not money itself, so they have a tendency to throw it around willy-nilly.

This person is likely to be a risk-taker, and will happily get involved in endeavours that would make other people faint with worry.

If you are a strong person who is determined to maintain separate bank accounts, and you don't mind surprises, and love people from all walks of life dropping in unexpectedly, then this butterfly of a human being could well be perfect for you.

<u>As the querent's Higher Self/Influences/Themes</u>: You might want lots of things, but you'll only get what you need. This life's lessons are about understanding give and take: give when you can, take when you must. 'Nothing in excess' is another phrase that springs to mind. There is an honesty and a warning here that is implicit. To take that which has not been offered, or freely given, is to invite disaster in the long run, because this card is about equality and balance.

You do not have to be from a poor background, or be hampered by poverty; you may have an excess of wealth to start with. But it is probable that you will lose any such excess through various calamities – such as a series of extravagant ex-husbands, or many, many children, stock market crashes, bad investments, or just plain old blowing your wad on frivolous fripperies and frills. Whatever the case, whatever your lifestyle, you'll have enough to meet your needs but very little more…there will definitely be times when you have to tighten your belt and rein yourself in to a significant, and possibly worryingly, painful degree. It is at these times that you will discover who your true friends are.

Through being placed in need yourself, you will develop compassion for other people who also find themselves in need during some point in their lives. The lesson, and *trial*, you go through may be quite harsh if you don't take the hint early and learn to see things from the less fortunate person's point of view during your life process.

The result is to teach you to give an olive branch as needed without any hope or thought of recompense from the other person, and to save for the proverbial rainy day: there'll be a few of these at the least. Planning, forethought, and timely action are also part of the lesson here; as well as the eventual wisdom and understanding that with effort and humility on your part, all your needs will be supplied with just enough to meet the crisis – as long as you put in the required effort in good time.

Keep your door open.

<u>*As the love interest's Higher Self/Influences/ Themes:*</u> This person will never have an excess of funds for long – something or someone will come along and eat up any spare capital. It could be that they give freely to charities, or it could be that they just never take account of the amount that they are spending. Either way, this person will definitely have

times in their life when they are caught short and will need a helping hand. While this might make them a drain on your wallet, the good news is that if you are ever in similar need, and you ask them for help, they should have learned the necessary compassion to be only too willing to help.

This card is about balance and equality – give and take. Needs are met, not wants.

This person is not necessarily poor, they could be very rich, however their assets are likely to be tied up in some way so that they are unable to access their extra wealth. Perhaps all that lovely cash which they earn is being paid out in alimony, or covers the school fees?

This person has to learn to give freely of their time, money and support to those who are in need. In return, when they are in need, they will find people who understand their pain, and who will give the aid required – although this may take the form of emotional rather than physical help, depending on where the real need lies.

This person must learn to open their heart during their life, and cease to judge those who they previously deemed beneath them.

Every one is equal; each one of us may go through a period of need at some point in life – king or pauper. That is the lesson of compassion that they are here to learn.

<u>*As the querent's link card*</u>: You are looking for someone who can satisfy your needs, particularly in regard to finance, a stable home environment, and lots of physical contact – probably in terms of walking hand in hand, and being hugged and caressed, as much

as anything else. You also want someone straight talking so you know where you stand at all times, and you need them to like the same thing in return. Surprises generally aren't welcomed by you unless they've been thoroughly planned, with your approval...Does that then count as a surprise?

You may crave someone who gives you gifts, but you will need to be equally generous with them: turn and turn about is the name of the game in this relationship.

You find emotional satisfaction in having the home comforts surrounding you, and you might find any kind of change in your home environment distressing, so ideally you are looking for someone who will help give you a structured, orderly, well-planned life, and who doesn't go around changing the furniture about every five minutes or changing the colour scheme just for the hell of it.

<u>As the love interest's link card</u>: This person is looking for a solid, organized person who can help them plan their life and their romance. They want plenty of physical contact: holding hands, hugs and cuddles, caressing, massage perhaps, as well as the other kind of physical intimacy that couples get up to.

This person needs a stable home environment where they can feel safe, away from the winds of change, and far from the unknown dangers of surprise.

Keep them informed of your activities, and always call if you are going to be late. Welcome them with a kiss and leave them with a kiss. The little intimacies and personal concern shown by such behaviour is very important to them.

If you want to give this person a surprise, I

recommend you plan it with them, or at least give them an idea of what you have in mind even if you don't tell them the small details, so that they can adapt to the concept and provide their input. Give them a date when the surprise will be sprung. Seriously.

This person needs a joint and equal relationship that both of you are fully involved in. Give and take, take and give. Balance, sharing and the stability of knowledge are the key here.

If this person becomes very upset they are likely to create the kind of storm that only happens once in a lifetime. Don't play silly buggers or mess with their heartstrings – you really will regret it.

As clarification: You may not get what you want, but you will get what you need. Check your love interest's Higher Self card for compatibility with your Personal card. Check your Higher Self card for compatibility with your love interest's Personal card. These influences should give you a better idea of whether you are supposed to attempt to proceed with a relationship or not. Either way, the universe and the forces of Karma are in charge here.

As a third party/obstacles: Money flows away leaving you financially embarrassed or at the least short of your requirements. A string of bad luck.

The two of you need to continue your journeys' separately, you can't continue on your current track. Neither of you is being honest with yourself or with the other, and this false front is impossible to maintain.

Seven of Wands

As the querent: You are likely to find life an enjoyable challenge, and you have been developing the courage needed to get out there and make the most of the opportunities that present themselves to you.

I wouldn't be surprised if you were in marketing, sales, or advertising, nor would I be surprised if you were keen to get higher in the organization you work for. Perhaps you've started your own company? Whatever the case, you want to be a leader in your field, and you want to win.

It can sometimes feel like a struggle, keeping up the strength and determination required for you to continually better yourself and beat your past achievements. But if you assert yourself and deal with each obstacle that rears its head one at a time you can overcome any problems you face.

As a competitive person, you are likely to want the best of everything; and that includes a partner who you can show off, or be proud of.

You are passionate about what you do, work or play, and you want to be with someone who can keep up, and who isn't afraid to give you a bit of a challenge.

You may not do so well with a successful partner who outstrips you in talent and achievements – perhaps you should question why that would make you feel insecure?

As the love interest: This person is highly competitive, and very motivated to improve themselves in all their areas of interest. They want to feel like a winner, and they want to do things their way.

The determination and energy required to keep up the level of fight that they put into their lives can be daunting to watch, and they may even find themselves struggling to meet their own standards of perfection occasionally.

This person needs a partner who can keep up with them mentally and physically in order to be satisfied, as they like a bit of a challenge. However, for them winning is likely to be almost a religion, so if you are better than them at something it may well cause them a lot of tears and frustration. If you earn more than they do, you might want to hide your paycheque, or find some gentle way of teaching them that there are more important things than winning. Good luck.

As the querent's Higher Self/Influences/Themes:
Courage, determination and purpose: these are the things you are here to explore, mainly in the arena of self-improvement.

You want success, but your main enemy is going to be your tendency to get bogged down in the details instead of keeping your eye on the bigger picture. A multitude of things will present themselves to distract you, and you need to make the choice to follow one path above all others until you are through that part of your journey and you are ready to look for the next path that you want to follow.

Prioritize, set your course, and then go for it!

Another person could provide you with a role model, or a whole lot of distractions, but you'll need to look at more than the surface appearances to discover which this person represents.

<u>As the love interest's Higher Self/Influences/ Themes</u>: This person is learning to stand up for themselves, fight the good fight, and forge ahead against the obstacles to find success. They need to develop the courage, determination and focus to follow one path. They need to find their purpose, and this is likely to involve self improvement of one kind or another.

Their life may be quite a struggle, and they'll be as much their own enemy as any external influences. They are likely to have a tendency to get lost in the details instead of clearing a path and forging forward to their goal.

This person has their own path in life, so let them follow it. They can't be second fiddle to your orchestra; they need to find their own way. If you have to be involved in every aspect of your lover's life, and control what they do, the two of you are not likely to last as a couple all that long.

<u>As the querent's link card</u>: This card is about meeting the challenges of a stiff competition, and learning to stand up for yourself, defend your views, and gain in strength through struggle.

Perhaps what you really want is someone with a strong will, who will never compromise, and who will pick you up on all your little faux pas, and provoke you into bettering yourself?

Somehow, you view this relationship as a competition – perhaps in terms of who has the best job, the highest salary, the nicest house, who is the most successful? Perhaps you view love itself as a competition?

Everything seems to be a struggle, or a race to win.

This can lead to some very inventive and productive methods of doing things both now, and in the future.

However, an intimate relationship needs to be a safe place for both of you to explore your individuality, and constant sparring – if perceived in a negative way by either of you – could be very damaging in the long term. So have a care.

In constantly testing the boundaries you may gain a deeper insight into your self-identity and your goals, as well as the true identity and goals of your partner.

It is possible that the person you are with has had many lovers in the past, and you might feel as though you are fighting to measure up, or struggling to be seen as a real person rather than just yet another conquest?

Whatever the case, this relationship may be daunting but it will have its benefits.

As the love interest's link card: This person is testing the boundaries to find out where their real strengths, and self-identity lies. They seem to view life as a test, and a loving relationship as yet another stage in the competition.

This person is looking for someone who has a strong instinct for winning, and who will stand their ground in the face of adversity. They don't want a roll-over-pussycat.

They may need to feel as though they have won through against all your other suitors to get top place at your side; if so, it's because they need that boost to their self esteem. They want to be a winner and they want to be with a winner.

If you want a quiet life, walk away. You won't get it here.

As clarification: If you want to achieve your goals you are going to have to up the anti. This is a time for hard work, ingenuity, determination and first class communication. The future is uncertain, so your dedication and approach are critical in this situation. Check your gut. Does this feel right?

As a third party/obstacles: Someone or something has put a very unexpected crimp on your plans. Act quickly and with determination if you want to be victorious.

Get a grip on your insecurities and stop shooting yourself in the foot. You can win through all difficulties if you approach the problems involved in the right way, even if you do feel that you have been conned into taking the necessary measures to see off defeat.

Ask yourself what is more important: feeling temporarily embarrassed over something silly, or having the love of your life walk out forever because you put your pride first?

Seven of Cups

As the querent: Too many choices, that's likely to be your problem. You spend a lot of time living in your head, perhaps even keeping quiet instead of speaking out in order to mask your real opinions on what is going on around you.

You have to learn techniques for grounding yourself, and bringing the thoughts you have out into the open. Your dreams and ideas have value, and if they can be made solid you are likely to get a great feeling of satisfaction. The obvious way forward is to force yourself to come up with a list of priorities, and work your way down it, concentrating on one thing at a time, getting it done, and *only* then moving on to the next item on your list of dreams to fulfil.

Sitting in the centre of a globe, surrounded by a multitude of ideas, seeing the potential in so many different things and so many courses of action; the effect can be paralyzing – to follow only one is to deny all the others, right? Not necessarily.

People tend to work in cycles, they seldom work at the exact same thing for their entire lives. Recognize that and take advantage of it. To deny one course of action now, doesn't necessarily mean that you can't do it ten years from now.

Make a list: prioritize, concentrate on one thing, take action, see it through to completion, then go to the next thing on your list of priorities and repeat.

As the love interest: This person has a tendency to dream, coming up with grand schemes that will never see the light of day, either because they are unrealistic in their breadth of vision, or because they will never pick one dream over the others and put in the effort to see that dream through to completion.

This person needs to come to understand the value of making a choice, planning a course of action, seeing that action through despite all the distractions that surround them, and creating something real in the world. The process of making a dream come true.

If you can help to teach them about focus, and about grounding their energy into form, you'll be doing them a huge favour. However they will resent the attempt if you try to force them to it. It's something they really need to find out through learning by watching someone else's example.

This person is looking for a light hearted partner who can take them on an adventure or two. People with no imagination need not apply.

<u>As the querent's Higher Self/Influences/Themes</u>: Of the many opportunities available in your life, which one will you choose? To choose one course of action is to deny another its place in that time, but to fail to choose one, is to do nothing – which could also be a choice, but isn't that a waste of the energy and options on offer?

When you make a choice, you are taking a responsibility on yourself to see it through until that choice results in completion or until it proves no longer tenable. So are you going to develop the skills, tenacity and focus to see it through, or are you going to allow yourself to sit paralyzed by indecision, wasting time and life?

You create your own reality, you've been told that before, yes?

<u>As the love interest's Higher Self/Influences/ Themes</u>: This person is learning the lesson which maturity brings, that life is what you make of it. When you make something it is a creative act that involves doing. The initial impetus is to imagine an outcome; then you need to act on that thought form, plan a way of making it happen, then set about doing the work involved in bringing the goal to fruition.

This person's imagination is fine, it's the rest of the process that they have trouble with.

Their dreams may be of a romantic nature, waiting for a knight in armour on a white steed to come and rescue them. In practise I have found that it is more effective to go search for a knight in the places where they hang out, like the jousting ring.

Dreaming versus doing. If you study this person in depth you'll find that it's not a case of them being lazy, it is in fact that they are paralyzed by the decision-making process, for to make one choice is to deny all the other options that are on offer.

This person is a talented dreamer who can probably turn their hand to a whole range of things successfully. Once they have learned to narrow that down and take action, they should be very successful. Question is, are you willing to hang around while they get around to working that out, or are you going to hang out with someone else who is a bit more focused on where they are in the real world right now?

As the querent's link card: You enjoy the world of fantasy and dream, and you enjoy sensuality and passion. You may have a yearning for control, or the desire to manipulate and possess. This will likely make you very open to adventures that other people might not contemplate.

Chances are you will need someone equally passionate and sensual, who has a good imagination. If your partner has a different level of sex drive it could be the death knell for the relationship. Also, if they are unable to share your capacity for dream or help you bring their fantasies to life, it could be that you'll grow bored and retreat into the world of the mind. If that's the case, you may not leave your partner, but there's a danger that you'll be looking for a kindred spirit outside the home.

You work from the gut and make your decisions based on instinct. Do that and you won't go far wrong.

If your partner tries to steer you on a different course, and you make the mistake of listening and going against your gut instinct as a result, then the two of you could end up in a world of trouble.

Follow your heart, follow your passion, follow your instincts, and help your partner share in your dreams. With a little work, the two of you could make them a reality.

As the love interest's link card: This person has a tendency to dissipate their energy by taking many lovers at a time, and keeping their relationships at a very shallow level. If they start talking commitment with you, they are going to have to learn to put aside all their other loving distractions and concentrate on obtaining a deep intimacy with you, and discovering the meaning of commitment. They do have the capacity to do this, if they want to.

This person's fantasies are many and varied, and they need to learn that if they want to make any of their whimsy and fantasies real, the first thing they have to do is concentrate on only one of them. They will need to restrict the output of their creativity and energy into bringing that one forth.

Otherwise their fantasies are the only things that they'll have to keep them warm in the long run; phantoms rather than solid fact.

As clarification: The dream of love, and so many possibilities. Fantasy is fine, but if you want to make something concrete you are going to have to prioritize and work on one goal at a time.

Do you really want one single, solid relationship, or would you prefer to cast your net wide for all those fleeting butterflies? Be honest with yourself, and the person you are with. Take a cold shower and then take a look in the mirror.

If you are in a relationship but financial worries are holding you back from making a commitment, or causing disputes, then this will be resolved soon.

As a third party/obstacles: Deception, and dreams being brought into the real world.

If the need for escapism and release exists, it may not be your fault but it sure is impacting on your life. The type of dishonesty involved shows a very deep underlying, possibly subconscious, problem that divides the two of you. You won't be able to bridge this gap successfully. Walking away is never easy, but in this case it might be the wisest course of action.

Seven of Swords

As the querent: You have more layers than a raspberry ripple ice-cream – you're not a Gemini are you? This card is all about working out who you are, getting to the honesty at the core of yourself. It is about finding the truth at the centre of chaos.

It's possible that your confidence and self-image have been seriously damaged by other people. If so, a relationship with someone lovely might be very appealing, but just remember that you need to take time out to look at your own personal development, and to heal those wounds that others have left in you. Instead of looking without, look within. Examine the pain and work to heal it. Another person could be very helpful to this process, if they are the right person.

If you are of the dishonest persuasion, this card is an omen that you will be forced to look at the way you behave towards others, both in terms of your callousness and deception to them, and to yourself.

What lies do you tell yourself to keep yourself feeling okay about what you do?

What is it within you that makes you feel the need to be false, and what can you do to heal that wound and repair your heart so that you can be happy about who you are once and for all?

Put your creativity to good use and find a legitimate outlet for your talents.

As the love interest: Tact and discretion may be this person's watchwords. If so, you might want to ask yourself, "Why?" What do they really think that they need to use tact? Are they very insecure about how you will respond if they give you their real opinion? If so why did they end up with such low self-esteem, and what can you do to help them regain their confidence? And, if they are being discrete, what are they up to that requires them to feel the need to cover it up or keep quiet about it?

This person could be perfectly innocent and just be an emotional and mental mess. But another meaning of the card can be deception, so it could be that they aren't in love with you at all, just your wallet or your other material possessions.

If this person is an emotional mess, their thoughts in a turmoil, then they are going to need some time by themselves coming to grips with who they are at the core of their being. If you are a psychologist you might be able to be of real help to them in their quest to regain their feeling of self, of confidence, and of wholeness.

They really need someone supportive, who can

hold their hand and bolster their self-confidence, and give them the sense of space, quiet and safety that they need while they try to make sense of everything.

If you aren't prepared to put this person's needs ahead of your own, you should walk away now.

As the querent's Higher Self/Influences/Themes: Life, the eternal onion. You think you understand what is going on, and then another layer is pealed back, and all you have in your hand is onion skin. Will you ever be able to make sense of it all?

Your life lessons are those of compassion, and of respect for self and others.

You need to be aware of the impact you have on the people who you interact with, and moderate your behaviour accordingly. Behaving like a bull in a china shop is not a productive way of getting the help and respect from others that you crave.

Honesty, with yourself and with others, is another aspect of this card. If you are dishonest in any way you should be willing to pay the price of being caught out, as the Universe is not going to let your thoughts, words, and deeds go unchecked.

If you can learn to consider how others are feeling as a result of what you say and do, that'll be a big step forward in your development as a social being.

As the love interest's Higher Self/Influences/Themes: Compassion, and respect for other people, are the themes here.

This person is learning the value of tact, discretion and diplomacy. If they haven't learnt it yet, you can expect them to be extremely blunt and tactless with regard to the feelings of others.

They are likely to be given lessons that show them how they are wrong about the way they perceive themselves, about the way they perceive others, and about the way they perceive the world. Depending on how harsh the lessons have become, they may have a pretty dented self-confidence.

This person may have learned the hard way to keep their mouth shut and be reticent about talking about their real feelings. If so, they'll need to find a way to knock the walls they've built down, and relate to people on a more sincere, compassionate and personally honest level.

Another possibility here is that the person is not strictly legit – they may even be downright fraudulent and criminal in their dealing with others. If so they're likely to be caught in the act.

Whatever the case, honest or dishonest, this person needs to be willing to pay the price, as they will have to come to terms with the consequences of their behaviour at some point in their lives.

<u>As the querent's link card</u>: There are three meanings for this card, "Unstable Effort", fraud, and lack of self confidence due to the actions of another.

There is a good chance that you are an emotional mess, splintered. You feel as though all the different aspects of your life are utterly separate. Basically either you feel you aren't worthy of a permanent relationship right now, or you are just so confused about who you are that you need to spend some time working on that, rather than dealing with another person.

Perhaps the person you are with makes you feel like you have multiple personality disorder, or maybe you are a bigamist?

The fraud option isn't such a nice one: it's likely you are being taken for a ride and will wake up one day without your shirt, or the person you love is being exceedingly unfaithful – perhaps they are the bigamist?

Whatever the case, you are not in a healthy place for a relationship right now, and if you feel that you are, then I would seriously question your love interest's motives – it is likely that all is not as it seems.

On the other hand perhaps you like sex, love to role play in all areas of your life, and want to experience as much of everything as you can. If so, you're probably after a short term fling, not a full on relationship. Perhaps even many sexual partners at the same time. Make sure the other person is aware of your intentions, or you could bring them a lot of pain.

<u>As the love interest's link card</u>: This person wants to experience a scintillating rainbow of sexual, emotional and mental situations. They are probably the type to want multiple lovers, and role play in bed, as well as elsewhere, and generally drive you nuts with their split personality games. If you like that kind of thing, hooray for you!

This person may be insane, they may be a sex addict, they may be a prostitute, or they may just be one of those people who leads multiple lives just because they are inclined to do that.

You might be able to have a fulfilling relationship with them, but I think this is a case of short term fling rather than permanent commitment.

There's a chance that this person might indulge in

deception on purpose, for material gain. If so, watch your wallet.

This person really isn't in the right place to be having a serious relationship with anyone right now, and there's nothing you can do to change that.

Chalk this one up to experience, one of life's little curveballs.

As clarification: Don't let on. Keep quiet about your feelings and intentions. Tact, diplomacy, and care are required now. There are unseen obstacles in your path. What you see is definitely not what you will get, as falsehood abounds.

Before you can proceed you need to determine exactly what it is that you really want, and your motivations for this. Any dishonesty on your part will be discovered and met with harsh retribution. Be wary of others' lies.

As a third party/obstacles: Someone is working against you. They have you chasing your own tail, while they steal your every last dime (and your lover). If you are getting divorced, you are going to lose your shirt. Wake up, take action, and clear the decks of obstacles – how can you avoid active deception by those around you if you don't have a clear field of view?

If you have been dishonest, then you are going to suffer the consequences.

Seven of Pentacles

As the querent: You find yourself in a situation in which you need to make a choice: whether to take the old, tried and tested path, or to branch out into something new.

Whatever you do, the path to success involves planning and hard work, but the hard work will be rewarded.

In terms of a permanent relationship the same is true: lasting relationships take constant work to keep them from falling into the rut of the same-old-same-old. Boredom and routine may be the biggest enemy you both face. But by taking the time to plan for your future together, and to manifest a creative, innovative, caring environment for yourselves, you are far more likely to last the distance despite any bumps you may encounter in the road.

Your choice: stay with something you are used to, or embark on the path of the new.

As the love interest: This person is in the process of going through internal revelation, which is likely to result in them making some big changes in their lives, setting out in a new direction, making important choices about their future. Chances are the path they take will be very different from the old one they were walking.

In going through the process of becoming more true to their inner heart, this person will be faced with the challenge of the unknown, which includes learning about: the need to settle down to planning, the steady application of hard work, and the realization that gaining successful results takes a bit more than just visualizing the outcome.

For opportunities to come to fruition, first they have to prepare the ground and sow the seeds, then tend the crop until harvest time comes. They have to make that choice to see things through from start to finish – rather than growing bored and walking away part way through.

As the querent's Higher Self/Influences/Themes: Life seems to be forever throwing decisions and choices at you. There's always more than one option facing you, and in the past you may have had difficulty deciding what it is that you want to do with yourself.

There are many testing points in life, where the choices you make can lead you on a new path to a truer expression of who you are – with maturity you begin to realize that in order to make the most of the opportunities on offer you have to plan what you want to do, stick to that plan and apply the hard work required over the long term in order to get to your goal: the successful outcome.

This card is about making a choice and then learning to see things through to the end. It's the difference between going rambling and then allowing your daydreams to drift you off the path into the wilderness, or concentrating on where you are now, sticking to the planned route, and getting where you wanted to go.

You can dream about what you want to happen in the future, or you can get off your arse and make it happen. You have a decision to make.

As the love interest's Higher Self/Influences/Themes: This person is learning about the value of putting dreams into action. They are likely to have many talents, many paths they could take in life, and they are constantly being offered choices as to what is on offer for them.

Their dreams don't have to be daydreams, they can become fact, if they put in the hard effort and stick-to-it-ivity required to make them come true.

Making the choice to put in the required hard work and turn wasted dream time into positive action that results in reaching their goal; this is a lesson we all have to go through. And it starts with dissatisfaction with where we are now and an undeniable desire to get to somewhere in our lives where we will feel fulfilled. Many times this requires a leap into the unknown, and overcoming that fear of stepping out over the edge of our normal bounds.

If you are already in a relationship with this person, expect them to start making dramatic changes in their lives. When they begin to talk about it, support them, or you could find your place at their side being one of the changes that they make.

As the querent's link card: Do you want to go out with the same type of person you've always plumped for, or do you want to make some changes and try loving someone who is very different from your usual choice?

You really need someone who can broaden your horizons and help you see life from another perspective. Question is: are you open-minded enough, and are you really prepared to put in the internal hard work required to make the changes inside yourself that this person is causing you to consider?

You need someone who will challenge you on all levels and blast your preconceptions out of the water. Such a relationship can be difficult and hard work to maintain, or it can be refreshing and remarkably joyful, depending on your outlook. So, how are you going to respond?

As the love interest's link card: This person is looking for someone who will challenge them into taking action instead of just dreaming about how things could be.

They need you to be the type of person who will draw attention to their assumptions, to their time wasting, to their delaying tactics and prevarication.

Of course what they want might be someone calm and quiet, who will pay the bills and let them carry on in their little patch of dreamland, eating up their partner's cash and never getting out in the world to make something of themselves.

It could be a rocky relationship if this person isn't fully ready for the internal changes that a demanding and growth provoking partner can bring.

If you are not the type to mind them lounging about on the sofa eating peeled grapes or crisps all day long, then – sadly – the relationship is likely to be short, as this person's internal clock is ticking away and their brain is nagging them louder and louder to find someone who will give them a metaphorical kick up the arse. Somewhere they'll find fault and look for someone else who can give them the challenges they need.

This person may take advantage of you if you allow them to, they need to learn about the constant effort that is required to make a relationship work in an innovative, enjoyable and fulfilling way for the long term. 'It takes two to tango.'

As clarification: It's time to make a decision as to

which path you are going to follow in your planning and strategy for how to obtain the person you desire. Should you use tried and tested methods, or a new and unfamiliar weapon in your arsenal of romantic moves? Nothing will come to fruition quickly, but it is how you go about achieving your goals – the method and work you put in – that counts right now. Eventual success is indicated, so keep at it.

As a third party/obstacles: It's hard work trying to maintain something that is over. And it won't help restore what was, it will just prolong the pain of the ending process. Mistakes have been made and decisions taken. Take ownership of the real situation and make the clean break you should have made some time ago.

Eight of Wands
As the querent: You feel like you are starting over, you have all the energy you need now to regenerate and take your life forwards in whichever direction you want. There's no need to limit yourself either, many choices are available, and each can be pursued at the same time if you have enough energy to cover all the bases.

You probably enjoy communication, travel and action, so any job that involves these things would suit your temperament well; you might consider being an air steward, a member of the rescue services, an officer in the armed forces, an adventure holiday guide, a camp leader, a diplomat, or a politician.

It's likely that you can think fast, make decisions quickly, and love good repartee. You want someone who can meet you on the same mental level, and who has a similar passion for life, and stamina, that you do.

Someone who wants to live in the same house for all eternity, and who has no desire to travel, and hates to party or go out and socialize, would not be the type of person you normally hang out with.

<u>As the love interest</u>: This person is a sparkling gem. Like a river, they never stand still, always on the move, circulating and scintillating. Can you keep up?

This person has the boundless energy of youth, and enjoys starting new projects and adventures. They love to travel and won't be happy if they get stuck in the same place for too long. Ruts bore them rigid, and routine eventually becomes an anathema to them. This is someone who wants to get out and about, live life to the full, and who has some great plans for the future.

Their life is a life of rebirth and new beginnings. This may also be true of their romantic life, so don't be surprised if all they are after is a short fling or just good conversation.

<u>As the querent's Higher Self/Influences/Themes</u>: The energy of renewal and rebirth is likely to be a powerful influence in your life. That burst of energy and restlessness that hits you every spring, demanding that you move on or start something new is likely to be a constant feature in your life. This comes with its price, as if you don't follow your instincts to get out of that rut you've fallen into, the Universe may well hit you hard to force you to get moving again.

You are going to wind up in countless situations that demand you think fast on your feet, and act or react just as swiftly.

Creativity, invention and new projects should be

easy for you to bring into your life, but the problem you are likely to encounter is one of 'lack of staying power'. Learning how to make use of the energy you feel when you come up with a new plan, so that you can harness it and complete the project before your passion for something new gets in the way, is likely to be your biggest hurdle.

The energy you work with is a healing energy that doesn't allow stagnation or disease to persist, however its action is swift and can sometimes only disrupt the surface. If you can learn to harness it and drive it deep, it can uproot or reinvigorate the toughest deadwood. It is an energy that can cause utter chaos and a lot of pain if it is not handled correctly, with due care and diligence.

<u>As the love interest's Higher Self/Influences/ Themes</u>: This person can get very restless, the Universe is constantly bombarding them with the desire to move on, and birth new projects and ideas.

They are very passionate, especially at the start of any endeavour, the danger is that they grow bored easily and then want to move on to something or someone different.

There are a multitude of different things that this person is capable of initiating, many of them at the same time.

Travel will likely be a feature of this person's annual cycle. Don't expect them to stay rooted in one place for any length of time. They may not be the one initiating the changes that happen in their life, but change will come all the same. They have no choice about this.

Be prepared to move house, country, or lifestyle at

the drop of a hat if you want to spend a lot of intimate time with them long term. You also need to be able to handle a fast pace of life, as when things get complicated this person will need to make lightning decisions and act on them immediately. Any changes that do occur in their lives are likely to be swift and come, pretty much, out of the blue. You can tell when one is on the way as this person will start to get antsy or restless. They're a bit like a barometer in that respect.

As the querent's link card: You want someone quick-witted and versatile who has boundless energy for new projects, travel and communication. You want someone who finds it easy to speak their mind and who can react quickly and innovatively to the situations the two of you find yourselves in.

A natural politician or diplomatic adventurer would be your ideal consort.

You also want the relationship to have an atmosphere that is open and free; you like to have many options, so you don't want someone who is going to pin you down or demand an itinerary that accounts for every second of your day.

Someone who is a stickler for control, or for routines, or for time alone gardening, or who has a need for the quiet life, none of these would be your idea of a perfect partner. You're looking for someone who will take you to Paris, London or New York at a moment's notice, someone who knows how to party and likes to mingle.

As the love interest's link card: This person wants to be with a partner who can provide sparkling conversation, think fast, plan fast, act fast, and get things up and running in the blink of an eye. If you are adaptable, flexible, have a passion for living to the full, and want to spend your nights out together exploring and partying, then this person wants you.

If you prefer to keep out of the limelight, detest parties, and hate acting on impulse then you won't get on very well with the lifestyle this person wants to lead. Look elsewhere for your homebody.

As clarification: This is a time for communication and travel. If you have been waiting, now is the time to act – but make sure whatever you do is guided by the inspiration and passion that motivates you. Not a time for dull, uninspired halfway measures. News travels quickly, you are going to have to think on your feet. A word of warning: business is emphasized more than pleasure.

As a third party/obstacles: Whatever is happening, you are feeling out of the loop. Frustration, delays and not being able to talk are all making you angry. If you put your feelings in writing or say the wrong thing to the wrong person, you are the one who is likely to come off worst. Being nasty about events is not the answer.

Release your aggression through a safe outlet like sports, and move on with your life.

Eight of Cups

As the querent: One of the skills you have, or will develop, is knowing when to cut your losses and call it a day. This is always more difficult when the part of your life you are trying to sever is something that has once been close to your heart: a relationship, a friendship that has run its course, or a project that was your 'baby'.

Being able to assess when something has reached the end of its natural cycle, or has just plain run out of steam is a valuable talent to cultivate. Any energy that is spent on a 'dead' project, other than the energy required to wrap it up, is energy wasted. Putting that energy into a new endeavour is far more productive in the long run.

You are likely to be in a stable and apparently successful situation, one which used to bring you joy, but now you are feeling discontent, the sparkle has gone and there's nothing left that you really value or want. There is a chance to move on, and it is likely that you will follow your heart and head out into pastures new.

It's time for a new beginning, as the past is likely to have lost its relevance or meaning for you. If you allow fear or laziness to prevent you from taking the paths that are opening to you, the result is likely to be a growing feeling of stagnation and boredom that pervades your home or work life.

One thing to be wary of is being overly reactive, chucking out everything instead of just the things that are holding you back. If you can possibly do it, you need to get to a calm place where you can see all the things that you have around you, and assess what needs to change without emotion clouding the decision. Some of your achievements are valid and can form the foundations of the new path that you are choosing to follow.

As the love interest: This person should be very

happy by all measures that society uses to determine success. But instead they find themselves bored and feeling hemmed in. Discontent has set in and they are getting itchy feet.

You can expect this person to leave their current situation, no matter how much of their heart they have put into it, and move on to pastures new. They have a deep need to get out of the rut they find themselves in and try something more rewarding and stimulating.

Many people might think that this person is mad for walking away from what they have achieved to date, but they would be wrong. Walking away is the most sensible course of action that this person can take right now. There is something calling them from the horizon, and if they don't follow the call they'll feel more and more trapped; depression may even set in. They need to get out, so don't be surprised when they make that break.

The one danger here is that when they make the move they "throw the baby out with the bathwater". Not everything in their past need be something that they should leave behind.

As the querent's Higher Self/Influences/Themes: Your life seems to be a series of realizations that what you have achieved to date is only a single step on the path that you are walking, and that you need to move on to the next stage in order to find satisfaction.

Each stage ahead of you feels like the final goal, but it always seems that way – until you reach it. Then you can see something new and better just a little further on. You are definitely beginning to suspect that your journey is actually up a metaphorical series of rising plateaus, where each has a better view the further you go.

Sometimes it can be quite upsetting to move on, leaving behind all that you have achieved, but if you don't do it voluntarily, events overtake you and force you to abandon your success and move on to the next thing. Usually, though, it's your internal demons driving you onwards. You wake up bored one day and know that it's time to move on.

As the love interest's Higher Self/Influences/ Themes: Either, this person seems to never be content with what they have, or, if they are content, something happens in their lives that forces them to move on. If they ever do stop and try to put down roots, eventually discontent sets in, and they find themselves looking to the next horizon instead of everything that they have around them.

In many ways this person is like a rolling stone, gathering no moss. They can't help it. It's their destiny to keep walking away from everything they've achieved to date, and set out to meet the next challenge. It's the process of achievement, rather than the achievement itself that draws them.

If you love this person, be prepared to move with them if necessary. But as we are looking at a card that symbolizes emotion here, it could well be that the success that is being left behind is a successful relationship.

This person finds it easy to fall into a rut, and get bored. Keeping them busy won't necessarily stop that pattern from repeating.

As the querent's link card: I don't think you are in the right place for a relationship right now? What once would have made you happy will now leave a taste of dust in your mouth and give you a feeling of dissatisfaction and laissez-faire.

You may start out fine, both of you happy, but you are looking for someone who can't fulfil your needs, or give you what you want. So, on what is probably an unconscious level, you are looking for someone who you will be able to walk away from, and tell yourself that it is the right thing to do. And it will be the right thing to do for you at the time. But make sure the other person is aware that you are not in it for the long haul or you could cause them considerable pain.

If you both have the right attitude, this will be a rewarding and fun relationship, but one that will come to an end sooner rather than later.

<u>As the love interest's link card</u>: This person, for some reason, needs some dissatisfaction in their love/home life. They need someone that they can walk away from and justify it to themselves as being the best move.

The reason they might spend time with you is because they know that you are the type of person who can't fulfil their needs in the long term, and that you aren't someone who they can make a life with for more than a short while.

The two of you might be ecstatically happy in the short term, and it may feel to both of you like you've finally found "the one"; but the card here suggests that this person is using you to meet their own needs and that they'll move on when they're done.

Another alternative is that instead of being the victim here, you are the one that's creating the dissatisfaction and driving them away. So be honest with yourself, do you really, truly love and honour this person, or are you using them just as much as they are using you?

I hope you aren't in love, because somehow, some way, this person is going to leave for pastures new.

If all you want is a short fling, then this is the person who it is likely to be the most fun to be with.

<u>*As clarification*</u>: If you are in a relationship, things are no longer bringing you the fulfilment they once used to. It's time to move on.

If you are looking at the possibility of starting a relationship, you should be aware that you have changed internally and no longer want the things you once thought you did. Don't make a mistake. This is your chance to recognize that it's time to put the past behind you and sort yourself out. Only you can do that for yourself, no one else can make the journey for you.

<u>*As a third party/obstacles*</u>: Stagnation. Events have overtaken you, you are alone, and yet you cling on desperately to that which no longer is. You are prone to massive errors of judgment, and all you want to do is run away and lose yourself in fantasy. This attitude is not helping you.

Take a vacation and get some perspective.

Eight of Swords

<u>*As the querent*</u>: You crave freedom, but you feel restricted. Perhaps your career is not fulfilling, or maybe your current relationship is tying you up in knots and dragging you down. Whatever the case, it is a difficult time for you at the moment. You may even be able to see the problems ahead of you but you feel

powerless to do anything about them?

A change of perspective and some clear thinking will show you a new path that is evolving for you. Perhaps it is something that you never would have thought of normally, but your current circumstances have forced you to totally reassess your goals, wants, and needs.

Ultimately, the changes you make should be liberating for you, but as to whether you can cope with a relationship right now – it may be a little too much to handle until you've found your inner space.

As the love interest: This person's life is likely to be in a mess. They are probably working in a job that doesn't suit them, or they may be living in a place or be in a relationship that makes them feel limited, frustrated and unfulfilled.

They probably aren't ready to embark on a relationship right now. Be very careful before you make any move in their direction, as you do not want them to see you as an additional source of stress or problems. They are confused enough as it is without an additional bunch of feelings getting in the way.

You'll do what you think is right, but if you do decide to make a move on them, please take care to assess the situation fully before you wade in – not everything will be immediately obvious. You could get hurt.

As the querent's Higher Self/Influences/Themes: This card indicates that you create a lot of the problems you encounter in your life yourself. You allow yourself to get into situations that need not happen; with a little due care and attention you wouldn't keep finding yourself in these constant quagmires.

In fact learning that extricating yourself from the limitations and restrictions that surround you is largely a matter of changing your perspective, is likely to be a revelation to you.

Think clearly before you act, and don't allow inaction to tangle you up.

<u>As the love interest's Higher Self/Influences/ Themes</u>: This person allows themselves to become confused easily; perhaps they are too literal, or perhaps they have a tendency to make erroneous assumptions or leap to inaccurate conclusions based on the flimsiest of evidence? They may worry needlessly, or imagine motives behind other people's actions that aren't there. Whatever inaction they perpetrate, or actions they take, what this person does is probably going to complicate or compound matters.

If you watch carefully, you are likely to see that most of the problems that beset this person's life are of their own making.

This person has to learn about perspective and emotional balance in order to free themselves of the limitations and restrictions that keep cropping up in their lives.

A stitch in time saves string.

Once this person has learned to count to ten, and to think clearly before they act, their life should become easier. Another of their Achilles' Heels is likely to be inaction in the face of events that need to be dealt with. Discrimination, sound judgment, paranoia, and self confidence are all likely to be issues for them.

As the querent's link card: Frustration and difficulty. The relationship is one that will leave you feeling trapped and powerless, confused as to what to do or how to feel. Clear thinking is called for on your part. You are only trapped if you hogtie yourself. A new perspective, or a timeout, should help you gather your thoughts.

If you try to hide from the reality of the situation it will only make you feel worse. The person you are with may be able to talk a good talk, and argue any point successfully; but when it comes right down to it, what do you know inside as truth? Love is about truth, not lies and manipulation.

As the love interest's link card: This person is frustrated, confused and upset. They have allowed themselves to buy into a lie, or have talked themselves into a relationship they didn't actually want.

Anything you do or say is likely to make this person feel more powerless, or create more obstacles for them to feel hemmed in by. Eventually they'll find their way to how they really feel underneath. And when they do, they'll likely leave.

Trying to force anyone to be someone they aren't, or to be with someone they don't love or want, is both negative and a futile waste of energy. It is energy that you could otherwise use to go out and find someone who actually does care for you.

Give it up before you cause yourself and them even more pain.

As clarification: It's difficult to know which way to turn, left or right, to embrace your emotion or to run and hide from it. Bottling things up doesn't help, but allowing strong emotions out sets you worrying about how they will be received.

You need to take a step back and find a new perspective on this whole romance thing, this will help you to find the solutions that exist. Right now you are confused, you need to apply some rational thought to clarify your position and your options.

Bad luck is indicated, but help is out there if you ask for it. The main thing to remember is that this is a time for thinking, not a time for action. Above all, don't panic.

As a third party/obstacles: You think you know what the obstacles are, so you go rushing off to take out your anger on all and sundry. This is not a good idea, as people who would otherwise help you will be hurt by your tirades and outbursts. Your frustration is unbearable, so the best course of action is to take a holiday, get out of town for a bit. Start thinking about the good things and freedom that a single future holds for you. The past is done, so move on.

Eight of Pentacles
As the querent: Your physical environment is changing. Perhaps you are going to move house, change career, re-educate yourself? Whatever the case, there is going to be, or has recently been, a big physical upheaval in your life which will pave the way for a new way of living and being.

This is a time of change which will lead to growth. It's going to take a lot of hard work and preparation to get where you want to go, but you believe the rewards are worth the effort.

It is possible to start a relationship now, but with

all the other environmental factors in flux, you might want to hold off until you are more settled in your home and work.

Any new relationship will take careful nurturing and will take a lot of time to flourish.

<u>As the love interest</u>: This person is more interested in changing their life than in having a relationship. They will be working hard to set out on a new career, they may return to education, or be taking night classes in order to get the skills they need to set out on their new life path. It is also likely that they may move house soon. They will be in the middle of major change and upheaval. A baby may even be on the way. While this person might be willing to consider staring a new relationship, they are more likely to be too busy to devote the time and energy required to a new lover.

If you are acting as a teacher for them, then they are probably only interested in the skills and information that you can provide rather than any long-term emotional commitment.

<u>As the querent's Higher Self/Influences/Themes</u>: A change in direction, the need for inspiration, the search for fulfilment: these are the constant themes in your life. You are *driven*. Whether you view this as a curse or a blessing is all a matter of perspective. It is likely to make you rather hard to live with though.

I wouldn't be at all surprised if you were an eternal student, a traveller, an actor, a jack of all trades. Your attitude is probably one of "been there, done that, what's next?" Always looking to the horizon; searching for the next conquest, eyes on the prize.

You are not afraid of hard work, your whole life has been about doing whatever's necessary to get to where you want to be, but as soon as you attain it, you feel that it is time to move on.

It is probable that you view your lovers the same way as you view your teachers or your many jobs – learn what you can from them and move on to the next. You're a bit of a butterfly: a long-term relationship may be beyond your scope.

As the love interest's Higher Self/Influences/ Themes: This person is a butterfly, they can never settle to anything for any length of time. Do not expect them to settle down with you, make a home, and remain your constant companion for all eternity. That's just not who they are. It's possible they might try to have a life with you, but you'd have to be some kind of magnetic multiple personality eccentric in order for them to stay interested in you for more than two seconds.

This person is driven to try the new. They are on a constant quest for knowledge and experience; they actively head out in search of a new horizon every day, and any time they do try to settle down, fate sees to it that they can't.

You will need to be open-minded in the extreme, and more tolerant than Buddha if you expect to put up with (and stay sane through) some of the life experiences that this person will put you through.

If you want anything more than a one night stand, my advice is forget it.

As the querent's link card: You are looking for a butterfly, someone who will stay just long enough to interest you, hook you, and then leave. Perhaps you're a masochist?

You are not looking for stability or permanence. You are looking for an experience; you want to learn something new every day.

You are either unfaithful, or you are looking for someone unfaithful. If you think you want to settle down with one person, you are deluding yourself.

You want someone who will constantly force you into different, unusual and totally new ways of living and being. One person can only teach you so much before their life experience/inspirational qualities get all used up and repetitive. The danger here is that you marry into a cult one minute, then wake up a week later and realize you've made a horrible mistake.

Accept the fact that you need a lot of different lovers, and be honest with all of them about that *before* you start getting amorous with any of them. That, or go get some serious psychological help for your abandonment complex!

As the love interest's link card: This person is looking for someone interesting, exotic, and out of the ordinary, who can teach them about life, the universe, sex and everything. Problem is, once they've got the hang of one thing they want to try something new, and there are only so many new experiences out there. They do not like to repeat anything once they feel they've mastered it.

You've got your work cut out for you if you want to have a long-term relationship with this person. It is also likely that in their quest for new experiences, they are unlikely to pay much attention to fidelity or even monogamy. They could cause you a lot of heartache before they are done.

This person is more suited to one night stands than relationships.

Either that or they have some serious emotional problems and are looking for someone who'll love them and leave them…but would you really want to be with someone who is that much of a mess?

As clarification: Internally you know what you need, and it is a radical departure from your previous way of doing things.

The need to regenerate, especially in terms of your career/work, is primary.

As a third party/obstacles: The person you love is more interested in work, training or study than in pursuing a relationship right now. It is something that they need to do, so get out of their way and let them do it.

If you help them, rather than hinder them by clinging to your desires and needs, then you are far more likely to receive recognition later on. Be the shoulder they lean on, the ear that listens to their woes; get clever: be open, provide lunch, let them come to you. Be a friend rather than a limpet.

Nine of Wands

As the querent: You are a survivor, and you're not afraid of hard work. Life has made some big demands of you, but you have met every conflict, each struggle or obstacle and come through it in more or less one piece, and wiser for it. You have reserves of inner strength that even you may not know about.

Success, winning, finishing the race: these things

are important to you, as is anything that makes you feel fulfilled. What drives you nuts is anything being left half done, or feeling that if you'd only gone that bit further you could have achieved your goals.

It's a bit of a blow for you when you get information, or a wake up call, that makes you aware that something you've planned will likely fail, but you are sensible enough to cut your losses and walk away from projects that you know are no longer feasible. Conserving your energy for the battles that you can win is something you've had to learn over time.

Ultimately the reason you do anything is because you enjoy it. Fulfilment and satisfaction are your primary goals.

As the love interest: This person wants to feel fulfilled; they do things because they enjoy them. Anything that doesn't give them a warm glow will be dropped, whether that is their high earning job, their latest acquisition, or you. This person can be hard when they need to, and they have massive reserves of inner strength. They are a survivor because they have had to be.

This person knows how to work hard, and they enjoy playing hard too. They are happy doing the tried, tested, sure-fire activities that they know will make them feel good, but they will also like to try new things: to see if they are enjoyable and to help keep them away from falling into any ruts.

He or she enjoys the sense of satisfaction that comes with finishing a project, winning a race, or succeeding at something they think is important in their life. Being forced to leave things partway through, or winning by default, drives them nuts.

People who flit from place to place, thing to thing, lover to lover are likely to annoy them or leave them feeling deeply unsettled or unsatisfied.

It is most likely that this person is looking for a long-term commitment when they do get romantically involved, but they will consider a one night stand if they think they are going to have a lot of fun…Just make sure they know it's 'one night only' right from the start or you could land yourself under a mountain of trouble.

As the querent's Higher Self/Influences/Themes:
Life is teaching you about inner strength, courage and determination, and tends to put you in situations where you have to find creative, imaginative and inspired solutions. In practical terms, this means that you are regularly engulfed by seemingly impossible situations, yet you manage to find a way through every time.

Your life can be very challenging at times, a real struggle. And yet these same forces that are testing you, are moulding you into someone who other people may assume is a miracle worker.

There is a Chinese curse that roughly translated says "May you live in interesting times". Did you annoy a Chinese sorcerer in your last life? I'm joking…kind-a.

You could view fate as having cursed you, but you could also view it as a blessing – find your inspiration, take control of your destiny, win past the opposition and achieve the impossible on a daily basis!

Finding that one piece of information that will turn a situation around and bring something really positive into being, is a primary skill for you. Observation, being open to messages of all kinds, allowing inspiration to find you: these things require a certain type of vulnerability and a high level of alertness – a rare mix which you can have in spades if you bother to work at it.

You may not realize it, but despite (or perhaps because of) the many setbacks you deal with, **you are capable of changing the world for the better**. Read that again, it's important.

One person can make a massive difference to the lives of others if they choose to, that person is you.

As the love interest's Higher Self/Influences/ Themes: Somehow this person navigates their way through impossible events, creating something positive from the worst personal disasters. Life constantly sticks them in situations where they have to struggle just to stay afloat, but it also gives them the information they need to come out ahead. When the chips are down, this person is capable of being a real winner – even if they don't always see it that way.

Need a miracle? This person has the best chance of helping you make it happen.

Fate has a strong hand in this person's life, which means they live through events that would finish off other mortals. On close inspection you'll notice that they lead a very interesting life, there's no chance to get bored if you hang around with them, but at the same time standing next to them may not be the safest place to be: they are a trouble magnet, a lightning rod.

'If you can't stand the heat, get out of the kitchen.' But if you can, knowing this person will change your life. You're a grown-up, you need to assess the risks for yourself.

<u>As the querent's link card</u>: You are looking for someone who makes you feel free and whole. You want someone who is true to themselves, confident, fulfilled, and who is free of the normal repressions and restrictions that society imprints upon people.

You need someone who will allow you to be yourself, and who will support you in your own search for emotional and creative fulfilment.

You feel a strong need to be free from the oppressive opinions of others, this includes any nagging or emotional demands from your lover. Which brings us to the inherent conflict between love and freedom: love can be seen as bondage by some, and thus on some level may be anathema to one or both of you.

The unbearable pain of loss is a potential outcome for you should the 'perfect' relationship fail.

<u>As the love interest's link card</u>: This person feels a strong need to be free from the opinions of others, this will probably include any good advice or guidance that you try to give them. Nagging will only drive them away. They want someone who can make them feel free and whole, rather than someone who makes constant demands of them.

<u>As clarification</u>: It might be a struggle for you, and seem impossible, but there is a chance of success. You are feeling the need for fulfilment, and this drives you forwards. Stand firm, trust your inner courage and the wisdom you have gained from past experience. Initial setbacks will pass.

<u>As a third party/obstacles</u>: A refusal to

compromise in a situation where compromise is the only solution. An attitude of obstinacy and a refusal to meet others half way is the cause of your feelings of separation and limitation, or restriction.

If it is the person you love who is being the brick wall rather than you, you're just going to have to accept your fate. This person's mind will not be swayed.

Nine of Cups

As the querent: You enjoy sensual satisfaction, feeling happy is very important to you. If you work, your career will be doing something you actively enjoy. If you don't work, your time will be taken up with doing things that make you feel good whenever you possibly can.

Life isn't always easy, but you know that you can make things go your way if you put in the effort. You're likely to be an optimist at heart, looking for the positive result in any action.

You're a bit of a hedonist – gourmet food, tasty drinks, massage, aromatherapy, fine clothes, good sex: you do what you can to make sure you get your full quota. Pleasures of the flesh are wonderful and help you feel emotionally satisfied.

You want the type of partner who will make you feel good, just remember it's a two way thing – satisfy them, they'll be a lot happier to satisfy you. And go carefully, your need for emotional fulfilment is so strong that you might end up with a whole string of unsuitable types before you work out what you really want from a relationship.

As the love interest: There are two options here,

positive and negative:

Positive: this person is a happy, optimistic type, they seem to spend their life walking on air. They enjoy life, and take pleasure in and from almost everything.

Their life isn't always easy, and they do have to work hard to achieve the things they want, but fundamentally this person is happy to be who they are and to do the things they do. Work, kids, house, husband, they are satisfied with what they have.

If they are already in a relationship they would probably be less than pleased with you rocking the boat; if they are single and they decide they like you, their world is your oyster.

Negative: this person is a hedonist, possibly a nymphomaniac. Celibacy and monogamy are likely to be nigh on impossible for them. Pleasures of the flesh – food, drink, sex – could be an addiction for them. Even if they are not an addict, this person is likely to be totally self-obsessed, and exceedingly fixated on their body and their bodily needs.

Looking good and feeling good, or more importantly, enjoying the pleasure they get from being themselves is their chief concern. Narcissism is a definite possibility.

If they do get involved with you, the relationship is likely to be rather parasitic. You get to do all the giving, they get to do all the taking.

<u>*As the querent's Higher Self/Influences/Themes*</u>: You may not think it, but you lead a very protected life. You don't have to deal with half the crud that the rest of us are forced to live through. Enjoy yourself, fate is on your side for a reason.

Having said that, don't get complacent. You may have a guardian angel looking out for you, but you'll still have to cope with the standard tragedies that beset all of us.

As the love interest's Higher Self/Influences/ Themes: Life is good to this person. Things may not always be easy for them, and they'll have their share of tragedy to cope with, same as the rest of us, but they are one of the lucky souls who is protected from the worst things that fate has to throw around.

Luck is on their side, and they have a guardian angel looking out for them.

As the querent's link card: You are looking for someone who can make all your dreams come true. That's a pretty tall order. Most folks don't qualify as a fairy godmother.

Human beings are human, warts and all. You might want to get a bit more realistic about what you actually need from a relationship before you make any kind of commitment to anyone.

Finding someone who can make you happy is what you really crave, so the question is, what mortal traits are you prepared to put up with to get that?

As the love interest's link card: This person wants to be with someone who can make them happy, but more than that, they have an ideal in mind that they apply to anyone they go out with. They are looking for someone who can make their every dream, and slightest wish come true. Their idea of love and marriage is based on romantic fantasy, so a real relationship stands about a snowball's chance in hell of being able to meet their expectations.

So maybe you are a god, or goddess, and can actually hover a couple of inches above the pedestal they put you on – good luck to you! If you can teach this person a bit about reciprocation, and a bit about love between mortals, you'll be doing well.

If you want a lasting relationship, you should probably look for someone else, as when this person eventually wakes up from the dream they'll likely hotfoot it out of Dodge.

<u>As clarification</u>: Get ready to purr pussycat, it's time to indulge your sensual pleasures. You feel the need to take it that one step further, make it more real, and now is the time when your wishes can come true. It won't be handed to you on a plate, but you can make it happen. Keep your mind open to new experiences.

Just remember precious moments such as these are to be treasured.

<u>As a third party/obstacles</u>: Narcissism and self obsession, dwelling too much in fantasy, or an overly active sex drive all have a negative impact. A relationship isn't about the satisfaction of one person only.

A difficult situation for anyone to deal with. When you and your partner have totally different wants and needs in sex, and vastly different sex drives from one another it can be difficult for a relationship to survive.

Nine of Swords

<u>As the querent</u>: You have a strong need for peace of mind, and you have to know what's going on. The

result is that you are both a problem solver, and you worry over the uncertainties in life. If you don't understand something, or can't see the cause behind an effect, or can't be certain what the results of a particular circumstance or set of actions is, then you worry. The issue will niggle away at you, possibly even causing sleepless nights and depression. Whereas, solving puzzles and finding a solution helps you to relax.

Any job that involves problem solving would appeal to you, for example: doctor, policeman, detective, trouble shooter, accountant, diplomat. However, any job that provides too much opportunity for you to worry would cause you extreme stress. So the jobs that appeal to you may not be the jobs you are best suited for in the long run, for the sake of your wellbeing…Stress management courses are a must.

You tend to invest too much of your time and energy in worrying over things that other people would ignore as trivial. Prioritizing which issues would actually impact negatively and severely on your life would be a good idea. Create a worry scale. Anything that features lower down on the scale can probably be ignored. Instead of dwelling on minor issues, learn to relax and chill out. Calming your thoughts and finding a positive mind space would be beneficial, so learning meditation or taking up an absorbing and relaxing hobby would be a good idea.

<u>As the love interest</u>: This person values honesty, and is willing to suffer a lot of pain and anxiety in order to get to the truth. However the pain and anxiety is usually created by their own inner demons niggling away at their fear of the unknown.

The cause of all the worry and despair they suffer is that this person is a compulsive problem solver: they have to know the answers, they want to understand the cause behind an effect, they have to puzzle through all the probable outcomes of an action or event. They want to be prepared for every eventuality.

They have a tendency to get hooked up on possible negative results, even if those results are the least likely of all the outcomes available. They waste a lot of time and energy worrying needlessly over trivial issues, or over things that will have no effect on them whatsoever.

This tendency to worry combined with the absolute value they place on truth, means that the slightest hint of infidelity from their partner, real or imagined, is likely to drive them to despair.

If this person is in a job that promotes the opportunity to worry about things, it will cause them a lot of stress – possibly to the detriment of their health and wellbeing; so a career in the police force, for example, may not be the best idea.

This person is likely to be controlling, anxious and accident prone (because they are worrying over something rather than looking where they are going). Learning to relax their mind and to live in the here and now would benefit them greatly.

<u>As the querent's Higher Self/Influences/Themes</u>: Life can seem cruel and painful when you look at it closely. During your dealings with this person that you love, fate is going to get involved and you are likely to suffer loss and despair, as well as cruelty at the hands of others. Your courage, and your ability to face the

truth without blinking, will guide you through these events and you'll come out stronger for it.

<u>As the love interest's Higher Self/Influences/ Themes</u>: During the time you know each other, this person is going to go through one or more emotional crises. What they are experiencing may be real, or it may be imagined, but their suffering will be utterly real.

Fate seems to have it in for them; life can be cruel. This person will probably reach the lowest depths of despair, but their courage and their ability to meet the truth head on will see them through the hard times. They will emerge from the other side scarred but stronger.

<u>As the querent's link card</u>: You want someone honest and faithful whose love is without question or doubt. You are willing to go through a lot of hardship and pain to be with someone like that, so if it turns out that they are a total sadist who enjoys making your life hell on earth you may just put up with it.

When someone said "love is blind" they were talking about you.

This person that you think is so wonderful, really isn't. Either they will destroy you if you allow them to, or they will leave, and that will nearly destroy you.

Save yourself a lot of anguish and walk away now.

<u>As the love interest's link card</u>: This person will fall in love with someone who they perceive to be honest and faithful.

Whether they fall in love wisely is another matter.

This person is willing to endure all kinds of cruel

and painful situations in order to be with the one they love. They are not a masochist, it's just that they make such a high emotional investment in the authenticity of their love for the other person (you?) that they are willing to walk through fire to preserve that.

Your callousness may nearly destroy this person, either during the relationship, or when you break up with them.

Do them a favour, don't get involved with them in the first place; and if you are already a couple and you are being cruel to them, seek help with your personality disorder. Or if the relationship seems fine, when you do walk out on them, for goodness sake try to be gentle and kind about it, and do it in person.

As clarification: Your thoughts and feelings are in turmoil. You are allowing your fear of something which is unknown to prey upon your mind to an unhealthy level. Impulsive action in response to the pain – which will pass in time – is detrimental. You need to find some calm and get back in touch with the real you.

Events are as they are, either the obstacles will be overcome, or they will not. Worrying yourself sick about it is a waste of opportunity and time. Accept the situation for what it is, and start making the most of what you have.

Determination, and a quiet appreciation for life, will see you through.

As a third party/obstacles: One, or both, of you are in a difficult and painful situation. Feelings of guilt, the desire for self punishment, and lost hope are understandable reactions, but you are nearly through this period of excruciating torment. After the long night comes the dawn, and this card shows that the Morning Star is on the horizon. Hold on, get support, you are going to come through okay.

Nine of Pentacles

As the querent: You feel a strong need for physical security and comfort, but your attitude towards money is one of detachment. The cold hard cash itself means very little to you. What you do have you may give away on a whim, or waste on an overpriced lifestyle or bad investments. But then, money seems to fall into your lap on a regular basis either through inheritance or through shear dumb luck.

The combination is one that can promote debt and bankruptcy; however you usually come up with a plan of action that'll pull your fat out of the fire, ready for you to start searching for that pot of gold at the end of the rainbow all over again.

Ultimately, once you get sensible about your quest for cash and get your spending under control, you should be able to achieve the type of lifestyle that you want.

It is probable that finding a supportive partner, who will be with you for life, will be on your list of goals. You're looking for someone who won't waltz out on a whim, or when the going gets tough; someone steadfast and reliable who'll stay with you through thick and thin. So take a careful look at that person you are interested in, do they have the inner strength and determination that that kind of commitment takes? As long as you realize that relationships take work you should do okay. The problems arrive as soon as you assume someone will be with you forever and start to take advantage of them; then they'll feel unfulfilled and be much more likely to leave.

If you want the relationship to last don't make assumptions, and remember that people change, and their needs change. So take account of that and nurture them accordingly.

As the love interest: This person needs a certain level of financial security and material comfort in order to be happy. They need to feel safe. Paying the rent and putting food on the table are their top priority, after that come the little luxuries.

In love, they are looking for someone who can provide or make a stable home. They are looking for something concrete and long term.

If you only want a one night stand, or a short fling, or an affair, or if you are not sure that they are 'the one', you'd better make that clear from the start, or you will really upset them. They will likely assume permanence, moving in together, kids, the whole ball of wax, unless you state otherwise.

This person is happy with who they are, they don't actually need anyone else in order to feel complete. If they are with you, it is because they genuinely like you/love you. You don't need to doubt their motives.

Financially, this person is a gamble. If you are marrying them for their money, you should be aware that they are capable of losing it just as quickly as they gain it. As far as they are concerned money is just a tool, other than that it has no real meaning for them. They know that they can live without it, they've done it before. So they have (misplaced?) confidence that they will survive any of life's lowest blows.

This person does have a tendency to be lucky and

they are good at convincing people to help them. In the end, they are likely to come through any hardship relatively unscathed, as for the people around them…they could be looking up from the gutter wondering how the heck this person managed to bounce back so quickly.

This person has staying power, they do not give up on something that means a lot to them, they are driven to attain security and comfort. Because of this they could be quite a gambler. Ultimately they will achieve their core dream, but getting there might be quite a rollercoaster ride.

<u>As the querent's Higher Self/Influences/Themes</u>: At the moment the constant need for more money in your life may be a cause of anxiety, but it is the Universe's way of trying to get you to trust your own skills at earning money and creating a pleasant environment to live in. You need to be more self reliant and understand the physical effort involved in making life work the way you want it to so you can live in the now and have the luxuries you crave.

The other part of the lesson here is that you can't expect other people to give you everything you need, even though they may have in the past. The process of growing up can be unpleasant – learning to stand on your own two feet without a net to catch you if you fall – but you will get help and guidance through the process if you keep calm and listen to your inner voice. There will also be a rare windfall (or two?) providing you with what you need to tide you over, possibly as the result of painful but necessary changes that you have to make in your lifestyle. But don't rely on getting a windfall whenever times are tough, you are being weaned off them so that you can stand tall and provide for yourself.

If you keep a level head and put in the required effort you will be able to create the financial security necessary to let you live the life you want to lead.

<u>As the love interest's Higher Self/Influences/ Themes</u>: When it comes to money, this person is having to learn to stand on their own two feet and provide for themselves. In the past they have lead a protected life and may be spoiled or expect a handout from everyone around them. The Universe is sending them a very strong message that they need to grow up and take control of their spending. It is also teaching them the effort and sacrifice that is required to earn the money they want for themselves, in order to lead the life they want to lead.

They may feel rather alone during this process and attempt to cling to any hand-out going, but the price they have to pay for continuing to rely on the generosity or gullibility of others is going to make this way of living untenable.

If you get in the way of this person's growth process the Universe is liable to slap you down and you may discover your finances are impacted negatively as a direct consequence.

<u>As the querent's link card</u>: Your need in a relationship is pretty specific. You need to feel secure.

This means that you have to feel that you can trust and rely upon the person you are with, and you want them to be with you for the long haul. You need a secure environment around you – a nice house in a nice safe location, no lighthouses for you thank you!

And you need your partner to have a steady income so that you know the mortgage is paid and you never have to worry about where the next meal is coming from.

As long as the physical side of things is good you can be happy.

A lack of security causes you stress and heartache. And may even cause you to leave the person you love in search of a more stable lifestyle.

As the love interest's link card: They want physical security, someone who is with them for the long haul who has a steady income and can provide them with a secure place to live in a nice safe environment. As long as you can tend to their physical needs of all kinds they'll be happy.

However, if life throws any stormy weather your way and you find yourself flat broke, no matter how much this person loves you the stress of uncertainty about the future and how you are going to survive right now may just drive this person away in search of a more stable environment.

They always like to know where they stand. So no gambling debts, remortgaging the house, or betting the farm on your fantastic new business venture (unless you have a nest egg that'll cover all the costs and 5 years worth of living expenses to boot). Not if you want a lasting relationship.

Stay faithful, steadfast, devoted and bring home the bacon, then this person will be 'happy as Larry'.

As clarification: Mixed messages. This card should indicate success, material comfort and emotional satisfaction. However I find it rather indicates a strong feeling of need for these things – no matter how much emotional contentment, wealth or success are currently present. Thus leading to the danger of throwing away what you have in an unsuccessful attempt to gain more. It is possible that instead of indicating success in amorous affairs, it hints at disappointment or dissatisfaction.

The feeling of wanting more.

Check the other cards in the spread for an idea of where the dissatisfaction may lie. Perhaps you are just a bit pickier now that you have reached a level where you don't actually need another person in order to feel satisfied in yourself and your achievements. You are looking for someone else who has that same inner light.

While you feel the need for someone, you don't want that someone to be just anyone.

As a third party/obstacles: Someone is being deceitful, whether this is you, the person you love, or another person altogether is unclear. What is clear is the loss of finances through either debt or theft.

An envy of what others have.

Also, possibly, a grasping desire to hang on to material things – which quite frankly is very unattractive, particularly if those things belong to other people and have been gained by fraud.

Basically the dark side of human nature is the obstacle to your relationship. Living on the pain, misery, and dashed hopes of others is no way to achieve a happy existence; why would anyone want to associate with someone who behaves like that?

Ten of Wands

As the querent: You work hard in order to be able to play hard, but you may find yourself shouldering all of the burdens you encounter on behalf of the people you care about. You tend to do the majority of the hard work, because you want your and their lives, work and relationships to be successful. "If you want something done right, do it yourself", seems to be the motto you live by. And this usually leads to very good results.

However, the danger with this approach is that you can sometimes find yourself feeling creatively stifled if you take on too much - stress overcomes joy; excitement becomes squashed under the burdens of responsibility.

The good news is that it is easy to regain your creative joyful self and bring the excitement back into your life, you just need to be able to step sideways and find a new way of approaching the problems or tasks that you take on.

You don't need to do it all yourself. Relationships are about sharing, and if you are with the right person the two of you should be able to find a good balance for working together in order to achieve great success.

You understand that life and relationships take work in order to be successful. Ensure that the person you love also understands this and to some extent shares your views and life's challenges won't be as hard as they may otherwise feel.

As the love interest: This person works hard in everything they do to try to achieve success. Frequently it works, but they tend to take on too much and may find their joy of life being smothered by the burdens they shoulder. They need to remember to take time out occasionally, or try to find a different way of approaching the issues in order to find their way through.

This person is creative and can be very exciting to be around as long as their joie-de-vivre is not squashed under the weight of the world. Maybe you can lend them a hand, or show them a new way of doing things that might be easier?

As the querent's Higher Self/Influences/Themes: You spend a lot of your life pretending there are no limits and that you can achieve anything – but life has a way of reminding you that there are boundaries and finite qualities to every aspect of being.

Your creative impulses and joy of life have a way of breaking up any carefully laid plans, and disrupting the walls you build around yourself with work and the obligations you set yourself.

You need to be able to find a balance between the two – work and commitment are necessary for success and happiness, but letting your hair down and allowing yourself to live in the moment and submit to impulse can be equally important to finding a satisfying life. Each time you step too far into one way of living, something happens that disrupts it and throws you into the other way of living. It can be a bit of a seesaw until you learn how to keep your balance on the axis.

As the love interest's Higher Self/Influences/ Themes: This person seems to spend their life seesawing between responsibility along with a level of hard work and burdens that make most people run for the hills, and a carefree abandon and spontaneity that is equally terrifying and breathtaking to most mere mortals. Life seems to force them to take responsibility or zap them with crazy times each time they settle too far into one way of living or behaving.

Everything this person does seems to have consequences and until they learn to balance their life somewhere between these two extremes, their life and the events surrounding them may be more interesting than anyone would want to handle.

As the querent's link card: You are looking for someone who can excite your passion and stimulate you mentally. Each new relationship starts out great, but quickly the other person tries to tie you down, puts pressure on you, it can all be too much. You're a romantic at heart. Don't they realize how sensitive you are?

You're looking for someone to be with for the long haul, but once the initial romance has calmed down you may start feeling overburdened by the mundane aspects of life and all the tasks that involves. Where has all the excitement and romance gone? The key is to not try to do everything at once, prioritize the important things, and don't let the other person take advantage of you.

You are likely to have a string of affairs or one night stands in your youth while you try to find that certain someone, and as you get older your need for something lasting will intensify and may lead to some wild behaviour. At this stage you will need to learn to prioritize your actual needs from the things you feel you might like. Work out the most important thing you want and set aside your other desires until you've achieved that.

You like to be footloose and fancy free in all aspects of life, especially love, but you should be aware that other people may see your refusal to compromise over your need for freedom as selfishness.

You are an exciting person to be around and a lot of people want that, so if you want to separate the wheat from the chaff and think you've found the right person to be with, make sure you are honest with them about your romantic and emotional needs right from the start – otherwise they may throw a fit when they find out later on in the relationship, "Aren't I enough for you?" and you'll need to start the hunt for a partner all over again.

As the love interest's link card: This person can be a little bit selfish, they believe there should be no limitations to their love life and relationships. They want to be free.

They are looking for someone who will stimulate their mind and imagination, but also someone who will not try to burden them with their problems or the banalities of life.

This person may have been married many times before. *If* they have managed to gain some wisdom as they flitted from flower to flower before they met you, they may realize the right relationship is worth sacrificing some of their immediate needs for if it means they'll benefit in the long term, however they will have had to learn to prioritize and concentrate on one thing at a time.

This person will gladly jump into a new relationship or marriage just for the excitement and the passion, but their ardour is likely to quickly cool once the day-to-day burdens of relationship or household upkeep kick in and then they'll look for mental stimulation and passion elsewhere, maybe by having affairs or perhaps you'll get home and they've simply gone.

This person burns brightly: just remember fire is hot and needs to be fed – smother it and it goes out. It can burn you just as easily as warm you.

As clarification: Biting off more than you can chew. To get to your goal you have to do a little bit at a time, you can't try to do everything at once and hope to be successful. Take your time, go slow. Prioritize. Don't let other's drain you of your power and resources. You will succeed if you change your approach to a more moderate one.

Even success has its price – just pay your dues by instalments or they'll hogtie you.

As a third party/obstacles: Mundane life is getting in the way. People keep laying obstacles in front of you, or piling on the pressure. Feelings of oppression, doubt, and dismissing your dreams as pointless or unrealistic all vie to make you want to give up. When other people are trying to reinforce your erroneous feelings of inadequacy in order to make you give them what they want, it can be a powerful cocktail that will do you no good.

Look after yourself; tell these other people to take a hike. If someone close to you is taking advantage tell them how you feel – if they are unrepentant, you might want them to back off too.

Ten of Cups

As the querent: You are someone who needs a solid home life. Comfort, happiness and stability are key things that you need to exist within your family life in order to feel content in yourself and your work. Like a tree, you put down roots, and these roots allow you to feel safe and grow tall and strong. As a result you are likely to have an aversion to anything or anyone that threatens this feeling of safety. Is there someone in your family that you don't get on with? Is it because they rock the boat, or undermine your feeling of safety somehow? Relax, every bird needs to spread its wings and practice flying.

You know that appreciation of the little things in life and gratitude for them, are part of the work involved in maintaining a happy home environment. The good life isn't something that just magically appears, it is something that you have worked hard for and that you know you need to continue to work for in order to maintain.

Domestic harmony, inner peace and lasting contentment within your environment are your main goals, and are very achievable. Live moment by moment and appreciate the good.

As the love interest: This person needs a lasting, safe, nurturing environment. They know how important it is to appreciate the little things in life and they are grateful for the good things that are around them as well as those that come to them.

This person does not want the boat rocked. They need safety and emotional harmony, and are looking for someone to share that with. Be who you are with them and they will appreciate you for who you are. If you are putting on an act they are likely to detect that and shy away, or if they fall for it and later in the relationship your true self starts to be revealed they won't enjoy the surprise.

This person lives life at face value. They are looking for someone who does the same.

Family is important to this person. They are willing to work hard to create a good emotional and physical environment for those they love, and they understand that it takes work to maintain what they have established. If you share that same understanding and value a lasting relationship, this could be the person for you.

If you are just playing the field or if you don't think you are looking for the same level of permanence, please don't play with this person's emotions; you will hurt them more deeply than you can imagine.

As the querent's Higher Self/Influences/Themes: Lasting contentment, pleasure and an enjoyment of the simple things in life is either the lesson that you need to learn, or with some effort on your part will be discovered by you.

It takes work to create and maintain the good life; and you have the opportunity to experience what is involved in making and keeping happiness. By being grateful for life's simple pleasures, appreciating the beauty in nature around you, and finding joy in the small things that bring happiness, lasting contentment can be yours.

Learning to merge with opposites; appreciating the play between Yin and Yang; finding the balancing point; selfless love; a brush with Zen.

<u>As the love interest's Higher Self/Influences/ Themes</u>: This person is learning to love life.

Their goal is to discover which blossom on the cherry tree is perfect, and thus attain lasting happiness. Even if you do not understand this, you may be able to help them on their quest just by being you.

This person is undergoing the healing process. They need support, and caring, and quiet acceptance. Are you able to give them these things? If not, maybe you should look for someone else - the Universe is watching.

<u>As the querent's link card</u>: You know who you are and you are happy within yourself.

If you can find someone to love who loves you equally well in return you will be very grateful. You know that successful relationships take work, and you're willing to put in that effort in order to gain enduring contentment with the person you love, but you'd appreciate it if they put in similar effort in return.

Not everyone is wise enough to understand the rare combination of stability and happiness that you can offer, but you should be able to spot the gadflies and charlatans without too much trouble and avoid them.

With the right person you can find a sense of completion and have a really good marriage, relationship, or partnership.

<u>As the love interest's link card</u>: This person is happy with who they are, and content within themselves. That by itself is a rare thing. This is a person you should be happy to know, be friends with, or to have any kind of relationship with.

Because they are internally sound, they are likely to be a solid, trustworthy partner who will also be able to provide you with shelter from the storms of life. And they want the same things from the person they love.

Boring? Not everyone sees it that way.

This person knows that successful relationships take work to create and maintain.

Treat them well, love them well and you could just discover that the secret of enduring bliss is being at their side.

As clarification: A solid relationship steeped in contentment. You may even wish to consider marriage. You've learned you need to work hard to make a relationship a success, and to keep it successful. Your dedication is reaping its dividends.

As a third party/obstacles: Your other half has found something that makes them happy. Right or wrong, you should respect their decision – they would only resent you if you try to force them to change their mind.

On the positive side, what they think they've found may not be all that good. If you keep the door open, they might come back. However, instead of waiting, you should get on with your own life. Make the best of a bad situation, and get on with your quest for personal fulfilment.

Ten of Swords

As the querent: Your life is changing big time. Any illusions you have been living with are over, it is time to face and accept the truth.

Abrupt change can be painful. It is time to accept what has happened, that part of your life is now over and you need to move on to the next stage – whether it is moving house, moving jobs, or moving out of the last relationship and getting on with your new life (possibly all of the above).

You need to sort yourself out first and foremost. (Check your attitude – it needs attention.) Clear away the confusion, and find a new goal. It takes time to start anew, so give it time. Find your balance.

Embarking on a new relationship at this time could be a very mixed blessing. Are you absolutely certain that this is what you want to do? You are very vulnerable right now. Do not hurt others or yourself needlessly.

As the love interest: This person has been living with lies and self-delusion for too long. They have now reached a point where they are being forced to change, their old life is over and they will likely be finding it very painful.

This person is vulnerable right now and needs time to re-establish themselves in their new way of living. It is not advisable to start any deep romantic or business entanglements with them at the moment.

They are on the path to healing now, so do extend the olive branch if you want to, just tread carefully. They are likely to need someone to lean on after the 'betrayal' they have just been through – but if you offer friendship and support, be truthful with them, and demand that they are truthful with you. They cannot slip back into the old ways and habits – this is their opportunity for growth now that the deadwood has been cleared out.

Friendship is more important than romance at this time. White lies are a bad idea. Be honest. This person needs to re-establish trust and truth in their life.

As the querent's Higher Self/Influences/Themes: Growth is needed. It's time to face up to reality. Your illusions are false, self-deception will no longer work. It can be a painful process when you are forced to face up to the truth of your situation. The way you have lived before can no longer continue.

One way through the pain is to separate your emotion out of the equation and deal with the situation in a purely rational way. Look the truth squarely in the eye, however uncomfortable this makes you. Thinking clearly will allow you to find a way to move forwards that makes sense, and provides the best opportunity for success in the future.

You feel betrayed; as though you have lost everything that matters to you, but once you have let go of the past you will be able to see that this change was necessary. It may be painful, but it will leave the way clear for you to find a new, more honest direction in which to take your life.

You are being given the chance to find out who you really are.

Old relationship patterns are no longer possible. If you try to follow the same route that you did in the past it will work out badly. You need to change. Another person may be able to help show you the way, but it is you who needs to change on a deep inner level.

As the love interest's Higher Self/Influences/Themes: Growth is needed. Any lies they have told, or that have been told to them will be coming back to roost. Their whole life is being melted in the crucible: home, work, relationships. Illusions are being stripped away, it is likely to be a painful process, but once it is over they will have the opportunity to rebuild their life from scratch.

This is their chance to make real changes, so they can live in a more positive and healthy way.

This person needs to learn the benefits of facing reality and living with truth and honesty.

Take care: if you help them with this process it can benefit both of you, but right now they are hurting and may well lash out instead of accepting help.

If you should take advantage of this vulnerable person and/or hinder their growth process, the Universe may well zap you with the same energy it is applying to them.

As the querent's link card: For some reason best known to yourself you are in a lot of pain at the moment and can be needlessly, possibly unknowingly, cruel to people who care about you or want to be with you. But that is likely to be for the best in the long run. Maybe you feel trapped by other people's emotional lies and manipulation?

You are in no place to have a relationship right now. Walk away.

As the love interest's link card: This person doesn't want a relationship at the moment, and they might be quite brutal in stripping away any illusions you may hold about yourself or about them.

Either your, or their, approach to romance has a falseness to it that any kind of relationship with them will shine a spotlight on for both of you.

This person is in pain and will be unnecessarily cruel to you as a result. There is nothing you can do to help them. Back off for the time being, or better yet walk away.

As clarification: Don't touch this relationship with a bargepole. Betrayal, or the rejection of your advances, will occur. It will be especially painful for you as you probably have deep feelings for this person.

At least with the certainty that things can no longer continue as they were, once you have regained your equilibrium, you are freed to set out on your own journey once more. Try not to dwell in the past, or on 'what if', the future lies before you.

As a third party/obstacles: It isn't going the way you wanted, and you are naturally upset. Devastated might be a better word. Every time you think you have a handle on things, they get worse.

You can't help but ask "Will this ever end?" The answer is, it will, just not quite yet. Don't allow despair to overwhelm you, the sun is on the horizon and the clouds will soon clear. You are going to come through okay, have courage.

Ten of Pentacles
As the querent: You work hard for your rewards, and you know that your success is proportional to the amount of effort you put in. You are very aware that patient nurturing is needed to get any endeavour to come to a successful and profitable conclusion, whether it be in love or business.

You are willing to put the lessons you have learned from family traditions to good use, which also helps with your success. You apply these lessons to both your emotional life and in your working life which results in success and happiness personally and professionally. You are happy to pass on these lessons to others, to help them achieve success too.

As the love interest: This person is successful both personally and professionally. Other people may be jealous of their inheritance – whether it be a family business, or wisdom passed on to them. But the reason they have got to where they are today is because they carefully plan out what they want to achieve and then they put in the hours and the work required in order to get it.

In other words, they create their fulfilment in life.

Another person could be handed the same opportunities as them and go nowhere, because they aren't willing to spend the time planning, nurturing, and seeing the endeavour through to completion.

This person can teach you a lot about being successful in relationships and successful in business if you are willing to follow their lead, and put in the effort.

As the querent's Higher Self/Influences/Themes: The lesson you need to learn is that success is not something that is handed to you (however much you might believe that), but that it is something that is earned through planning, nurturing and continual work.

Even the most beautiful garden becomes choked with weeds if no one tends it.

If someone is handed a fortune, they can spend their way through it until one day nothing is left, and then they cry, "Woe is me!" Make sure that isn't you.

Take what you have been given, learn the lessons previous generations have to give, and instead of frittering away what others have built up over time, add to it and build further. Create a legacy for you and your family.

As the love interest's Higher Self/Influences/ Themes: This person is learning the amount of planning, work, persistence and nurturing that goes into both business and personal success.

They may have been handed a gift, or inheritance, or have the chance to learn traditional skills; this can be the basis for success in the future, but only if they put in the work and nurturing required for that success.

This person can provide you with a lot – either in terms of life lessons, or family, or even financial security – even if they may appear to have nothing that you want or need right now. They can be a beneficial, positive influence.

As the querent's link card: You want someone who is successful and who is ready to start a family.

You feel a need to belong, and to pass on what you've learned to future generations. You are looking for someone to settle down with and make that long-term commitment to.

As the love interest's link card: This person is going to take time to get to know, and wants someone who is willing to put in that effort to get to know them in return. This is likely to be because they want someone who is serious about a long-term relationship.

They've worked hard in life, and now they want a family and children who can continue their legacy.

This person needs a successful long-term union. If that's not what you want, you'd best keep on moving. If that is what you want and you're prepared to put in the effort to make it work, I wish you many fat, happy children.

As clarification: The indication is that it is time to get married, time to start a family, time to buy a house. Basically you are ready to set down something solid, physical and real for the future. Somehow this will link to the continuation of family traditions. Happiness, contentment and 'family' support will be available for your romantic endeavour.

As a third party/obstacles: Divorce is in the offing, and it may lead to financial disadvantage – certainly the splitting of assets. Whether it is you or your other half who initiates proceedings, it actually comes – surprisingly – as a bit of a relief.

It is time to make a new start, to head out on another adventure. All the old family stuff is stifling you. It's time to make a break.

Page of Wands

As the querent: You are a creative person who continuously explores new ideas, you are eager to learn, and passionate about making the most of your life; you have great potential. Impatient and impulsive, the danger here is that you can easily get distracted by your next project or passion before you have completed the last one.

You keep yourself very busy with all your creative projects: plenty of communication and messages, urgent matters require your attention – but you do need to take time out to plan your strategy for your next endeavour. A meeting with an old friend could be an important past of this.

You are the type of person who needs recognition of their skills, so you are likely to work in one of the creative fields that requires collaboration to at least a small degree, and/or you will gain your plaudits from your fans.

It is quite important to you that the person you love recognizes your talents and gives encouragement and appreciation when it's due.

As the love interest: This creative whirlwind is constantly on the hunt for inspiration. They are passionate about their work and about the people they value. They can be impatient and impulsive, and can't stand being bored. They need people around them who recognize their talents and appreciate their skill.

Doom merchants and naysayers are not required, thank you. They are already well aware of the level of risk they are taking even if it does seem like they have their head in the clouds permanently.

If you are a positive person who can keep up, and you like what this person does, then find a way to introduce yourself – messages or a mutual acquaintance may be the best method. However, if you have flare and a certain je ne sais quoi this person has likely already noticed you.

<u>As the querent's Higher Self/Influences/Themes</u>: You need to shake things up a bit and get some inspiration and passion back into your life. You will be receiving messages and communication that all point to your need to get out of the rut you are in and put some fire back into your life.

Art and appreciation of art – whether it be pictures, books, movies, sculptures, etc – will somehow be an important part of the process that you are going through, or are about to undergo.

Keep on the look out for a messenger or an old acquaintance bearing news. They may be able to shine some light on your situation. It is time to explore the real you, so be prepared to take the opportunity when it presents itself.

<u>As the love interest's Higher Self/Influences/Themes</u>: This person has somehow lost their way, and is now being asked to rediscover their true self. They need to find passion and inspiration in their lives once more, and the path to this will likely be through one of the fields of art.

A messenger or old friend may bring them news that can help them change and get out of the rut they are in.

If you are a creative, inspirational, positive person, you might be exactly what they need. Introduce them to movies, books, sculpture, art … see if you can get them to explore and blossom. Maybe they have a hidden talent?

<u>As the querent's link card</u>: You need an encouraging partner who will applaud your efforts and provide honest, constructive feedback about your

artistic efforts in life as well as in the bedroom.

You're looking for someone with a positive outlook on life, a sunny disposition, and a desire to experience new things and encourage you to do the same.

If you find yourself feeling constantly exhausted and you avoid talking about your feelings, it probably means you are depressed because your partner is not supporting you in the ways you need. Have a heart to heart with them, and if they remain a stick-in-the-mud it's probably time to move on to find someone who can love you the way you need, and deserve, to be loved.

As the love interest's link card: This person is an innocent, looking for someone who will inspire them, encourage their artistic endeavours, and stimulate their imagination in life as well as in the bedroom.

They are looking for an appreciative audience. If you're it and you're open and honest and willing to support their efforts, then the relationship could grow into something really special. If however you are a negative wet blanket, or don't provide feedback, they'll clam up about their feelings and may exhibit signs of exhaustion which is likely a symptom of depression. Nurture them and introduce them to lots of new experiences and they'll be 'happy as Larry'.

Possibly demanding, impatient and impulsive; but this person's charm and innocence along with their quest for constant stimulation will never leave you bored.

As clarification: You may have been surprised at finding someone you like, and in turn, it seems that they also like you. This card is a good omen of something small that can become important and lasting. Relax, be yourself, and allow things to blossom. Messages need tending to, and good news is likely.

As a third party/obstacles: Someone is stirring up trouble, or bad news is headed your way.

It is likely that selfishness and a spoiled attitude combined with a holding back of true feelings is leading you and your other half on separate paths. Things may not be over yet, but if you both don't start talking sensibly about how you really feel, then the relationship will suffer.

Page of Cups

As the querent: You are an insightful, imaginative, artistic and sensitive person, who can tune in to the emotions of others – either on purpose or by accident. It can be quite draining at times.

You need to find someone who will nurture you, and allow you to be yourself, and maybe even provide a little inspiration to spark your creativity?

You have a lot of creative and emotional potential which has not yet found proper expression. But you are in the process of creating a meaningful life. Once you have decided on your path you need to take the time and effort to study the skills you will need to excel. Picasso didn't become a master overnight. Learn the tools of your trade and the skills you need to use them well, and the results you achieve could amaze you. Your energies tend to dissipate when not contained, the hard part for you is sticking at it. The right person can help motivate and inspire you. It's important you choose the right one. They do not have to be a lover, they could easily be a friend or business partner who can help mold your dreams into reality.

As the love interest: This person is imaginative, sensitive and has deep emotions. They may appear to be a dreamer but they are able to apply themselves when needed. They just prefer to feel their way through life, find its heart gently, artistically; rather than drive a stake through it – which is the way some people try to tackle life, head-on at full speed.

This person is insightful and intuitive, and quite an innocent in all the important respects (no matter how outrageous their life may be). They need protection and nurturing. All they need is a little inspiration and they can go far in their chosen field.

As the querent's Higher Self/Influences/Themes: Outside influences, and deep internal influences are guiding you to experience a change of heart. You need to allow yourself to explore your emotions, and how you feel connected to the world and the people around you. Birth is a key concept here – the birth of something new within in you, or maybe the birth of a child?

You will discover that new emotions are coming to the fore, and you need to spend time with them. This is not a time for judgment or analysis; this is a time for feeling and being.

You are being prompted to study a new way of life, to use your creative gifts, and to embark on a new loving relationship, with yourself, or with others.

<u>As the love interest's Higher Self/Influences/ Themes</u>: This person is experiencing a subtle change at the deepest level of their intuition and emotions. They are faced with a totally new experience of life, and they need time to absorb the feelings they are going through. In some respects they are being born again, or perhaps a new baby is forcing them to change their experience of the world.

This person needs gentle nurturing and may need guidance – although their heightened intuition is probably already prompting them in the right direction. They need reassurance that they are correct about what they already feel emotionally.

If you are looking for a quick one night stand you may end up with a very different outcome than you bargained for with this person.

<u>As the querent's link card</u>: You are possibly still discovering your true sexuality, and your wants and needs in a relationship. If you are a woman you are likely to be a tomboy, and if your are a man you will have some strong feminine qualities that can be very appealing to the right person.

You really need someone who wants you for who you are, rather than a lover who wants the socially ideal partner. You're too creative to fit neatly into that mould.

You tend to find it difficult to separate your mind from your emotions, and you have an intense imagination which can fool you into thinking things are different to the way they really are – which can be quite painful when your are forced to confront reality as it is, rather than reality as you wish it was.

Practical matters do need to be addressed, so make

sure emotion isn't consuming you or clouding your judgment.

You need a lover who is supportive and can give you reassurance as well as guidance, otherwise you tend to let your energies dissipate through lack of focus ... feeling everything can, in a strange way, lead to feeling nothing, and vice versa.

As the love interest's link card: This person is looking for a new start in love. In their innocence they may have made some mistakes in the past, but now they are ready to move on and find a beneficial and fulfilling relationship with someone special.

They view love as a gift, and won't take it for granted; they need someone who feels the same way.

This person may not seem like the perfect partner at first glance, but give them time, avoid making any judgments and they'll surprise you. They need support, reassurance and guidance from their lover. At times you may find them reacting like a petulant, spoiled child, but this is usually because their dream of "what could be" has clashed with reality in a painful way.

This person tends to live in his or her emotions. They will also share a lot of traits in common with members of the opposite sex: if they are male they'll have a strong feminine side, and if female they'll probably be a tomboy.

Love them for who they are, not who society wants them to be.

As clarification: This card bodes well for a new relationship, or for feelings of love. It is nice to drift away, allowing your feelings to take you where they will, but remember to keep one eye on practical matters – love won't do your chores for you or pay the bills. Make time for both.

As a third party/obstacles: Reality is imposing itself into your dream world. Thinking clearly about things may reveal information you'd rather not know, but at least if you are thinking clearly you can make proper plans. Try to see what's what in amongst all the make-believe.

Page of Swords

As the querent: You are dedicated to your cause, and you intellectualize your motives, but you are far more driven by your feelings (including the darker ones: revenge, jealousy, fear) than you are willing to admit to yourself.

You are adept at observation and use idle chit-chat to seek out knowledge. You give little away about yourself, but can be subtle about finding a way past other people's defences. You enjoy intrigue, and have enough mental agility and eloquence to be able to charm others, or to act as a successful go between in settling other people's differences.

You are driven by curiosity, and can be an ingenious ally.

Your thoughts tend to be based upon what you see happening around you, but you should avoid leaping to conclusions until you have delved a little deeper into the motives of others and found out the true facts.

Try to avoid getting involved with negative people and their arguments as this will not improve your self-esteem, however much you might think you're helping.

As the love interest: This person has a tendency towards fanaticism and obsession, they have a keen mind and are very good observers, they can winkle out the best kept secret if they put their mind to it.

They intellectualize their motives and actions, but they tend to act more from emotion and assumption than they care to admit even to themselves. And if they leap to the wrong conclusions, or feel slighted, they can be very caustic and vindictive in their pursuit of revenge.

This person is very secretive about themselves, while appearing to be gregarious and chatty. They are driven by curiosity. They need to know everything about the people around them, so that they can meld into the crowd more effectively.

This person will take time, patience and understanding to get to know, and you will need to engage them both intellectually and emotionally if you want to get closer than scratching at the surface.

As the querent's Higher Self/Influences/Themes: You need to learn how to interact with others and you also need to conquer your anxiety in unfamiliar situations. As a result you are being prompted into new situations or meetings with new people where you get to practise communication, body language and learn how to relax with strangers. After all, most people are friendly – even the big scary ones that are covered in tattoos.

Don't allow your prejudice and fear to close you off. You have the chance to make new friends, learn new skills, and evolve as a social animal. Let your curiosity tempt you out of your shell.

Studying people, appraising others, learning to tell

truth from lies – these are all skills you are likely to get to practise now.

<u>As the love interest's Higher Self/Influences/Themes</u>: This person is learning how to reduce their anxiety and communicate successfully in new situations or with strangers, so if they come across as uneasy don't be surprised.

Eloquent and with a keen mind, they are more than capable of holding their own once they are relaxed, or think they have a grasp on a situation, however they can be obsessive to the point of fanaticism.

They are very curious and are mentally adept. They are great at observing people and deducing secrets, but they can also leap to conclusions and take offence before they have all the evidence and facts.

However rational and objective they proudly claim to be, they frequently base their decisions on emotional judgments and tend to allow the darker side of their emotional nature to rule their mind whether they realize it or not. They can be jealous, vengeful and vindictive if they haven't learned to mellow out yet. They could probably use someone calm to explain to them the benefits of keeping an even keel when navigating deep water.

<u>As the querent's link card</u>: You are learning about what it means to be involved in a lasting loving relationship, but as yet you may not have grasped the idea that it takes work on both sides, and real communication between yourself and your partner.

Try to keep your jealousy in check; don't just leap to assumptions because you saw the person you love talking with someone else.

You are looking for a confidante, a 'partner in crime' so to speak, who you can share other people's secrets with, discuss their habits and peccadilloes, someone to gossip with. However if you take this trait further and start spreading gossip about your lover; talking about their faults and foibles with others – no matter how annoyed with them you are, or how harmless you think it might be – is unlikely to lead to a quiet life of loving togetherness, unless you can find someone tolerant, or someone who really doesn't care what others think about them.

Your insecurities mean that a lot of the time you react as a result of emotion, rather than thinking things through. You also tend to use cold clinical detachment as both a shield and a weapon, perhaps without realizing that's what you're doing. From another person's perspective you may seem to go from gossip to brick wall at the turn of a dime, which may leave regular folk unsure how to deal with you.

Relationships are a challenge, a test of your ability to compromise with another person's ideals and emotional truth.

As the love interest's link card: However old this person is, they are probably still learning that it takes a lot of work on both sides to create a lasting, loving relationship.

They will also need to learn how to communicate clearly with the person they love; or else you will need to learn to read them and translate their emotional responses to the situations they are in, which will take **patience** and **deep understanding** on your part. For harmony, it will probably take a bit of both.

This person can be tempestuous, a bit of a drama

queen, but this is only because they feel rather than think their way through life (no matter how clever they are). On top of this they may tend to allow their jealousy or desire to control their words and actions, so they can be quite a handful. Don't expect a quiet life. If this person appears touchy and emotional it is their insecurity in play, they need reassurance and a good cuddle far more than they let on.

They also enjoy gossiping and tend to seek out other people who like the same thing. If you dislike having your personal life (real or imaginary) splashed all over the grapevine, this person may not be for you.

This person can be a joy to be around much of the time, they are quick-witted and always looking for the next entertainment or activity. Life can be hard work with them, but it will never be boring. See to their emotional needs and you can both have a lot of fun.

As clarification: You are allowing yourself to be driven by emotion. If these are positive emotions, then a nice little romance could evolve from day-to-day occurrences and chit-chat; however, negative emotions such as fear and pain are, sadly, what drive most people to act as they do – a relationship forged from fear will not stand the test of time, and will do neither of you any good.

Take care to be sure what drives your motives before you engage in a union.

As a third party/obstacles: Someone is trying to split you up on purpose. There is an underhanded person here who is being malicious for their own reasons. They have likely wormed their way into the good graces of one or other of you – it could even be an old friend. Do not react in anger or pain when there is no way to tell if your suspicions are founded. Check things out properly before you act in any way. Nothing can be trusted right now. If you start being nasty, you will regret it.

Page of Pentacles

<u>*As the querent*</u>: You know the benefits of being prepared. You are someone who builds foundations, so that the following work can grow and prosper without being undermined by avoidable flaws.

You know that anything worthwhile in life takes careful planning, then you can start the process, nurture the process, and once it has matured you will have something special that needs continual tending if it is to continue to thrive.

You prefer to avoid high risk, and are uncomfortable around people who walk the high wire without a net. Sure they're dazzling to watch, but do you really want to be around to clear up the mess after they inevitably slip and fall? No one else brought a bucket.

<u>*As the love interest*</u>: This person doesn't tend to take leaps of faith without having a good idea of where they are going to land. So don't be put off by their hesitance. They want something solid for the future, so they are assessing potential, planning how to get what they want, and then once they are ready they will set about bringing their plan to fruition.

If you understand that this person is 'long-term results, commitment oriented' their plodding methodology starts to make sense.

They put in the work and they achieve their goals

more often than not. Discounting them because they are a slow starter would be a mistake.

As the querent's Higher Self/Influences/Themes: You are learning about the importance of firm foundations being at the core of any successful enterprise – remember if you build on sand, the building will collapse, whereas if you lay a proper base the walls should be able to weather any storm.

The universe is testing your mettle – it won't send you anything you can't handle, although it may feel like it. So dig deep and find those foundations, if they're not there then build some.

As the love interest's Higher Self/Influences/Themes: This person is going through the ringer at the moment, and if they're not, then they're about to. The universe will be challenging them, testing their mettle.

Although they may need help, ultimately they'll have to deal with the battle on their own. Facing your inner demons and fears is never fun.

They are being asked to find their inner strength; examine their beliefs; find their true self. If they need support, give them support, but don't interfere with the process, this is something they have to face. Allow them the space to do this.

As the querent's link card: You are really looking for someone who can help you in your work, or teach you about things that will help you in your career. Possibly you are just looking for an investor? You need a business partner first and foremost, if they also happen to be your lover that could be the icing on the cake – or your worst nightmare if things should go wrong in the relationship and they want to take their 50% and go their own way. A pre-nup is strongly advised here.

You see love as a contract with each of you having specific roles in the relationship; you need to ensure that the other person is aware of what you expect from them and in turn what they can expect from you right at the start. If both of you are honest about this, and negotiate any changes in your roles with adequate warning as you go along, you should both be very happy.

You need someone who is as fascinated by the world as you are, who wants to create growth and nurture life in all its forms. You also need safety and an element of predictability from your partner. Someone you can unite with under the same goal. If you have that you can flourish and build something really special with your life.

As the love interest's link card: This person is looking for someone who can help them with their career – they see a partner or a lover as an investment for the future: as a financier, a contact in the industry, a mentor, or a teacher. To put it bluntly they will see you as an asset as much as a lover. So get a pre-nup if you have money or any chance of gaining money – just in case. They won't mind, they see the sense in it. And don't let any of the above put you off, this person might just be the foundation stone you need in your life.

They are very rooted and want to create something meaningful with their life. For that to happen they need someone solid and reliable to support them and lean on in times of stress.

If you have a good head for business, the two of you could start a very successful relationship – either as their adviser, while pursuing your own career, or as a partner in a joint venture.

Family with this person is likely to be both fruitful and lasting, as long as you are honest with each other, and if you provide the stability and support that this person requires.

Discuss your needs and goals, make sure you are both working from the same page before you get serious. This person won't thank you if you run off part way through them living their dream.

As clarification: Study and finance have the floor right now. If love can figure in that mix somehow, then great, because this card is a foundation stone of future success, and solid reality. Of course, a foundation stone is just that, it takes a lot more work to build anything from it. Hard work and attention to detail in matters you enjoy, is what is required. Whether love of another person has anything to do with it would just be an additional benefit; but it is not one that is guaranteed.

As a third party/obstacles: Whimsy, distraction, and the ability to eat other people's money without any concern for their penury all add up to extreme dissatisfaction on the benefactor's part.

Two people have to work hard to make a relationship work. If one of them is sat on their bottom eating chocolate, or gallivanting about town with all and sundry, while the other one works hard to try to keep the couple financially buoyant, it is not likely to make for a happy home life, specially not if the debts are piling up.

'Shape up or ship out' is the phrase that springs to mind.

Knight of Wands

As the querent: You like a bit of an adventure, and you have the energy, passion and imagination to turn the ordinary into the extraordinary. You're not afraid to throw yourself into any exciting opportunities that come along which catch your interest.

A positive attitude is the key to your fearlessness. And if things should go wrong, you pick yourself up, brush yourself off and head on to the next adventure with few regrets – at least you took a chance and tried.

Good humoured, loyal and adventurous, you are governed by your instincts and desires and trust your gut over what other people tell you.

As the love interest: This person makes up their mind quickly, so you will only have the first few seconds when you meet them to make an impression.

This person doesn't like to stand still, there is far too much out there to experience and be inspired by to waste time lurking about or sulking.

They have a passion for life and cannot be called a shrinking violet. They make quick decisions usually based on gut instinct. They seem to throw themselves into their next adventure with barely a moment's thought, and they seem willing to try everything – because they don't want to regret doing nothing. Missed chances seem to be the only thing that causes them concern, as a result they go out of their way to embrace every opportunity for a new adventure or experience that comes along.

If you want to take a ride on the whirlwind this person may be the one for you. But don't be shocked if you suddenly find yourself dumped on the side of the road once they've had their fun with you. Keeping this person's attention is more difficult than catching it was.

You can tell who this person really is by how they respond to and behave in a situation. Their initial reaction will tell you how they feel. Of course as time goes by feelings can change and their initial response will reflect that internal emotional progress towards or against.

<u>As the querent's Higher Self/Influences/Themes</u>: You are being forced into situations where you have to trust your gut instincts, and fly by the seat of your pants. Life seems to have become a bit of a whirlwind adventure, with plenty of chances to experience new things, and little time to catch your breath.

Have courage, have fun, and if you fall over just get up, dust yourself off, and get back on that whirlwind – at least you are experiencing life.

The Universe is asking you to take a chance and learn to laugh with others and at yourself. Make the most of the new opportunities that present themselves.

<u>As the love interest's Higher Self/Influences/ Themes</u>: This person is being forced into situations where they have to trust their gut instincts and make quick decisions. They need to put aside brooding, regret and caution and find some excitement, anticipation and courage in their lives.

The potential for adventure and new experiences are strong now, as this person needs to learn to live a little more lightly and enjoy themselves.

If you are a positive go-getter you may be able to help them with this.

As the querent's link card: You are looking for an imaginative adventurer, someone creative and courageous with a positive outlook who can liven up your life and add some bounce to your step.

You feel the need for someone impulsive who acts on their desires: a creative knight errant who will sweep you off your feet, rather than the standard white knight. You don't need prim and proper; you want someone who is free enough within themselves to be able to show you their path of liberation.

Your lover will need to be able to stand up for themselves and their lifestyle, someone who will give voice to their opinion and stand up for what they believe is right against all opposition.

As the love interest's link card: This person needs someone who is positive, outgoing and imaginative who can bring a bit of magic back into their life.

They want an impulsive knight errant who acts on their desires to sweep them off their feet, rather than the standard prim and proper white knight that less physical idealists dream of.

Action, dancing the night away, trips abroad – they want romance and love to be an adventure, rather than a quiet night in with your feet on the sofa.

If you are impulsive, courageous, outspoken, positive and believe actions speak louder than words then you might just be the breath of fresh air that they are looking for.

As clarification: Take a chance, if it doesn't work out you know how to pick yourself up and keep right on going – confidence and optimism have never been obstacles to progress for you. Just remember, not everyone is ready to leap right into the thick of things without testing the water first. Patience is a virtue, remember?

Faint heart never won fair lady. If you don't at least try, how can you hope to get what you want?

As a third party/obstacles: A person who acts on impulse and has a fiery temperament that gets them into arguments, trouble and strife on a regular basis. Perhaps even violence. Now whether this is someone else, your lover, or you who behaves in this way, the effects will be the same – to drive you and your lover apart.

Shouting and fighting solves nothing. If you burn your bridges you may regret it in the future, so be tactful.

You got yourself into this mess either by action or inaction, now get yourself out of it. Inspiration, listening to your heart, clear thinking about the issues, and positive action will help you resolve things and take them to a conclusion; either reconciliation or separation – which depends upon the underlying truths of the relationship the two of you share.

Knight of Cups

As the querent: You may appear calm, but that's only because you're trying to keep your intense, passionate nature under control.

You used to wear your heart on your sleeve, which generally resulted in a lot of pain in the past, so now you try to keep the intensity of your emotions hidden. Despite the calm surface, you are a raging torrent underneath.

You are driven by your feelings, and love to experience the world when it loves you back. But the conflicts of everyday living, and the contrasting emotions, opinions and feelings of all the other people you meet can leave you reeling and exhausted.

You long for romance, and you are willing to sacrifice a lot for love, or rather for the ideal of love. You need commitment from the people you love, especially from your partner. You are an idealist and a dreamer, but can move mountains when you have to.

As the love interest: This person may appear calm on the surface, but intense emotions churn underneath. They are driven by their feelings, and don't tend to spend time thinking, they follow their heart and their gut instead.

If they appear secretive, or uninterested, it is just a mask. They have been hurt many times before and want to be sure of you before they say or do anything.

They are seeking commitment, probably marriage.

The best way to break through this person's armour is with a romantic gesture, followed by quiet sidling and shy looks. Once they get the message and if they're interested they'll probably knock you off your feet in their rush to embrace you. If they're not interested they'll probably storm off, all affronted that you took the risk, but they'll appreciate your romantic gesture nonetheless.

As the querent's Higher Self/Influences/Themes: Cups represent water and emotion, Knights represent action and challenge, so this card represents the disturbance of emotional calm. Emotions in action. Active emotions. Surging passion or flooding pain.

The quiet and calm in your life is about to be broken, or is being broken. Allow your heart to rule your head and follow the torrent of emotion. It will finally settle back to the calm you crave, but first you will undergo a sea change that will force you to reassess your place in the world and how you live in it.

<u>As the love interest's Higher Self/Influences/ Themes</u>: The universe is using this person's emotions as a catalyst for deep inner change. It is in the process of challenging them, either with passion or pain – probably both. Internally they are suffering a tempest.

Their everyday life is likely in the process of being reduced to tatters, forcing them to face their buried emotions. It they act irrationally rather than rationally, this will likely be the cause.

<u>As the querent's link card</u>: You are looking for someone romantic who desires marriage and who will create a snuggley nest of pink cushions with an endless supply of rose petals for you to live in for the rest of your life. You need romance and the chance to live in your feelings, rather than cope with the day-to-day hard realities of life.

<u>As the love interest's link card</u>: This person is likely to be a dreamer who longs for romance and marriage, and they are looking for someone who feels the same way. They want someone who lives in their feelings, rather than someone who spends time

thinking about how to get by in the world.

If you are that romantic dreamer and if you are lucky, this will be a practical person who can take care of the day-to-day nitty-gritty so that you, their lover, can concentrate on creating a romantic life for you both. If you are unlucky, they too will be a dreamer who puts heart before head in which case the hard realities of life can be a very painful experience for you both as they jolt you from your dream of love and force you to face survival.

As clarification: A good time for loving relationships and positive emotion. The heart rules the head. This means you risk getting more hurt than someone who lets their head control their decision-making process. However, if you test the waters you may be pleasantly surprised by the response of the other person, as a calm surface could belie the roiling passions underneath. Take care how you present your suit.

Someone new will enter your life.

As a third party/obstacles: You are being deceived, quite ruthlessly. Your lover will soon depart, and though you may not like it at this second, ultimately it is a good thing as while this person might look handsome or beautiful they are not actually very nice. Good riddance to them.

For you, parting from someone is usually filled with stress and pain – in this case you should let your head have its say before you allow your heart to go "Ah, poor me." It might find it's not so poor after all.

Knight of Swords

As the querent: You enjoy gathering new facts, words, just for the sake of it; but you don't like spending too long on a subject – you have quite a short attention span if you start to get bored. The most important aspect of your information gathering is the fun of it – the feeling of achievement from obtaining the information, and from knowing things that other people don't. It's an exercise in power in some respects: proving your intellectual superiority.

You view life as an adventure, with challenges to be met, obstacles to overcome. You can be eloquent when needed, and prefer any conflicts to be fought with, or resolved with, words.

You crave intellectual stimulation.

You detest being bored, patronized, or treated as mentally inferior.

As the love interest: This person is likely to be very intelligent. They crave knowledge and will seek it out just for the pleasure of knowing things, and also for the feeling of power – knowing things other people don't.

They enjoy games with words, and will likely be an eloquent and charismatic speaker treating debate as a sort of game.

They prefer conflicts that can be fought with words, or resolved with words.

This person gets bored easily and craves constant intellectual stimulation.

As the querent's Higher Self/Influences/Themes: Life is facing you with new opportunities, the challenge is to study abroad, or learn new lessons in new environments. Any conflict, adventure, or obstacle you face will be linked to intellectual matters or communication.

Intellectual stimulation will be at the heart of the lessons here: have fun while learning the facts. Boredom is your enemy.

Learning how far is too far to push matters.

Blaming others for your lies or bad behaviour will have consequences.

As the love interest's Higher Self/Influences/ Themes: If this person tends to indulge in negative behaviour like lies, or blaming others for the things that this person has done, then they will be forced to face the consequences now.

If they are a more positive person then the challenge they are being faced with is either studying abroad, or learning new things in new locations.

Travel, intellectual challenges and mental stimulation will be a feature of what this person is living through now.

This person needs to learn when to charge ahead and when to apply caution.

As the querent's link card: You get bored quickly and want someone who can stimulate you mentally; preferably someone charming as well as eloquent. You want them to be interested in everything, and happy to move quickly on to the next subject or adventure as soon as you've had enough of it.

You want someone who knows their own mind and is willing to tell you what you are both going to be doing next, or help you plan your next adventure.

As the love interest's link card: This person is looking for someone both forceful and intellectual who is unafraid of voicing their opinion or arguing their point of view.

They are easily bored and want someone fun who can teach them about a lot of new things, quickly. They want constant stimulation and if they can't get it here, they'll move on to the next person / party / adventure.

As clarification: This person could turn your life upside down, but that's probably no bad thing. Change and chaos are there to keep life interesting.

Attractive, charming, eloquent and a virtual force of nature. This person will provide a lot of stimulation, but needs a lot of it as well. If they get bored they'll leave. Can you handle it?

As a third party/obstacles: Someone has fallen under the spell of a treacherous but attractive and plausible liar. This person is no good and will cause a lot of damage before they are through.

Caution, in this case, is the better part of valour. Hold back and try to view the situation from a distance, objectively. This person will talk you in circles until you don't know night from day if you let them. Leave your chequebook and credit cards in the safe.

Don't even bother trying to argue with them: just don't open the door when they come knocking, let the answer machine get the phone, return their post to sender unopened.

Harsh? This person will wipe the floor with you given half a chance.

Knight of Pentacles

As the querent: You know that if you study well, work hard, maintain focus, attend to the detail, stick to the plan and keep going no matter what, you can achieve your goal.

Slow, steady progress is better than hurtling ahead and falling headlong over the unexpected bumps in the road.

You are willing to sacrifice a lot to get what you want, because you know that the end result will be worth it.

You are passionate, and enjoy having fun on your journey through life. You never give up on anything, or anyone, that you value. You're in it for the long term.

As the love interest: This person may be quite methodical and have a single-track focus, but they are also happy to learn new things and set out on adventures. They enjoy movement, and you won't find them standing still or doing nothing. They are always moving forward towards their goal, they just won't be leaping after it blindfolded. It was the tortoise that won the race in the fable, the hare lost because he got bored and his attention drifted. Some people might consider the safe route boring, but this person finds it comforting, because it very frequently leads them to success.

They believe in staying the course and seeing through their goals to completion. This can make them appear quite obstinate at times; but if you can show them a good, solid reason to change their mind on the matter at hand then they are not afraid to admit when they are wrong and try it your way – but they will really need to believe that you are right. You can't bully them or seduce them into it; you will need to give them solid proof.

This person is in it for the long haul, and they'd love to have some fun on route.

<u>As the querent's Higher Self/Influences/Themes</u>: You need to pay attention to the details when it comes to people: some are kind hearted and are trying to help, others are only in it for themselves – you need to learn which is which. This is very important, because one of the main tests you will face is learning when to compromise and when to fight on to the bitter end.

Compromise is likely to be something you've avoided in the past, but you are going to be faced, again and again, with situations where it may be necessary. Alternatively, if compromise is something you frequently practise, now is the time to learn to stand up for yourself and your goals, and do it your way.

If you want to be seen as trustworthy, you need to be seen to keep your promises.

<u>As the love interest's Higher Self/Influences/Themes</u>: This person is either bull-headed and is being given a lesson about the value of compromise. Or, they compromise all the time and need to learn to stand up for themselves and their goals.

If you want to learn which lesson they face, then just ask what they would like to do today, when they give you the answer, say that you would like to do something else instead. Their reaction will tell you which lesson they are needing. If they are bull-headed about doing what they want to do, they need to learn to compromise; if they try to negotiate a compromise, or cave to your will, then they need to learn to stand up for themselves and their goals.

As the querent's link card: You are looking for someone solid and reliable who sees things through to the end. A finisher rather than an uncommitted butterfly.

You are looking for kindness and honesty in your lover. Someone practical and down to earth who will fight their corner, or fight for a goal, a cause, unwavering in their commitment.

You don't like taking risks, and you want someone with the same attitude.

As the love interest's link card: This person is looking for commitment, a lasting relationship.

They need someone honest and reliable who keeps their word and will see things through until the end.

If you don't like taking risks, and you are willing to work hard to achieve your goals, you might be exactly what they want. Show them a bit of kindness, pay attention to the details and they'll start paying attention to you.

As clarification: Work is more important than love right now. You need to concentrate on the task at hand; it is important for your future welfare, and you cannot allow yourself to be distracted.

If you can balance both work and love, that's great. But remember, if you leave this project incomplete it could have a profound, lasting and negative impact on your life.

As a third party/obstacles: If you are getting married, check the other person's gold-digger status. Do it now. I'm not kidding.

You need to look at the situation with a clear eye and take a proper note of what is going on. You have the chance to change things if you act immediately.

Cancel your travel plans; do not invest in that grand scheme. You are wasting your effort and you will lose out in either case. Other people are trying to part you from your cash; can you really afford the downside?

Queen of Wands

As the querent: You take joy and inspiration from life: be it the countryside, or the people around you. And you want to share that sense of wonder with others. But you are also shy.

You have a fully developed understanding of the process of creative inspiration, and a deep intuitive knowing of how to express it in a way that other people can appreciate. The combination of mind and emotion that you bring to your art – whether it's sculpture, painting, writing, or life – is a rare and effective mixture that can move people profoundly.

You can find opportunity in the unlikeliest of places, but you are unwilling to take risks unless you are sure you can succeed.

You feel a deep need for success but you tend to back away from the attempt due to fear. ... Fear of ridicule? Fear of failure? Fear of success? Fear of being seen for who you really are? Fear of being mistaken for someone you're not? How silly is that.

You are a strong, caring, intelligent, well organized person, and you instinctively know how to inspire others. You probably need to socialize more.

As the love interest: This person has a deep intuitive understanding of the creative inspirational process, and is likely to be very artistic.

Well organized, inspiring, generous, practical and kind to others. This person sees the wonder in life, and wants everyone to live in joy the way they do.

This person may come across as shy or retiring, unwilling to take any chances when they are uncertain of success; but they can shine brightly in an environment where they feel safe and loved.

As the querent's Higher Self/Influences/Themes: The universe is challenging you to face your fears and quit being so shy and reluctant to take risks.

Or alternatively, if you take too many risks, you will be paying the price now: losing, both things and people. You have to learn your limitations.

You can find happiness and creative inspiration in the world and people around you if only you'll look. You know how to inspire others, you just need to feel safe in order to shine. Now is the time to renew your spirit and start living a healthy, positive life.

You are being urged to find a good relationship and create a happy home life.

As the love interest's Higher Self/Influences/Themes: This person may be losing a lot, perhaps both things and people, because of their risk-taking. They need to learn their limitations. Alternatively they need to conquer their shyness, face their fear and allow others the chance to get to know them – possibly through their art.

This person should be concentrating on creativity, art, inspiration and their very real need for a safe, fulfilling relationship and happy home life.

<u>As the querent's link card</u>: You are looking for someone ambitious, with a positive outlook, enthusiasm for life and art, and a need for family. You want to find yourself inspired by their intuitive, creative know-how. But you also prefer someone who is risk averse and knows their limitations.

<u>As the love interest's link card</u>: This person is looking for someone who can help them create a loving home life. They need someone who can inspire them both creatively and emotionally – someone with a love of the artistic qualities of life – who also has a strong sense of wonder and amazement in nature and living. They also need someone who knows their limitations and who prefers to avoid risk.

<u>As clarification</u>: Socialize as much as you can, ask them out on a casual date; a picnic, a hike, a museum trip, a play or the opera – something intimate but social. Do not rely on the advice of others so much, go with your gut and do what feels right to you. With luck they'll lead and take the guesswork out of it; you'll know exactly where you stand.

<u>As a third party/obstacles</u>: I think you may have just woken up next to a dragon – the fire breathing, seriously nasty kind. You might want to change your phone number, your address, your hair colour….

This person is vengeful, jealous and possessive. Obsessed. They could even be a stalker.

If your other half is being stalked, quit making a joke of it, it's not even slightly funny. This person is going to cause you both serious problems. They will hang on stubbornly too; unshakable. You'll have your work cut out, as a couple, if you are going to find a way through this to less hostile shores.

Queen of Cups

As the querent: Water of water. You feel everything so strongly, you want to control your emotions, therefore you tend to hide how you feel from others – perhaps even from yourself. What is this accomplishing for you?

You are very sensitive to the events and emotions swirling around you. You know strongly who you are in yourself. But you find it easy to get swept away by the currents and eddies of life's emotional peaks and troughs.

You are intuitive, psychic even, and know that you need to follow your gut when you get that 'itch' in your senses.

Follow your 'knowing' and you are unlikely to steer yourself wrong.

As the love interest: This person is very deep, and their depths are enigmatic. They know far more than they will ever tell. They are an oracle, a holder of secrets.

Deeply emotional and intuitive – they will trust their gut over logic; which given the level of sensitivity and psychic ability they have is likely to prove the correct choice.

They feel their emotions strongly and will want to control this surging sea within them, so they may totally hide their feelings from the outside world.

Outside events and other people's emotional focus can pull this person off balance. Water of water, they flow with the tides.

This person knows a lot about love, but their real need is to experience deep and lasting love.

Never take them for granted – never assume anything about their feelings or state of mind. Never try to force them into a mould.

As the querent's Higher Self/Influences/Themes: You are beginning to experience the world in a different way. You need to find your inner voice – that 'knowing' – that tells you the truth of a situation.

You are being taught to trust your instincts and follow your gut. They will get you out of trouble more times than you want to admit to yourself.

You are also being challenged to connect to your emotions and dwell in the world of feeling and intuition.

This is something that you need to do at the deepest level within the core of your being. It's not something you can talk about with others, because there are no words to adequately describe it. Only people who experience this way of living can truly know what you are going through. And there are many of them. You are not alone.

Perhaps it is time for you to consider some new concepts about the way you live your life?

As the love interest's Higher Self/Influences/Themes: This person needs to access their emotions, and trust how they feel about things and people and events. They react the way they do for a reason, and they need to fathom out what emotions drive their action or inaction, and why they feel the way they do.

This person also needs to learn to trust their instincts and to follow their gut. Their inner 'knowing' can guide them far better than logic or reason at this time.

They think they know about love, but they have a very strong need to experience real and lasting love.

Love is selfless and deep like the ocean – it's not the storm that tosses the waves about on the surface. This was something that confused them in the past.

Relationships of all kinds are highlighted, now.

They may have the chance to investigate their own psychic abilities. I would suggest meditation as a starting point, because the first step is to connect to their Higher Self. Other sources and skills can be a distraction from their inner Truth.

As the querent's link card: You are looking for someone who feels as strongly about relationships as you do. You feel the need to be with someone passionate and deep, mysterious and seductive. Maybe someone slightly enigmatic, who understands more about feelings than they ever reveal, and who gives the impression that they know a lot more than they ever tell.

You need someone with quiet strength and the stamina to survive the occasional tempest you may put them through.

Anyone who tries to dominate you and is critical of you can wound your feelings deeply, it would be best to remove yourself from their attempts to crush you.

As the love interest's link card: This person feels

the need to have relationships with people who understand love, and who know more than most the importance of passion and romance in keeping the inspiration of love alive. They desire someone deep, seductive and mysterious to lose themselves in. Quiet strength and stamina will be a bonus.

Shallow surface-types and domineering critics need not, and should not, apply.

As clarification: The person you like has a serious thing for romance. Rose petals, velvet, champagne and strawberries – the important stuff like remembering what they wore on your first date. Make the effort it'll be worth it for this person. Tactile and sensory pleasure are of primary importance, give them what they want and they'll respond like the cat that got the cream. You like purring, right? Teach them massage, you'll never regret it. And get a garden with that house; you need room for all the flowers to grow.

As a third party/obstacles: It is possible that the person you are with has not been honest with themselves or you about their feelings. Fear may lead them to grasp whatever they can get, whether they have feelings for it/you or not. They are so wrapped up in the need to satisfy their own desires and whims that they will seek gratification wherever they can get it.

Perhaps they are afraid to go too deeply into the emotion of love, afraid to let go and be controlled by their heart rather than their head?

Perhaps the fantasy of love they hold in their mind cannot survive in the face of reality?

In any event the thing that is driving you apart is a

lack of honesty. However, it may be this very lack of honesty that is keeping you together? Assess your situation and work out whether you are willing to compromise or not.

Queen of Swords

As the querent: You are capable of hiding your feelings and maintaining a pleasant façade even in the face of serious pain. But why suffer other people with dignity? You may not want to create an emotional scene but you can walk away, you don't have to put up with their negative attitude, bad behaviour, rudeness or attempts to control you.

When it comes to love you need more than sex to make your heart beat faster. Mental stimulation is an important part of your enjoyment of life and relationships.

You are perceptive, logical, intelligent, and enjoy music and reading. You fill every moment with mentally stimulating activities, especially those that you also find emotionally satisfying.

You are capable of detaching yourself from emotion and looking below the surface of words and actions to understand what makes people tick.

You are very independent and capable of making decisions and acting quickly when necessary.

Some people may see you as brilliant but aloof and detached, however this is only because you are a rationalist and you don't want to waste precious time in the messy drama which that type of person lives in.

As the love interest: This person enjoys mental stimulation and prefers to avoid emotional mess, so if you are into chess and Chopin and dislike arguments and public emotional scenes you might be who they are looking for.

This person tends to look on new situations and people with rose-tinted spectacles: they may initially perceive you as being the ideal lover, a god amongst mortals, and only later look analytically and realize that in reality you are a human being with all the faults and flaws that make life interesting; faults and flaws that may have them remove you from the pedestal they put you on and throw you out of Mount Olympus. So take care to explain your foibles to them at the start of the romance – there's no point trying to hide them, this person is very perceptive and will notice the true you eventually.

This person is capable of great courage and can suffer pain of all kinds without giving the faintest glimpse of the agony they are going through. They are highly independent so attempts to dominate them and criticize them will cause pain whether you know it or not.

If you want to offer this person feedback, be tactful, sincere, and find a way to phrase it positively, they respond far better to a carrot than a stick.

As the querent's Higher Self/Influences/Themes: You are being challenged to look at the underlying cause of the situation; perceive what is real dispassionately and rationally, and then take swift action to extricate yourself, or to solve the problem.

Arguments and emotion will not help you at this time.

If you are being dominated and criticized, you need to determine this person's motivation – what is driving them to behave in this way? It's not your fault that they can't see clearly or deal with their emotions.

If you have been looking at a person or situation as you would wish them to be, rather than as they really are, then you are waking up to reality now. Are you going to suffer quietly, or are you going to discuss this rationally; find a solution.

You know the truth so don't succumb to any flimflam. Take swift, decisive action.

As the love interest's Higher Self/Influences/Themes: This person has been living in a world of ideals rather than the real world, and they are being challenged to find the truth underlying the situation they are now surrounded by.

They are going through emotional turmoil, and may be living in suffering, quietly enduring the pain. Either they have been bereaved, or someone they thought loved them is being cruel, domineering and critical because they feel they can get away with it.

This person needs to look at the situation rationally and dispassionately and then take swift action in order to alleviate their suffering.

They may have been living in a bad situation, wasting time on useless emotion, and now it's time to get rational and take charge. They need to assert their independence and find a more truthful relationship; look with new eyes at what is going on under their nose. They know the truth, if they are willing to face it.

As the querent's link card: You are looking for a gentleman or lady, someone refined and cultural who shares your love of mentally stimulating activities. Someone you can share a proper conversation with.

You have a tendency to look at only the good things about a person when you start a romance, and only later start to notice the warts and flaws which may turn you right off. Try to be more realistic when assessing a person at the beginning, don't put them on a pedestal or treat them as an ideal of perfection which they will be unable to live up to.

You are looking for someone independent who is also perceptive and intelligent, who prefers to avoid messy emotional scenes and arguments, and will not be hyper-critical of your flaws or inadequacies (stop putting yourself down so much! Find the positive.). Everyone has interesting wrinkles; you need someone who can see the real you and accept you for who you are.

<u>*As the love interest's link card*</u>*:* This person's idea of love is more of an ideal. They tend to go into relationships wearing rose-tinted spectacles. Their vision of who you are, and the reality of who you are, will undoubtedly clash at some point in proceedings.

This person wants their lover to be a gentleman or lady: polite and civilized no matter how ruffled their feathers may get. They are looking for someone who is a master at disguising their pain, and who can remain calm on the surface even if they are seething underneath. If you are the bottled-up, tragic hero/heroine type who likes to have discussions rather than arguments or (*shudder*) fights, they'll probably adore you.

Mental stimulation is a must for them. If you are an academic genius all the better, as far as they're concerned. They want a partner who can teach them something new every day, either through talking, or through direct experience. Where you confidently lead, they will happily follow.

Excitement of the mind is probably at least as important, if not more important, to them than sex. And when it comes to making love, they need clean sheets, and they are likely to claim that they hate mess.

So, if you are a genius, a martyr, utterly self-contained, independent, confident and plain old-fashioned socially acceptable at all times – then you might have a chance for lasting happiness. Good luck maintaining the façade: you'll need it, because they'll probably spot any deception in short order. This person is a sharp cookie despite their tendency towards idealism.

As clarification: Analyzing a situation for potential clashes and problems is wise, specially before getting emotionally involved with someone else. However the rational brain prevents the emotional brain from working. At some point you have to let go of what you think, and just get downright messy and emotional in love. Your intuition will guide you, so trust your inner process.

As a third party/obstacles: This person may have already detached themselves from their relationship with your lover, but that won't stop them from being manipulative and cruel. A tough cookie who will out manoeuvre you both at every turn, especially if you try to rationalize their behaviour. Chances are this person will never take their claws out of the person you love.

If you can handle putting up with an ex in the mix,

then stand up for your relationship. If not, then walk away, your lover isn't going to let go of this third party – that person's hold over them is too strong.

Queen of Pentacles

As the querent: You are likely to be a bit of a hedonist. You enjoy life's luxuries, and try to make the most of what you have. You are not afraid of a bit of hard work in order to get what you want. You probably don't like to take risks unless you are fairly certain of the outcome. Safety is important to you. You want a roof over your head, and food on the family table; the pursuit of luxury comes a very close second.

How you live your life, is likely to be as important to you as your quality of life. Settling for imperfection, or less than optimum, disturbs your equilibrium. Similarly, you firmly believe that if a job's worth doing, it's worth doing well. Mainly because you know that you are the one who will ultimately benefit from high quality craftsmanship.

It is possible that you measure love in terms of money and gift-giving. If so, this isn't always the healthiest approach as it can attract leaches to you. In addition, children need plenty of hugs, as do lovers; the latest gadget is no substitute for love. You have a sensible head on your shoulders so hopefully this confusion over *giving equals loving* is something that you have already faced in your psyche.

As the love interest: This person probably has a good head for business. Certainly they know what they want from life – quality and enjoyment. Family and physical safety is also important to them. The drive to have a roof over their head and food on the table means that they are prepared to work hard to get what they want, especially if it means that they can indulge in their love of luxury. Good food and pleasant surroundings are important to them.

This person does not like taking unnecessary risks. They prefer to be reasonably sure of the outcome of any gambles they may take. However, sometimes their need for personal fulfilment may drive them to extreme actions – like suddenly changing careers or moving house in order to gain a better quality of life, as they see it.

This person may sow quite a lot of wild oats in their youth, but the desire for family and commitment in a sexually satisfying relationship is likely to tame them as they get older.

This person may confuse love and giving gifts as being the same thing. Certainly they are generous, possibly to a fault. You may need to explain to them that togetherness and physical closeness are more important in maintaining a loving relationship than expensive presents. Hopefully they have already learned the difference.

As the querent's Higher Self/Influences/Themes:
Know thyself. You need to learn who you are if you want to be fulfilled and happy. Basing your self-image on the opinions, biases and agendas of other people is a sure-fire recipe for unhappiness.

In business you need to take the time to do your own research, and learn everything there is to know about a potential investment – there are a lot of conmen out there, and they all seem to be lining up at your door. Better yet, invest in yourself rather than the harebrained schemes of others.

Another lesson life has for you is that quality is more important than quantity: craftsmanship produces unique and lasting individual things, mass production stamps out carbon-copy simulacrums.

The key words for you? Hedonism in a safe environment: Spending yourself in frivolity, or living in denial can be equally damaging. Finding the balance between self indulgence and a healthy physical environment will improve your life. Prioritizing the important things in life, like a roof over your head and food on the table, ahead of spending money like water on drugs, alcohol, or gambling could be a major lesson for you.

As the love interest's Higher Self/Influences/Themes: This person needs to discover that all that glitters isn't gold. They may get taken for a ride by a few conmen before they learn to do their own in depth study before committing any assets for investment. Their own business ventures are likely to be more lucrative for them than other people's.

Their quest this life is to discover the balance between indulging themselves and prioritizing the important things in life. They need to discover that quality is more important than quantity, and that a roof over their head is better than exposure to the elements.

This person needs to learn that gift-giving and love is not the same thing. A loveless marriage to a person of wealth will not bring them the happiness they thought it would. And if they are wealthy they are likely to suffer at the hands of a false partner; pre-nup is the name of the marriage game.

This person also needs to learn to appreciate the

awe-inspiring glory of the natural world. Greenery and peaceful surroundings will help them find their centre, and be beneficial for them. Gardening is a good stress reliever.

Their mission in this life is to appreciate themselves for who they are, and thus other people for who they are; and to learn how to smile again.

As the querent's link card: You are looking for someone who can keep you in the luxury you desire. Plentiful food, and great furnishings are a must for you.

You desire a world of shimmering silver. And they do say that every cloud has a silver lining; just because someone doesn't have the means to keep you now doesn't mean they won't in the future. You limit yourself too much. What you really need is someone who will love you for who you are, why isn't that more important than the cash in their wallet?

Someone lacklustre in bed will not do it for you – however many other good qualities they have: e.g. good looks, a perfect credit rating, a palace, a personal chef.

You need someone grounded who enjoys indulging in the pleasures of life; you need a person who knows about finance and hard work, who values stability and family and home, and who has the money to keep you both safe and warm with a roof over your head and food on the table. Practicality and earthly pleasures.

In terms of astrology, someone with a strong Taurean influence is likely to fit your needs well.

As the love interest's link card: This person is happiest when their physical needs are met. They know all about hedonism and pleasure. They enjoy good food, plush furnishings, financial security, and they want someone who understands the subtleties and knows the techniques of earth-shatteringly satisfying sex.

If they aren't responding to your caresses, chances are they are either worrying about money, or your lack of ambition. Alternatively it could be that you have to get a little more adventurous in the sack. Don't be afraid to ask them what they want, they'll be happy to show you (even if they would prefer you to be fully accomplished already). Take the lead, they want someone strong and refined who knows what to do in all situations. For this person actions speak louder than words, so brush up on your skills and practical knowledge. What type of wine should be served with fish? If you don't know you need to find out quick.

As clarification: Take pleasure in the world around you, enjoy the luxuries.

This card speaks of the fertility of earth; motherhood is likely to feature somehow.

If you are looking for family, and a partner who pursues their own course in life while remaining deeply committed to the people around them, then this relationship could be a good one. If that's not what you're after, you might want to head back out and keep looking, as this person won't hesitate to show you the error of your ways if you toy with their emotions. And if you do provoke them into action, the lesson they teach you will be one you can't erase from your memory.

As a third party/obstacles: Someone who can't let

go. They'll cling on no matter what. You will find yourselves as the centre of attention, as they are likely to involve all their friends in their quest to avoid letting go, or to avoid change at all cost.

Behaving like a miser who won't part with cash, or belongings, or emotion.

If it is you who is clinging to the past, upset by the unfair events that have overtaken your life, take a bit of time to treat yourself to the nice things in life. You can't live your life through someone else, you need to step out on your own path – it may be scary but you can cope, you really can.

King of Wands

As the querent: Busy, busy, busy. You are an inspirational leader who is constantly active, and impatient when things get delayed or sidetracked. Your positive enthusiasm and passion for a new project engages the imagination of others and leads them to follow you in bringing your dreams into reality.

You love putting on a show, holding centre stage, proclaiming to the crowds...but when people come to you with routine questions, and look to you for answers if things crash and burn – it can make you feel restricted and tied down. You hate limitation or naysayers pouring cold water on your dreams. In fact, reality can be a real pain in the bottom sometimes.

You are ambitious, but wise due to practical experience, and this combined with your confidence allows you to maintain your success – though you always have your eye on the horizon and what is new, you also hire the right people to see the current job through to completion. This forward thinking and practical application can make you a leader in your field of endeavour if you have the right team of people with you.

Other people can find you exhausting to be around, and when you are pissed off you can be belligerent and arrogant. But you are also a good mediator, so if you want to calm a situation, you know how.

As the love interest: Honour and etiquette are important to this person. Romance and passion are likely to be instinctive, or second nature, to them. They have strong feelings about art and know what they like.

This person is always the centre of attention, and very good at persuading people to get involved in their projects and plans. Always on the go, they are not someone to stay trapped at home – specially not if there is a soirée, art exhibit, or new big thing in town. Expect them to be out until all hours, most likely they will have been working late, and then come home expecting you to give them the red carpet treatment, or at the very least a comfortable shoulder on which they can lay their weary head.

You may be quite surprised to discover how wide your paramour's social circle is. This is a good thing, it gives them less of chance to get bored if they have lots of people to talk to about many varied things.

If you anger this person you can expect short shrift and some pretty selfish behaviour.

As the querent's Higher Self/Influences/Themes: Life can be a bit of a performance – sometimes you find yourself looking around to see if you can find the script lying around on an abandoned chair.

All you really need is creativity, art and that new horizon. Getting that seems to be about persuading people to give you the goods you need to pursue your goal. Thus your charisma and confidence are your biggest assets in achieving what you want.

Your life is about the experience of passion, in all its flickering, fleeting forms. The pace that the world throws these objects and subjects of desire at you can be quite exhausting, and you frequently find yourself involved in many projects at the same time – keeps life interesting.

The danger is that you gloss over the important experiences because there is so much going on that you don't realize the depth and relevance of what could be, until it is past and you are up to your elbows in something else.

Learn to focus on one person at a time in the area of romance, as lovers tend not to appreciate discovering that your affections are shared with others.

As the love interest's Higher Self/Influences/Themes: This person is one of life's natural speakers, a mediator who can hold an audience with the power of their charisma, and the intensity of their confidence. They have a lot of experience to back up their words, so people will trust them.

Their life tends to throw them to centre stage, and you may have trouble keeping up with all the constantly changing events, people and situations in their life.

When things happen to this person, they happen quickly, totally encompass their every waking moment, and then pass just as swiftly.

Your lover may be a tad obsessive, or alternatively a total gadfly. Either way, whatever they are involved in, however short or long the process, they will be into it one hundred percent – and if you are their lover that will include you too. Just don't necessarily expect that when they say they love you they mean they will love you forever. Life doesn't let them work like that, it can force them into unbearable situations that make them have to leave at a moment's notice…so you will need to be able to pack up and move faster than they can – and they are well practiced at it.

If you like soap operas or politics this is one person to keep track of.

As the querent's link card: You are looking for a show – a theatre performance – in your love life and relationships. You want someone magnetic who can hold you spellbound with their stories and rhetoric.

You require constant change, and interesting events and people, so that you can increase your experience of every aspect of life, and of all the passions of life.

You want to hold every moment tight to you, you hate letting go of something or someone – until you are finished with them. Therefore if your lover walks out on you it is quite devastating, but you've done that to so many other people that you really have to get some perspective in this regard.

You need someone who will surrender themselves to you totally, and feed the myth of romance that you harbour in your heart. You need a heroine or hero to sweep you off your feet and whisk you away to paradise. This attitude can make you vulnerable to opportunists.

As the love interest's link card: This person wants a romantic hero or heroine to sweep them off their feet. They will appreciate games, stories and acting in a relationship, to magnetize them and keep them interested in the kaleidoscope of emotion you present them with. They need you to be there for them one hundred percent and, when you are with them, they will not tolerate you thinking about something else, especially when you are getting intimate with them – if your eyes glaze over they will freak.

They want you to talk to them constantly and enlighten them with your experience. I suspect that they are looking for an older lover (older in emotion and attitude) who can constantly teach them new things and whisk them to new heights of experience.

If you are a natural speaker and mediator with a flare for the stage, you could be just what they are looking for. They require that you provide inspiration and charismatic leadership in your adventures together.

As clarification: As long as you come at this from a realistic perspective you should have a lot of fun and get swept up in the excitement of new experience, new people, and new things to do.

However, if you put your loved one on a pedestal and imagine the sun rises at their command, you are liable to get disappointed – and when you are disappointed you get irritable and stop listening to reason. When you are like that no one wants to know you.

I guess the warning is make hay while the sun shines…but it should be a long, fine summer.

As a third party/obstacles: Bullying and belligerence are not appealing qualities in a relationship. Obstinacy and a domineering attitude are a turn off.

Relationships are about give and take. When one person takes everything and acts like a brick wall when questioned, the prognosis is loneliness.

If the person you love is being bullied by a third party, the best thing you can do is help them find a way to tell the bully the harsh truth – or help them pack and take them away from the cause of trouble.

If you are the control freak who drove their beloved away because of your tyranny, then shame on you. Quit your hassling, and go take a look in the mirror. If you can't iron out this behaviour you will wind up in a repeating pattern of people getting riled by your selfishness and leaving as a direct result. Learn to relax and chill out.

King of Cups

As the querent: You have experienced a lot in your life, your emotions may even have been run ragged in the past, which is why you are now a little hesitant about getting closely involved with anyone. Cutting yourself off from other people doesn't work – you need the love and personal attention they are able to bring, more than you can fully explain. Social relationships for you may be few, but they are very important. A true friend is of great value to you.

Your strong need for love can mean that you get involved with the wrong people: that wall that you have built up is a good thing, in that it keeps you safe from the scoundrels and unscrupulous harridans of this world. But in an intimate relationship that wall has to come down, otherwise the right person may shy away thinking that your intentions are not deep or serious.

When someone says that they love you, that is the point at which you have to trust them to mean what they say. Go with your instincts, they are always right. Don't let fear get in the way or cloud your judgment. Let your passion out now and again.

As the love interest: This person has been hurt in love and is now reticent to get close to anyone. They have had a tendency to make bad judgment calls about people in the past, and have been badly used as a result. Even if they are new to the dating game, there is something in their past that makes them loath to commit, no matter how serious they are about someone. You could be the love of their life, but they'd try hard not to show it. They'll let you know they love you, but talk of marriage would have them running for the hills even though that's what they really want in their heart of hearts. Let them do the proposing, they'll get around to it when they are ready.

If they give off an air of disinterest around you, then it is probably just that – they're not interested.

If they do like you, they'll let you know it in a way you can be sure of, as this person is exceedingly passionate and will follow their heart in all things. They aren't shy.

As the querent's Higher Self/Influences/Themes: Life surrounds you with opportunities for love and disappointment. Whether you have been disappointing others, or they have been disappointing you is unclear.

Life keeps throwing new emotional experiences at

you, which means that you have been through quite a lot for someone your age and have a deep understanding that other people may not share or comprehend.

As with many things, a person has to go through an experience before they will fully comprehend what it means or how to respond to someone else who is going through the same thing. Your understanding means that you can help others effectively, and life may be trying to get you into the position of working with those who need aid.

Love and personal relationships are a very important part of your life, and mould the way you live as well as your life choices. Therefore choosing the right people to share your experience becomes more important for you than for most people: with the right people at your side you can achieve pretty much whatever you want – you are a great team leader when you are fully in tune with your environment, doing the work destiny has called you to. In the wrong environment you will be deeply unsatisfied and feel like a fish out of water.

<u>As the love interest's Higher Self/Influences/ Themes</u>: This person seems to be a sponge for the universe – they have lived through all kinds of emotional events, and come out of the other side. Because of all that they endure they can be standoffish, but they can also be the most accommodating of people because they understand what pain and real need are.

This person is likely to be psychic, and they will certainly work with people in their daily job. Human interaction is very important to them.

If they are working in the wrong field, or with the wrong people, the universe is likely to smack them around most viciously until they 'wake up' and go do the work they are supposed to be doing.

This person will go through quite a lot of trauma in their life, but they are also better able to cope with it than many people. This is because they have a depth of character and self-understanding that most people their age have not yet achieved.

If you are interested in humanitarian issues, this person is someone you could be happy walking with through life.

As the querent's link card: You need love and permanent commitment on a deep level that you do not quite understand. You may even be unwilling to look at that heart-need within you, because you have been let down in the past and want to avoid any more feelings of loss or abandonment. The fact remains: you need a spouse, family, love, and commitment – their absence is an ache in your soul. You may fear it, but you need it even more.

The love interest's personal card should tell you everything you need to know about their worthiness and suitability as a life partner. If not, you need to ask why – check for obstacles.

As the love interest's link card: This person is afraid of the depth of emotion, and also the possibility of abandonment, in a loving relationship. This makes them reticent about words like 'marriage' and 'children'. However, this person has a deep need for permanent commitment in love: a loving spouse and family are the only things they really, totally and utterly want in life. They would never admit it though.

If you aren't interested in marriage or lifelong commitment, then stay clear of this person. It would not be fair to them to deceive them on purpose, as their feelings are very strong and when they do fall in love they fall hard.

If you do want a one night stand, for goodness sake, make sure they realize that is all it is. They want more. A lot more.

As clarification: The opportunity to both give and receive love. Both parties may be deeply committed to each other and be passionate in their desire, however the fear of commitment/marriage will hinder each from expressing the true depth of their feelings.

This card is telling you to take a chance. If you don't even try you will never allow yourself the chance to succeed – "A life lived in fear is a life half lived." You have so much passion that I know you will never settle for a half-life. Why wait?

As a third party/obstacles: An addictive personality, or someone deeply unhappy with their own life who forces pain upon others in an attempt to mitigate their own inner agony. In either event, the person indicated is afraid to face their inner demons, emotional darkness and fears, and thus instead of growing into a well-rounded personality they keep themselves down in a rut of despair, pain and weakness.

If it is you that is afflicted, you must realize that each of us has demons, darkness and fear – facing this side of ourselves is what makes us human, and incidentally it is not until we have done this personal work that we are ready to become involved with another person in a permanent and healthy relationship. Find a support group and get help; you aren't the only person who feels the way you do, trust me on this.

If you or your partner is afflicted, it will take hard work by that person, and understanding and support from the other person to help them get through it. If it is a third party who is inflicting themselves on your relationship – possibly even a family member – you need to find a way to gently disentangle them from your intimacy and get them in touch with the support group they need for their particular emotional trauma.

If the person is very destructive it might be necessary for you to walk away to preserve your own sanity and life.

King of Swords

As the querent: You find that you are most comfortable when everything has its place, and is in its place. A well ordered world is what you aim to create in your environment and in your life. However, once everything is as it should be, easy to access at need, fair and equally divided, then you get bored. And when you get bored you tend to over analyze things, or set out to find new horizons, or poke at things you know should be left well alone – just to get that unpredictable response.

Your realm is the boundless world of the mind, and you find structure in law – whether scientific, social or otherworldly. Injustice upsets you, as do needless displays of intense emotion.

Sometimes you feel the need to be around messy or

emotional people just to be in a different environment. Doesn't mean you want to live like that permanently though.

People and children will not conform to your ideal standards, they are messy and emotional most of the time. Learn to love that about them, or revel in your bachelor/spinster status. The alternative is being seen as a tyrant, which goes against your need for fair play.

As the love interest: This person can be controlling and domineering – although they would be very upset if you accused them of such unfair conservative behaviour. They like their world to be ordered so that they know where everything is and what they can expect to happen in their environment.

This person wants a lot of mental stimulation, and may even go out of their way to get into scrapes or new situations, just for the experience. They are likely to drive you nuts talking about it afterwards – or write the definitive book on the subject.

They should achieve a lot in their life and can be incredibly single minded about their goals.

If you annoy them, or set out to hurt them somehow, you can expect a retaliation of the like you have never witnessed before. This person can be cruel, unforgiving and merciless if given sufficient cause for disquiet.

As the querent's Higher Self/Influences/Themes: Your life appears to have a distinct order. It's like there is a street map that you live by, or a particular route that the universe is forcing you to travel along. Events will happen to you that give pause for thought, as you digest a new way of thinking about things, new cultures, new environments. The street map of your life is an interesting one, even if it can occasionally seem too well ordered.

The only real problem for you comes when your goals in life conflict with those that fate or destiny has planned for you. Fate will always manage to win out, so be prepared to be flexible or you could get very cynical and disappointed by the events and people in your life.

Things fall into place around you much of the time, usually because you have worked hard for the very result that is now manifesting. Any goal that you do set out to achieve, will usually find the outside help needed to complete it in one form or another.

Never limit yourself, something new is always around the corner and if you don't go to it, it will come to you.

<u>*As the love interest's Higher Self/Influences/Themes*</u>: This person seems to be at the heart of a network of influential, powerful, and sometimes ruthless people. Mental achievements surround them, pushing them onwards to explore the new, and to catalogue and file all their discoveries.

This person may work in the field of law, or a museum or library – any kind of ordered environment that will provide mental stimulation and the chance of contact with other 'great' minds.

Expect them to be in charge of their life, and to have a set place for you in it. Sometimes they may give the impression that everything else in their life is more important than you are – this is not true, it's just that life has a way of forcing them into situations where they have to take action. There is no easy way around this, because if they don't follow where their heart and mind leads, the consequences tend to be very unpleasant. It's a fate thing.

As the querent's link card: You need someone who can provide order in your life, as well as mental stimulation. If the love interest's personal card is The Magician, they could be just what you are looking for.

Perhaps you want a control freak who will dominate you? Your sexual preferences may even lean towards the bondage end of the spectrum.

Be careful to ensure that you are with someone who will respect you as a person and as a lover, or you could end up living in a nightmare that you would rather not be a part of.

Check the love interest's cards carefully. I would also recommend drawing an obstacles card for them – just to check that they are not the type to mangle you.

As the love interest's link card: This person is looking for someone who can provide interest and direction in their lives. They enjoy being kept busy mentally, and want someone who likes intellectual pursuits, so that you can have fun together. They need someone fair and just to point them in the right direction.

It is possible that their ex may have been a bit of a tyrant; while they like a certain amount of authority and pointed suggestion in their lives, bullying and total domination are not something they enjoy.

As clarification: The rational mind thrown into turmoil by emotion. Talk is the key, a meeting of minds. As to whether you are suited to each other check the other cards in the spread, the interactions between them should reveal any beneficial or problem areas.

There is a lot of potential indicated by this card – your first impressions and subsequent cool analysis should give an accurate reading of the other person.

Get talking, it's your best way forward; stimulation of the mind is a priority you both share.

As a third party/obstacles: Someone in authority who you really don't want to mess with. This person could talk for their country in the Olympics – if it was a sport – and they will bring to bear their considerable knowledge and weight of personality to control and dominate any interaction you or your lover have with them. Browbeating is a definite possibility.

Legal difficulties, a confidence trickster, or a manipulative authoritarian may be tying you up in knots. Walk away. Or if the two of you wish to stay together (make sure your lover isn't the confidence trickster first) then you will probably have to elope – even then the problems will be waiting for you when you get back.

If it is a legal issue, possibly to do with the age of you or your lover, then you are just going to have to wait until you are both old enough to legally commit to each other.

King of Pentacles

As the querent: You are an ambitious, hard working person who needs stability and financial security to feel safe in your life. You know what it takes to be successful and you are a first class provider when you want to be.

The danger in any relationship is that you may place more emphasis on your work life than your home life. Emotions and relationships need to be nurtured, this takes time, work and effort too. If you neglect this area you may end up with a top notch home, running your own successful company, only to discover a divorce petition in amongst the post on your desk when you check in to work as usual on a Sunday morning.

Marriage and family are important to you and will provide much of the stability that you crave in the landscape of your personal life.

As the love interest: This person needs stability in their life the way normal people need air. This doesn't make them stodgy, not in the slightest, they will happily get on that surprise flight to Tibet with you – as long as they know that their business/work is covered by someone trustworthy and that the home they love so much will still be there when they get back. Planning and homework required: you can't just buy the tickets for a three month trip and expect them to leap joyously on board without a backward glance.

This person will work hard and play just as hard, because they want to enjoy the fruits of their labours as much as you do. Thing is, this person might put too much emphasis on material gain if they think that is what you want or if that is what is required to have a 'perfect' life.

Before you talk them into buying that mansion that they can't really afford, you must realize that they will spend every waking hour earning the money required to pay for that mansion so that you have a roof over your head – because they think that that is what you want them to do. This means that you will not get to see them much, and when you do, they will be exhausted and unable to cope with much more than falling asleep in a chair in the living room when they do get home. If you want them to be the bright, sparkling person that you loved when you first met, you need to make a note to yourself to ensure that you don't expect them to give you the world, otherwise, like Atlas, they will take it on their shoulders in order to make it yours.

As the querent's Higher Self/Influences/Themes: The universe is teaching you to be at one with yourself and with your way of life. It is possible that your family background is one of money or worldly power, or perhaps a family tradition or trade such as farming or fishing...either way you will be comfortable with that landscape, learning your expertise through hard work, or having that hard work forced upon you.

Your life lesson is that if you want to achieve success you need to put in the constant hard work and effort required to build solid foundations, and then continue to build on those foundations to create your success, and once you have that success to continue the hard work in order to maintain the success.

You will get what you want from life, if you work for it. That includes relationships and family.

When you have times of serious need in your life the universe is likely to provide for you, but you cannot rely upon this and you must put in the ground work for any aid that does come your way. Seed won't grow on barren land.

As the love interest's Higher Self/Influences/Themes: The world, and the universe, seem to expect a lot from your love interest. This person is the hub of activity, opportunities are presented, or worked for, and will lead to great accomplishments if this person follows their heart.

Stability is a feature of this person's life, along with the mountains that surround them and require being moved. Work is a constant for them. Things may run smoothly for a while, but something will always crop up that requires their undivided attention before it is resolved – driving them to try to achieve more, to reach further.

They are likely to be in the public eye, somehow, and will need someone trustworthy at home to rely on for support, encouragement, love, and most importantly a stable home life.

As the querent's link card: You need someone constant, stable and hardworking who can provide for your needs. Your greatest desire is to feel safe at home and in your relationship. You are looking for 'Petra or Peter, the Rock' – a person who will always be there for you and who can be relied upon.

The slightest question over the other person's fidelity, or their ability to provide you with what you need, is likely to send you into emotional turmoil. Check your love interest's personal card for compatibility, if this is not a perfect match you may wish to check the clarification card. If both are ambiguous you should think twice about engaging in a relationship with the person.

As the love interest's link card: This person requires stability, reliability, and someone with the financial wherewithal to provide the hedonistic little luxuries of life that they value. If they are a stay-at-home husband or wife, they will require an allowance that enables them to get these 'necessities'. They need someone who is emotionally and physically faithful to them, who will never give them cause to doubt.

All this may seem selfish, but this person understands the work involved in making for a perfect home life, and they will be happy to talk about what you need from them in return. Whether they do that or not depends on their personal and Higher Self cards.

As clarification: You both know the hard work involved in making something lasting and successful, and you both enjoy reaping the rewards of your hard earned labours. This card bodes well for a productive and equal union where both parties respect and trust one another. You work hard and you play hard; and you enjoy both because you are doing what you want to do. Why aren't you married already?

As a third party/obstacles: Someone is after your cash, or your status – either, they are jealous of your achievements, or they are so materialistic it is just painful. Possibly there is a gambling problem, or associates who are nefarious grasping individuals. Whoever is indicated by this card, they are a person who wishes you ill, and their actions will cause you and your lover to be separated if you are not astute enough to deal with the interference solidly and immediately.

If it is your lover who is after your cash, I'm sorry – they are not the person you thought they were. They probably don't love you, maybe they never did. They know what they are doing, but a clever lawyer and some fancy footwork should disentangle you from this mess without too much financial pain.

Afterword

I trust that you found this book useful, and that it gave you food for thought with regard to what you are, and are not, looking for in your life partner.

We are all creatures of free will, with hopes and dreams, patterns of damage, or sensitivities, which are different from one another. The dawning realisation of this may allow you to investigate your own flaws and the behaviour patterns you exhibit in particular situations, or with particular types of people. One of the clues is: anything which irks you in another person is very likely something that you unknowingly do yourself. Is this your Higher Self's attempt to nudge you into self-awareness?

You cannot change another person, no matter how hard you try. You can only change yourself, and that change comes from deep within – constantly monitor your own thoughts and behaviour, then adapt accordingly. Continuous practice may help you iron out some of your glitches. The mind, like the body, falls into habits. Retraining is possible, and regular exercise of new, positive thought patterns to replace the familiar painful negative ones will lead to success.

Even so, no one will get on with everyone they meet. This is part of the colour and flavour of life. If we can leave happiness and peace around us, making life less stressful and richer for others, then I feel we have achieved something worthwhile.

      In light,
            Eleanor

www.ingramcontent.com/pod-product-compliance
Lightning Source LLC
Chambersburg PA
CBHW071852290426
44110CB00013B/1110